THE TRANSNATIONAL VILLAGERS

THE
TRANSNATIONAL
VILLAGERS

PEGGY LEVITT

UNIVERSITY OF CALIFORNIA PRESS
BERKELEY   LOS ANGELES   LONDON

University of California Press
Berkeley and Los Angeles, California

University of California Press, Ltd.
London, England

© 2001 by the Regents of the University of California

Library of Congress Cataloging-in-Publication Data

Levitt, Peggy, 1957–.
    The transnational villagers / Peggy Levitt.
        p.   cm.
    Includes bibliographical references and index.
    ISBN 0-520-22811-1 (cloth : alk. paper).—ISBN 0-520-22813-8
(pbk. : alk. paper)
    1. Miraflores (Dominican Republic)—Emigration and immi-
gration.   2. Boston (Mass.)—Emigration and immigration.
3. Dominicans (Dominican Republic)—Massachusetts—Boston.   4. Globalization.   5. Transnationalism.   6. Emigrant
remittances—Dominican Republic—Miraflores.   I. Title.

JV7395.L48   2001
304.8′744610729373—dc21   00—55172

Manufactured in the United States of America
10   09   08   07   06   05   04   03   02
10   9   8   7   6   5   4   3   2

The paper used in this publication meets the minimum
requirements of ANSI/NISO Z39.48-1992(R 1997)
(Permanence of Paper). ∞

Portions of chapter two appeared as "Social Remittances: A
Local-Level, Migration-Driven Form of Cultural Diffusion,"
in the International Migration Review 32 (124), winter 1999:
pp. 926–49. Portions of chapter six appeared originally as
"Local-Level Global Religion: The Case of U.S.-Dominican
Migration," in the Journal for the Scientific Study of Religion (3),
1998: pp. 74–89. Parts of chapter seven were published earlier
as Transnationalizing Community Development: The Case of
Migration Between Boston and the Dominican Republic," in
the Nonprofit and Voluntary Sector Quarterly (26), 1997:
pp. 509–26.

For my mother and father

Contents

Acknowledgments

My first thanks go to those who guided this project from its inception. The late William Alonso, Susan Eckstein, Martin Rein, and Mary Waters all provided invaluable assistance. I am especially grateful to Gary Marx for his unconditional support and wisdom, which he has shared with me so generously over the years.

Many friends, family, and colleagues read and reread parts of this manuscript, helped me to make field contacts, offered encouragement, and pushed me to think in new and different ways including Ricardo Arias, Jill Block, the Cárdenas-Tovar family, Jim Ennis, Rosario Espinal, Robert Fogelson, Nancy Foner, Herbert Gans, Philip Genty, Helen Glikman, Steve Gold, Barbara Greene, Sarah and Murray Greher, Luis Guarnizo, Pedro Guzmán, Georgia Kaufmann, David Laws, Mary Lou Levers, Juana and Claudio Liriano-Feliz, David Luberoff, Sarah Mahler, Kitty Margolis, Lynn McCormick, Edwin Meléndez, Patricia Moger, Sharon Neuman, Kathy Newman, Lisa Peattie, Patricia Pessar, Alejandro Portes, Seth Racusen, Rubén Rumbaut, Naomi Schneider, Harry Sellin, Yasemon Soysal, Diane Stratton, Jody Tannenbaum, Reed Ueda, Judith Waksberg, Miriam and David Weil, and Debbie Wengrovitz.

Colleagues in the Dominican Republic also provided invaluable support including Lourdes Bueno, Walter Cordero, Wilfredo Lozano, Radhamés Mejía, Tirso Mejía Ricart, and Hugo Tolentino Dipp.

Many institutions generously funded this project, including the Ford Foundation, the Social Science Research Council, the Spencer Foundation, the American Sociological Association Fund for Advancement of the Discipline, the Aspen Institute Nonprofit Sector Research Fund, and the Wellesley College Faculty Research Fund. My special gratitude to Connie Buchanan and Josh DeWind. The initial idea for this study grew out of my work at the Institute for the Study of Economic Culture at Boston University—my thanks to Peter Berger and Marilyn Halter. The Center for Population and Development Studies gave me a MacArthur Fellowship and a place to write my dissertation. I especially thank David Bell, Lincoln Chen, Winifred Fitzgerald, Chris Cahill, Sue Carlson, and Miriam Orenstein. The Weatherhead Center for International Affairs and the David Rockefeller Center for Latin American Studies at Harvard University both supported this project—Jorge Domínguez and John Coatsworth deserve my gratitude. To my colleagues in the InterUniversity Seminar on Migration, particularly the late Myron Weiner, and at the Department of Urban Studies and Planning at the Massachusetts Institute of Technology, I also extend my appreciation. Thanks also to numerous colleagues at Wellesley College and Harvard University, including Susan Silbey, Lee Cuba, Jonathan Imber, Tom Cushman, Pam Bauer, Michael Jones-Correa, Chris Winship, Theda Skocpol, Werner Sollors, Marcelo Suárez-Orozco, and Peter Marsden. Erin Collins, Jay Dater, Miguel Salazar, and Rafael de la Dehesa also played an invaluable role in the preparation of this manuscript.

Sixto Escobar took me on my first tour of Jamaica Plain. Enerio Barros and Orlando Antigua guided me through much of this project. Numerous Dominicans opened their homes and hearts to me and inspired me with their generosity and goodness, including Ramona, Chita, Silsia, Mindris, Ping, and Freddy Peña-Medina; Onilio Sánchez and his family; Juan Cabral; Sócrates Tejeda; Milciades Tejeda; Nelson Brea; Marina Soto; Leonelo Cabral; Hector Cabral; La Rubia and Mercedes Nova and their family; Moreno Tejeda; Juan Castillo; Wilton Guerrero; Carlos Betancourt; and Milton Castillo.

My deepest gratitude is reserved for my husband, Robert Levers; our children, Dylan and Wesley; and my parents, Fred and Claire Levitt, whose love, confidence, and understanding have never failed me. I could never have done this without them.

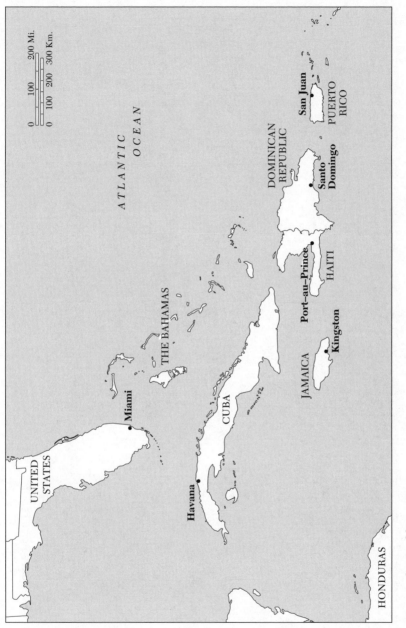

Map 1. The Caribbean

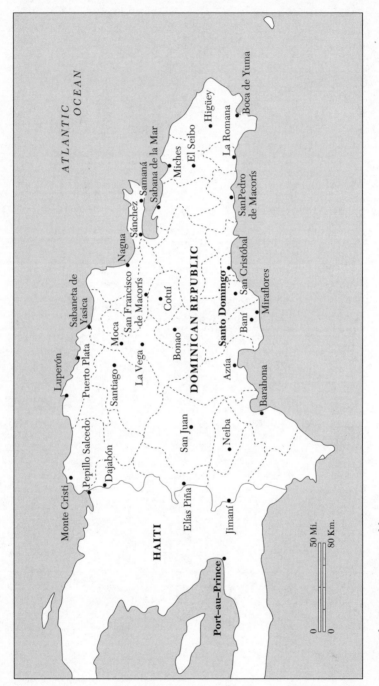

Map 2. The Dominican Republic

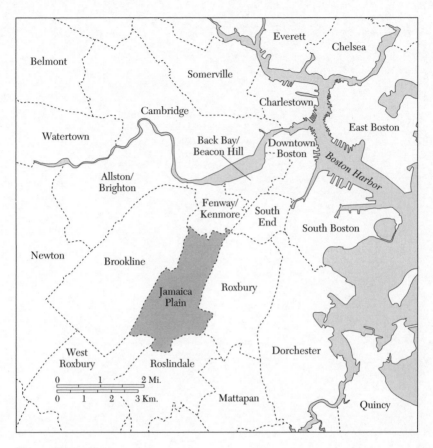

Map 3. Boston Area

Introduction

The top part of the avenue leading from the Dominican city of Baní to the village of Miraflores is bordered by thick, leafy mimosa trees. Throughout the year, they are covered by orange blossoms and blanket the street with a delicious shade. On the way out of town, the sidewalks are busy with women shopping and children returning home from school. The streets grow quiet as the beauty parlors, small grocery stores (*colmados*), and lawyers' offices closest to the town square gradually give way to residential neighborhoods. On one corner is Mayor Carlos Peña's feed store, where he and his coworkers from the Partido Revolucionario Dominicano (PRD)[1] meet to talk about politics every late afternoon. Farther down the street, members of the Partido Reformista Social Cristiano (PRSC)[2] also sit in front of their party's headquarters, drinking sweet cups of coffee and discussing the current election campaign. At the edge of town, the buildings end abruptly in overgrown fields. The avenue goes silent except for a lone motorcycle driver. The countryside is overwhelmingly beautiful.

A few hundred yards ahead, two sights unexpectedly interrupt this peaceful landscape. On the right side of the road, four partially complete mansions stand behind large iron gates. Their crumbling marble pillars and large cracked windows, so out of character with the rest of the scene, mock onlookers from the street. A little farther down the avenue, at the edge of a large, uncultivated field, a billboard proclaims, "Viaje a Boston con Sierra Travel"—Travel to Boston with Sierra Travel. Telephone numbers in Boston and Baní, coincidentally beginning with the same exchange, are hidden by grasses so tall they almost cover the sign completely.

A small restaurant, its rusting metal chairs and tables glinting brightly in the sun, announces the entrance to Miraflores. Turning off the road into this village of close to four thousand residents reveals further discontinuities. While some of the homes resemble miniature, finished versions of the empty mansions along the avenue, one out of five families still lives in a small, two-room wooden house. Four in ten use outdoor privies. Though the electricity goes off nightly for weeks at a stretch, nearly every household has a television, VCR, or compact-disc player. And although it takes months to get a phone installed in Santo Domingo, the Dominican capital, Mirafloreños can get phone service in their homes almost immediately after they request it.

What explains these sharp contrasts? Who is responsible for these half-finished homes that differ so completely in style and scale from the other houses in the area? Who is the audience for the billboards in the middle of fields that advertise international plane flights? How is it that people who must collect rainwater in barrels so they can wash when the water supply goes off are watching the latest videos in the comfort of their living rooms?

Transnational migration is at the root of these contradictions. The billboard speaks to the nearly two-thirds of Mirafloreño families who have relatives in the greater Boston metropolitan area. These migrants pay for the home improvements and buy the appliances. They create such a lucrative market for long-distance phone service that CODETEL (the Dominican phone company) installs phone lines in Miraflores almost immediately after they are requested. And some built the dream palaces on the avenue, which they completed only halfway before their money dried up.

Mirafloreños began migrating to Boston, Massachusetts, in the late 1960s. Most settled in and around Jamaica Plain, traditionally a white-ethnic neighborhood until Latinos and young white professionals replaced those who began leaving the city in the 1960s. Over the years, migrants from the Dominican Republic and the friends and family they left behind have sustained such strong, frequent contacts with one another it is as if village life takes place in two settings. Fashion, food, and forms of speech, as well as appliances and home decorating styles, attest to these strong connections. In Miraflores, villagers often dress in T-shirts emblazoned with the names of businesses in Massachusetts, although they do not know what these words or logos mean. They proudly serve their visitors coffee with Cremora and juice made from Tang. The local *colmados* stock SpaghettiOs and Frosted Flakes.

Many of the benches in the Miraflores park are inscribed with the names of villagers who moved to Boston years ago. And almost everyone, including older community members who can count on their fingers how many times they have visited Santo Domingo, can talk about "La Mozart" or "La Centre"—Mozart Street Park and Centre Street, two focal points of the Dominican community in Jamaica Plain.

In Boston, Mirafloreños have re-created their premigration lives to the extent that their new physical and cultural environment allows. Particularly during the early years of settlement, but even today, a large number of migrants lived within the same twenty-block radius. There are several streets where people from Miraflores live in almost every triple-decker house.[3] Community members leave their apartment doors open so that the flow between households is as easy and uninhibited as it is in Miraflores. They decorate their refrigerators with the same plastic fruit magnets they used in Miraflores, and they put the same sets of ceramic animal families on the shelves of their living rooms. Women continue to hang curtains around the door frames; these provide privacy without keeping in the heat in the Dominican Republic but are merely decorative in Boston. Because someone is always traveling between Boston and the island, there is a continuous, circular flow of goods, news, and information. As a result, when someone is ill, cheating on his or her spouse, or finally granted a visa, the news spreads as quickly in Jamaica Plain as it does on the streets of Miraflores.

Many Americans expect migrants like Mirafloreños to sever their ties to their homeland as they become assimilated into the United States. They assume that migrants will eventually transfer their loyalty and community membership from the countries they leave behind to the ones that receive them. But increasing numbers of migrants continue to participate in the political and economic lives of their homelands, even as they are incorporated into their host societies. Instead of loosening their connections and trading one membership for another, some individuals are keeping their feet in both worlds. They use political, religious, and civic arenas to forge social relations, earn their livelihoods, and exercise their rights across borders.

The proliferation of these long-term transnational ties challenges conventional notions about the assimilation of immigrants into host countries and about migration's impact on sending-country life. But how do ordinary people actually manage to stay connected to two places? Who participates, where, and with what consequences? Under what circumstances is this a recipe for long-term social and political marginalization, or can participation in two polities result in a case of "two for the price of one"?

This book is about everyday life in a transnational village. It is about how ordinary people are incorporated into the countries that receive them while remaining active in the places they come from, and about how life in sending and receiving countries changes as a result. It explores the costs and benefits of transnational practices by detailing who engages in them, who the winners and losers are, and why. The book also examines how economic and political globalization shapes local-level dynamics, showing how transnational ties at the village level create—and are created by—ties at the municipal and national levels of each country. Local-level transnational activities are also reinforced by the growing numbers of global economic and governance structures that make decision-making and problem-solving across borders increasingly common. Consequently, in this era of heightened globalization, transnational lifestyles may become not the exception but the rule.

How Do Transnational Lives Actually Work?

The United States at the turn of the twenty-first century is much more tolerant of ethnic diversity than it was at the beginning of the twentieth century. We acknowledge that there is no monolithic "American" culture that immigrants assimilate into. Migrants adopt some values and practices but not others, and they do so at different rates.[4] They gain access to some social and economic institutions and are blocked from integrating into others. They may exhibit structural assimilation without cultural or residential assimilation, or they may assimilate into different segments of U.S. society.[5] They often use their identities symbolically or instrumentally, tailoring them to fit particular settings.[6] Nevertheless, many Americans continue to view assimilation as incompatible with transnational participation. We expect newcomers to renounce their membership in their home countries in exchange for full social and political membership in the United States.

Parallel changes have also occurred in conceptions of political integration. Marshall (1950) and Evans (1988) distinguished between civil, political, and social citizenship. They argued that not all people achieve these memberships simultaneously and that they could assert or be allowed to assert one form without the others. They also assumed, however, that migrants would not continue to participate in their countries of origin; where one resided ultimately determined where one belonged.

More recent work calls into question the meaning of citizenship and its relevance for social and political participation. Yuval-Davis (1997) views citizenship as a multitiered construct that categorizes people's memberships in a variety of local, ethnic, national, and transnational communities. Individuals' rights and obligations to specific states are mediated by and dependent upon—but rarely completely contained by—their membership in specific ethnic, racial, or religious groups. Baubock (1994) and Soysal (1994) propose the notion of postnational membership. They argue that international legal regimes and discourses now guarantee certain human rights within a globally accepted framework regardless of citizenship. They suggest that new forms of participation and representation are emerging that do not require citizenship and that newly emerging supranational institutions guarantee a set of basic rights, thereby superseding the nation-state.

In this book, I argue that the case of Miraflores, and others like it, suggests yet another kind of experience. Here migrants' social and economic lives are not bounded by national borders (Pessar 1999). They do not shift their loyalties and participatory energies from one country to another. Instead, they are integrated, to varying degrees, into the countries that receive them, at the same time that they remain connected to the countries they leave behind. Citizenship is only one of several bases upon which individuals form their identities or exercise their rights. New forms of representation and participation are emerging that do not require full membership or residence. In contrast to a postnational view, however, the state is not superfluous. Rather than disappearing or being subordinated to international regimes, states play a major role, along with other civic, religious, and political institutions, in creating and reinforcing lasting transnational involvements. From this perspective, transnational practices are not just another way station along the path to assimilation. Rather, assimilation and transnational practices are not incompatible. Many first- and possibly second-generation immigrants will continue to be active in their countries of origin from their firm base in the United States.

Scholars from a variety of disciplines use the term *transnational-ism* to describe this contemporary complex of migratory activities.[7] But this term has been used to delineate such a wide variety of connections at so many different levels of social interaction that it risks losing much of its analytical power. Several scholars have made important strides toward clarifying what is meant by transnationalism with respect to migration. Basch, Glick Schiller, and Szanton Blanc define it as the "processes by which immigrants forge and sustain multistranded social relations that link together their societies of origin and settlement" (1994, 6). Guarnizo argues that it is a "series of economic, sociocultural, and political practical and discursive relations that transcend the territorially bound jurisdiction of the nation-state" (1997, 9). He and his colleague M. P. Smith (1998) juxtapose "transnationalism from below," or the everyday, grounded practices of individuals and groups, with "transnationalism from above," or global governance and economic activities. Portes et al. (1999) use *transnationalism* to describe those economic, political, and sociocultural occupations and activities that require regular, long-term contacts across borders for their success. They propose the individual is the appropriate unit of analysis for assessing the extent to which transnationalism occurs. Finally, some scholars suggest using the term *transmigrant* to describe those individuals who engage regularly in cross-border activities (England 1999; Glick Schiller 1995; Guarnizo 1997).

Many questions remain unanswered. Are transnational practices primarily economic, or are other aspects of life also enacted across borders? How does their impact vary by type and level of social activity? Are transnational migrants only those who regularly engage in cross-border activities, or do those who remain behind also become embedded in the transnational social fields created by migration? What forms do different transnational communities assume? And, finally, what are the consequences of these arrangements for sending and receiving country life?

To answer these questions, this book focuses on the transnational practices that individual migrants and nonmigrants engage in and on the transnational social groups and arenas within which they carry these out. To do this, I insert the intermediary level of community between what M. P. Smith and Guarnizo call "transnationalism from above and below" and what Portes et al. call "high" and "low" levels of institutionalized transnationalism. The kinds of transnational practices migrants and nonmigrants engage in, and the impact of these activities, are a function of the kinds of organized social groups within which they are carried out. Individual actors cannot be viewed in isolation from the transnational social fields in which they are embedded. The economic initiatives, political activities, and sociocultural enterprises they engage in are powerfully shaped by the social fields in which they occur.

Adding community to the analysis helps clarify several things. First, communities are one of several mechanisms mediating between "high" and "low" levels of transnationalism. When individual actors identify and organize themselves as transnational communities, the state or international religious groups from "above" are most likely to respond. When national political and economic actors reach out to local communities on both sides of the border, they encourage individual members to maintain dual loyalties.

Second, the communities and organizations that emerge from transnational migration offer migrants a variety of ways in which to distribute their energies and loyalties between their sending and receiving countries. When transnational communities establish many diverse organizations across borders, membership in both places is easier than when there are fewer, more narrowly focused organizational arenas. Third, a focus on community provides a constant reminder that the impact of transnational migration extends far beyond the migrant to the individuals and collectivities that remain behind.

A combination of political, economic, and social factors stimulates transnational migration. Many contemporary transnational actors are former subjects who settled in the nations that colonized them. Political and economic relations established under formal or unofficial colonial rule, as in the case of the United States and the Caribbean, for example, stimulated labor migration and the emergence of transnational ties. Other transnational migrants are refugees and former Warsaw Pact residents who migrated in response to the political aftermath of the Cold War. A third set of transnational migrants are the exiles, ethnic outsiders, and other stigmatized communities who have been cast out by nationalistic and repressive states (Gold 2000). Members of this last group, in particular, are often keenly interested in remaining active in their homelands because they want to bring about regime change.

The globalization of production and consumption, or the height-

ened mobility of people, goods, ideas, and capital, also creates transnational communities and generates a demand for the skills and out-
looks these communities offer. Global markets create a permanent
demand for highly skilled technical and professional workers and for
unskilled laborers willing to work for low wages with little job stability
(Massey et al. 1993; Piore 1979). Uneven development and the industrialization of traditional economic sectors in sending countries create
large, mobile pools of underemployed labor. The countries sending
the greatest numbers to the United States tend to be those with the
longest history of economic, military, and political ties to this country
(Rumbaut 1996).

Once begun, migration spreads through social networks. Social networks are the sets of cross-border interpersonal ties connecting migrants, return migrants, and nonmigrants through kinship, friendship,
and attachment to a shared place of origin. Once a network is in place,
it becomes more likely that additional migration will occur. The risks
and costs of movement for subsequent migrants are lower because
there is a group of "experts" already in the receiving country to greet
newcomers and serve as their guides. Because these well-established
migrants help new arrivals find jobs and housing, they also increase
migration's economic returns (Massey et al. 1993).

These social networks do not develop further among some immigrant groups. They do not deepen, grow more extensive, or become
more institutionalized. Over time, they may even begin to unravel as
migrants transfer their economic and political loyalties to the countries that receive them or as they become less beholden to claims from
those who stay behind. Transnational social networks also weaken
when there are no new arrivals reinforcing them.

In other cases, continued contacts and social network development
between migrants and nonmigrants create a transnational social field
or public sphere between the sending and receiving country (Mahler
1998; Fraser 1991).[8] The many social connections and organizations
that tie these individuals to one another create a border-spanning arena
that enables migrants, if they so choose, to remain active in both worlds.
This arena has multiple levels. A political party, for example, links nonmigrants and migrants through their membership in local sending and
receiving country chapters. These local, personalized ties often form
part of the party's national-level operations as well. In an increasing

number of cases, the state also plays an active role in creating and sustaining this transnational social space.

The transnational social fields that migration engenders encompass all aspects of social life. Though they generally emerge from economic relations between migrants and nonmigrants, social, religious, and political connections also constitute these arenas. The more diverse and thick a transnational social field is, the more numerous the ways it offers migrants to remain active in their homelands. The more institutionalized these relationships become, the more likely it is that transnational membership will persist.

Many migrants and nonmigrants described in prior research engage in some kind of transnational activities, but not all are embedded in transnational social fields, nor do all belong to transnational communities. A distinction must be made among individuals who travel regularly to conduct their routine economic and political affairs; those whose lives are primarily rooted in a single setting, though much of what they do involves resources, contacts, and people in the places that they come from; and those who do not move but who live their lives within a context that has become transnationalized.[9] The entrepreneurs who travel regularly to get the money, information, and supplies they need to conduct their business on both sides of the border are transnational migrants (Portes and Guarnizo 1991; Smart and Smart 1998). The political party official whose job it is to coordinate activities between the United States and the home country also falls into this category. The parent who leaves a child behind to be raised by a grandparent and the leader of an immigrant religious group who travels periodically to his homeland to consult with superiors are individuals who are based physically in their host countries but who engage in numerous activities and social relationships spanning borders. Many of their social ties and practices are transnational, though they themselves may only travel once or twice a year. Likewise, the individual who never migrated, but who is completely dependent on the economic remittances she receives each month and who lives in a sociocultural context completely transformed by migration, also inhabits a transnational social field. To understand the relationship between transnational migration and development, we must assess the impact of transnational practices on all those embedded in these transnational spaces.

Some scholars describe social fields spanning entire sending countries and embracing all migrants living in an important place of reception. Glick Schiller and Fouron (1998), for example, argue that Haitian young adults, who have never migrated, live their lives within a social field connecting the United States and Haiti because so many aspects of their lives are permeated by Haitian immigrant influences. Transnational social fields, however, are multilayered composites, with numerous sending-receiving country ties at each level. Though there may be large, overarching fields between the United States and Mexico, the Dominican Republic, and El Salvador, for example, these encompass smaller fields between particular sending and receiving villages and cities. Brazilian migrations to the United States have created transnational social fields between nonmigrants in the city of Governador Valadares and migrants in New York City; Pompano Beach, Florida; Danbury, Connecticut; and the greater Boston metropolitan area (Margolis 1994). Transnational social fields also unite Dominicans in Venezuela and Spain and those who stay behind.

In many cases, numerous individuals embedded within transnational social fields engage in high levels of transnational practices, but few communal activities emerge. Colombian migrants in New York have created a complex web of multidirectional relationships, but their mistrust and fragmentation impede community organization (Guarnizo et al. 1999). Often, however, certain sites within transnational social fields become sufficiently organized and institutionalized to give rise to some kind of transnational community. In such cases, it is not merely that numerous individuals live their lives within a social formation that crosses borders; it is that a significant number from a given place of origin and settlement share this experience collectively with one another, transforming the way they think of themselves as a group.

Since transnational communities emerge from the social networks that first encourage migration, members tend to know one another personally or have family members or acquaintances in common, at least initially. They acknowledge that they belong to a collectivity constituted across space and express some level of self-consciousness about this membership by forming groups like hometown organizations that manifest their transnational character. In the receiving country and at home, their social lives continue to be so entwined with one another's that those who do not send money to their families or do not "do right" by the community feel the consequences. Transnational communities are generally small and personalized enough that values like bounded solidarity and enforceable trust still work (Portes 1995). Furthermore, many migrants still use their sending community as the reference group against which they gauge their status. One of the reasons so many Mexicans, Dominicans, and Central Americans contribute to development projects or help organize and participate in beauty pageants and patron-saint celebrations in their communities of origin is to affirm their continued membership in these transnational groups and to demonstrate their enhanced position within them (Goldring 1998; Smith 1995; Berry 1985). These organizations stimulate and are stimulated by the institutionalization of transnational practices at other levels of the transnational social field.

Miraflores is just one type of transnational community, which I call a transnational village.[10] Transnational villages have several unique characteristics. First, actual migration is not required to be a member. Migrants' continued participation in their home communities transforms the sending-community context to such an extent that nonmigrants also adapt many of the values and practices of their migrant counterparts, engage in social relationships that span two settings, and participate in organizations that act across borders. This is not to say that those who migrate and those who remain behind live in an imagined, third, transnational space. Instead, they are all firmly rooted in a particular place and time, though their daily lives often depend upon people, money, ideas, and resources located in another setting.

A second characteristic of transnational villages is that they emerge and endure partially because of social remittances (Levitt 1999). Social remittances are the ideas, behaviors, and social capital that flow from receiving to sending communities. They are the tools with which ordinary individuals create global culture at the local level. They help individuals embedded in a particular context and accustomed to a particular set of identities and practices to imagine a new cartography (Appadurai 1990), encouraging them to try on new gender roles, experiment with new ideas about politics, and adopt new organizing strategies. Once this process has begun, daily life in the village is changed to such an extent, and migrants and nonmigrants often become so dependent on one another, that transnational villages are likely to endure.

A third feature distinguishing transnational villages is that they create and are created by organizations that themselves come to act across borders. These political, religious, and civic organizations arise or are reorganized to meet the needs of their newly transnational members, enabling migrants to continue to participate in both settings and encouraging community perpetuation. This also means that migrants have multiple channels through which to pursue transnational belonging. Dual citizenship is just one way to be a transnational actor. Religious, civic, and political groups allow migrants to express and act upon dual allegiances.

Migrants organize groups across borders in several ways. They may establish hometown associations, like the Miraflores Development Committee, with chapters in the sending community and in the areas where migrant residents cluster. They may form receiving-country divisions of national political parties. Or, as in the case of the Catholic Church, they may extend an already established international institution to incorporate new connections resulting from relations between migrants and nonmigrants.

Groups that are organized and act across borders do not always aim to produce transnational effects, nor do they always succeed when they set out to do so. Though resources, money, or ideas from both sides of the border are harnessed to achieve transnational goals, the impact of these efforts may be felt primarily in either the sending or the receiving country. In this study, Mirafloreños participated in three types of transnational organizations: a political organization that acted transnationally but did not achieve its transnational goals, a religious organization that acted and accomplished its goals transnationally, and a community development organization that acted transnationally to benefit one direction only.

A fourth feature characterizing transnational villages is that they are studies in contrast. Material well-being increases at a high social cost. Some community members used the social and economic resources available to them across borders to their advantage, while others returned to Miraflores not much better off than when they first set out. Class, gender, and generational divisions sharpened at the same time that community members' reliance on and commitment to one another increased. Transnational villages endure because they are constituted flexibly enough to be able to tolerate heightened power and status differences and the increased economic and emotional attachments that accompany them.

Other types of transnational communities arise between sending and receiving countries. Looser, more flexibly defined place-based communities form when migrants leave one urban area for another, though norms of bounded solidarity and enforceable trust still hold sway. Because cities encompass greater numbers, whose social ties to one another are weaker, not all potential members chose to belong (Levitt 2000; Roberts et al. 1999). Migration from the city of Governador Valadares in Brazil to the greater Boston Metropolitan area is a case in point. Elite community members who articulated a vision of transnational community, and tried to organize around it, received only minimal support from ordinary community members (Levitt 2000).

Other communities grow initially out of members' shared attachments to a particular place but then mature into groups based more on the identities, occupations, or values that people from a particular region share with one another. Members of the Patidar community in Massachusetts have ties back to Gujarat State in India where their families orginally came from. But because this group has such a long history of migration to East Africa and England, their sense of community grows less out of their common roots than on the norms and values they have in common. Similar transnational communities have formed between Mixtec Indians in Mexico and Northern California, who also share geography but organize themselves around their mutual ethnic identities and experience of oppression (Rivera-Salgado 1999). Turkish immigrants throughout Europe have created transnational groups to press for greater religious freedom (Kastoryano 1994). These individuals come from multiple sending areas but, again, their shared norms provide the basis for transnational community formation.

By using the term *community,* I do not wish to imply that all members feel a sense of affinity or solidarity toward one another. The divisiveness and hierarchical nature of all social groups also characterizes transnational communities. The costs and rewards of transnational community membership are not more equitably distributed than they are in communities rooted in one place. Long-standing patterns of privilege and access do not disappear merely because they are re-created across borders. In fact, though some predict that transnational migration allows its participants to rebel against global capital and the nation-state (Kearney 1991) or elude essentializing national identities (Bhabha 1990), this has not been the case for most Mirafloreños. In this community, transnational migration re-creates patterns of gender and class inequality and creates new frictions between parents and children, men and women, and poorer and more advantaged community members at the same time that it opens up opportunities for others.

A distinction must be made between transnational communities, the less organized social fields within which they are embedded, and the overall context of economic and cultural globalization that produces these different social forms. Migration-driven transnational activities at all levels are different from those arising from globalization, though economic and political globalization often precipitate migration flows. Globalization refers to the political, economic, and social activities that have become interregional or intercontinental and to the intensification of levels of interaction and interconnectedness within and between states and societies (Held 1999). Global processes tend to be de-linked from specific national territories, while transnational processes are anchored in and transcend one or more nation-states (Kearney 1995).

Globalization also transforms relationships at the local level, but these changes differ from those transnational migration brings about. The Mirafloreña woman who tries to establish a more equitable relationship with her husband does so not only because Dominican women in general are gaining more independence, but because she is inspired by the kind of marriage her migrant sister has with her husband. In such cases, transnational migration and globalization are both changing gender relations. The impact of transnational migration differs from, but must be understood within the context of, the heightened globalization in which it is embedded. Changes prompted by migration and globalization mutually reinforce one another.

Finally, I want to locate transnational communities with respect to the term *diaspora*, which has also been used to describe a range of contemporary migration experiences. Diaspora traditionally referred to groups who were forcibly expelled from their homelands and who remained socially marginal in the societies that received them as they waited to return. The classic examples of this were the Jews, Greeks, and the Armenians. Of late, researchers have begun using this term more broadly, defining those "dwelling in the diaspora" as individuals who have been exiled or displaced to a number of different nation-states by a variety of economic, political, and social forces (Tölölyan 1998). Laguerre describes these individuals as residing "outside the formal boundaries of their states of origin but inside the reterritorialized space of the dispersed nation" (1998, 8). Cohen suggests different types of diasporas, distinguishing among those who are victimized, form part of imperialistic projects, seek to trade or labor, or "form part of a cultural diaspora, cemented as much by literature, political ideas, religious convictions, music and lifestyles as by permanent migration" (1997, xii).

Transnational communities are the building blocks of diasporas that may or may not take shape. Diasporas form out of transnational communities spanning sending and receiving countries and out of the real or imagined connections among migrants from a particular homeland who are scattered throughout the world. If a fiction of congregation takes hold, then a diaspora emerges. Dominicans who identify themselves as belonging to a diaspora might be transnational community members or isolated individuals who, wherever they are, share a sense of common belonging to a homeland where they are not. Similarly, the Garifuna diaspora consists of transnational communities connecting New York and Honduras, or Belize and Los Angeles, and the many individual Garifuna migrants who live throughout the world (England 1999; Matthei and Smith 1998).

Miraflores Is Not Unique

Studies of transnational migration evoke passionate responses. Some argue that Miraflores and villages like it are isolated examples that do not represent the experiences of other groups. Most immigrants, they say, will not stay as connected to their homelands as those from Mexico, the Caribbean, or Latin America. These migrants continue to participate actively in their homelands because their countries of origin are close to the United States and have long been dominated by U.S. political and economic interests (Jones-Correa 1999b; Suárez-Orozco 1998; Waldinger 1997).

Clearly, the strength of the relationship between Mirafloreños on the island and those in Boston is, in part, a function of certain special characteristics of the Dominican–United States connection. The Dominican Republic is a mere 1,200 miles from Miami and even closer to Puerto Rico. It takes only five and one-half hours to travel from Boston to Santo Domingo. During the off-season, plane tickets can cost as little as $500. The national pastime in the Dominican Republic is baseball, unlike most of Latin America, where it is soccer. Is it any wonder that such strong, durable connections would emerge?

Despite these particularities the Miraflores case is not unique. Instead, it reflects a growing tendency among people from a number of countries to maintain strong ties to one another. Several trends suggest that migration from countries other than the Dominican Republic produces similar attachments. Table 1 (Appendix A) estimates the proportion of the sending-country population from certain Latin American and Caribbean countries living in the United States. These figures are low because they do not include migrants who are in the country illegally. In 1990, Dominican immigrants represented almost 9 percent of the entire Dominican population.[11] These figures were matched by Mexicans (9.4%) and surpassed by Salvadorans (16.8%). The numbers of immigrants from parts of the English-speaking Caribbean, such as Jamaica (23%) and Trinidad and Tobago (16%), also exceeded double digits. Long-term transnational ties are more likely to occur, and to be encouraged by sending states, when such large numbers migrate. They are also easier to sustain when large concentrations of migrants from one sending-country city or region live near one another in the receiving country.

Villages from Mexico, El Salvador, and Jamaica, to name a few, also send large percentages of their populations to the United States. Like Mirafloreños, these individuals tend to settle close to one another and to maintain strong ties to their communities of origin.[12] In some cities in California, links to particular towns and villages in Mexico can be traced back to the Bracero Program (1942–64) and extend over generations (Massey et al. 1987). The population of Chinantlá, Mexico, is equally divided between Mexico and New York, though community members still consider themselves part of the same community (Sontag 1998). Twenty percent of the small Salvadoran town of Intipucá was living in the Adams-Morgan section of Washington, D.C., in 1985 (Schoultz 1992). These individuals often contribute large sums of money toward development projects, invest in small businesses, and sway political outcomes in their home countries. Mexican migrants from the village of Ticuani who live in Brooklyn, New York, for example, not only funded a potable water project but flew back to Mexico for the weekend to confer with contractors and authorities during its construction (Smith 1995).

Migrants and nonmigrants from other parts of the world also form transnational social groups. The social and political context of the new European Union is particularly favorable to long-term home- and host-country attachments. The E.U. has granted new rights to non-residents, is generally more tolerant of ethnic diversity than some of its individual member countries, and offers incentives to those who organize themselves transnationally (Favell 1998; Faist 1997). Entrepreneurs and elites have been quick to capitalize on this because their continued success depends upon their ability to shift toward transnational governance and organization and away from national and state institutions. But there is also evidence of transnational participation among ordinary individuals. Sonja Haug (1998), for example, found Italians living in Germany for three generations who continued to return to Italy to find marriage partners, to send their children back to be educated, and to go "home" after they retired. Turkish Muslims throughout Europe are mobilizing across borders to protect their religious freedom and to advocate for change in their homelands (Amiraux 1998). There is also some evidence of transnational group formation among migrants and nonmigrants living in areas that are geographically and culturally farther apart. Bangladeshi migrants from the Chittagong District who have settled in the Central Square area of Cambridge, Massachusetts, continue to send remittances and support development projects in their sending communities.

Migrants' attitudes and practices are not the only factors that determine the strength of the transnational group connecting them to those who remain behind. Strong ties also develop because the lives of so many nonmigrants are also touched by migration. Here again, the numbers are striking. Phillips and Massey (1998) found that more than 40 percent of all household heads and 20 percent of all persons in western Mexico had been to the United States at least once in their lives. All told, 73 percent of household heads from that region had social ties to someone living north of the border and 81 percent knew at least someone who had lived in the United States. Similarly, despite more than thirty years of restricted contact, high levels of social connectedness are said to link Cubans on the island with those in the United States. Rumbaut (1997) estimated that at least a third of Cuba's 11 million residents have relatives in the United States and Puerto Rico. A culture of migration and a reliance on its rewards are more likely to arise when so many of those who remain are influenced by migration. These, in turn, encourage stronger, long-term transnational attachments.

Another critique raised about transnational migration is that these ties will not last. They will either wane as the first generation spends more years in the countries that receive them, or they will be of little consequence to immigrants' children. Several factors, however, reinforce first-generation migrants' continued attachments to their sending communities. The first is that many migrants today play a critical role in their sending countries' economies. Sending states need the large sums of money that migrants send home. In 1995, remittances to Mexico totaled $3.7 billion. Salvadoran migrants sent home $1.1 billion. Dominican reliance on remittances is particularly strong. According to the country's Central Bank, in 1999 Dominicans living abroad sent home $1.4 billion (Rodriguez 1999). As a result, an increasing number of sending states are making concerted efforts to reach out to their expatriates to ensure their continued contributions.

A second factor suggesting that dual memberships are likely to continue is that unlike migration to the United States at the beginning of the twentieth century, which was followed by a forty-year period of highly restricted entry, present-day migration is likely to remain strong. The conditions that precipitate migration, such as wage differentials, labor market segmentation, and the globalization of the economy, are unlikely to disappear soon (Massey et al. 1993). After the U.S. government enacted severely restrictive immigration laws in the 1920s, the number of new migrants introduced into the ethnic mix declined sharply, "ensuring that whatever ethnic identities existed would be predominantly a consequence of events and processes operating in the United States" (Massey 1995, 642). The experiences of the second, third, and fourth generations in the United States shaped the meaning of ethnicity because few new immigrants arrived who introduced updated models of home-country life to challenge those already in place. Because entry today for migrants is much less restrictive, and migration has continued unabated since the 1960s, homeland elements are continuously infused into the receiving-country context.[13] According to Massey, "New arrivals will tend to exceed the rate at which new ethnic culture is created through generational success, social mobility, and intermarriage. The character of ethnicity will be determined relatively more by immigrants and relatively less by later generations, shifting the balance of ethnic identity toward the language, culture, and ways of life in the sending society" (Massey et al. 1995, 645). While for some, this suggests that ethnic attachments will persist beyond the third generation (Alba and Nee 1997), it could also signal an ability and willingness among particular groups to sustain various types of multigenerational transnational involvements.

The third factor encouraging durable ties is the growing number of countries that officially sanction some form of dual membership. States do this because they need the economic remittances and political influence that migrants offer. In 1996 the Dominican House of Deputies passed legislation allowing dual citizenship. The government also granted citizenship to children born abroad to Dominican parents. In 1997 the Dominican Senate approved an electoral reform package allowing migrants the right to vote and to run for office, including individuals who are naturalized American citizens of Dominican descent (Sontag 1997).[14] There is currently a proposal being considered in the Dominican Congress to create a legislative seat that would represent migrants. By putting these policies in place, Dominican leaders created an official, institutionalized way to sustain dual involvements and extended those to the second generation.

Here again, the Dominican state is not alone. Mexico, Colombia, Brazil, Ecuador, and Portugal, to name a few, have all amended their constitutions to include migrants as official members of their political communities, though each country grants them different political rights. Since 1998 Mexicans have had the right to hold Mexican nationality as well as U.S. citizenship. Dual nationals cannot vote in Mexican elections or hold high office, though these restrictions may be repealed. In Trinidad and Tobago dual nationals can vote only if they have lived in-country for a year prior to elections, whereas migrant Colombians and Brazilians can vote at polling sites set up by their consulates. Colombians living abroad have their own special elected "expatriate" representatives in the Colombian legislature, but they can also run for regular office (Sanchez 1997). If Jesús Galvis, a travel agent in New Jersey who ran for a Colombian Senate seat in 1997, had been elected, he planned to hold office simultaneously in Bogotá and in Hackensack, where he is a city councillor (Sontag and Dugger 1998).

Finally, migrants remain active in their homelands because they are unable to achieve full social membership in the United States. Because increasing numbers of contemporary migrants are people of color, they often experience blocked mobility, racism, and discrimination. They are not allowed to become completely "American" even if they want to. In some cases, transnational practices grant migrants access to valuable resources that enable them to circumvent these barriers. The money, training, and labor power they harness across borders allow them to achieve economic gains they would not be able to achieve otherwise. Transnational practices also enable migrants to recoup their sense of purpose and self-worth. Though they may feel isolated and unwelcome as immigrants, they are still treated as respected and valued members of their sending communities, a fact that also encourages their continued membership.

Some dissenters acknowledge that while the first generation remains strongly connected to its homeland, the second generation will not sustain these ties. Several recent studies support this view. Rumbaut (1998) and Waters et al. (1998) found that the second-generation individuals they surveyed were well integrated into U.S. economic and social life, though they had achieved varying degrees of success. Their respondents expressed little connectedness to their ancestral homes. Though they enjoyed visiting and continued to uphold many of the traditions and values that were passed on to them, they had no plans to return to their homelands to live. They also exhibited high levels of language and socioeconomic assimilation. Most preferred English and spoke it better than their ancestral tongue.

Other studies, however, suggest that for some children of immigrants the picture is more complex than it first seems. Such high benchmarks as wanting to repatriate or achieve language fluency miss the many ways in which some individuals engage in transnational practices.[15] These vary according to the characteristics of the transnational social field in which individual actors are embedded and its level of institutional completeness. Children born to parents who are members of tight-knit transnational villages or who participate in transnational organizations that keep them firmly connected to their ancestral homelands are more likely to remain active in the countries their parents come from (Levitt 1998b; Smith 1998b; Glick Schiller and Fouron 1998). People of color also seem more likely to engage in transnational practices. They do so to circumvent the social and occupational "glass ceilings" they experience and because they view their homeland ties as potential economic or social tools (Kibria 1998; Louie 1998; Portes 1999). Finally, transnational activities seem to ebb and flow at different stages of individuals' life cycles. Though Irish American young adults engaged in few transnational practices, their middle-aged counterparts forged more ties with Ireland, because the diminishing demands of their careers and families made it easier for them to do so (Levitt and Collins 2000). Since so many children spend their preschool years, summers, and even parts of their adolescence in their parents' homelands, the customs, values, and traditions of these countries become ingrained in their everyday vocabulary and can be activated or deactivated at different stages of the life cycle, as is most expedient.

Is Keeping Feet in Both Worlds New?

Living transnationally is not new. Migrants in the past also participated actively in the economic, political, and social lives of their sending states.[16] They returned to their homelands to visit and many actually went back to live. Between 1910 and 1920, for every 100 immigrants who entered the United States, a little more than one-third returned (Foner 2000). Between 1880 to 1930, an estimated one-quarter to one-third of all immigrants to America repatriated (Wyman 1993). Even an estimated 15 to 20 percent of Russian Jews, one of the groups most likely to settle permanently because so many came to escape persecution, were said to have returned to Russia between 1880 and 1890. Many individuals also circulated between their home and host countries, working seasonal jobs during the warmer months and returning to Europe during winter layoffs. The majority of Slavic and Italian migrants, for example, meant for their journeys to be temporary. An estimated 30 to 40 percent went back to live, and between 15 to 30 percent made frequent visits back to their countries of origin (Morawska 2001a).

Migrants also sent back significant remittances to their sending communities. They saved money to buy land, build homes, or support family members who remained behind. Hometown clubs funded improvement projects, provided famine relief, and aided communities that were ravaged by war. In the Italian case, remittances reached such high levels between 1900 and 1910 that the secretary of the Society for the Protection of Italian Immigrants claimed that Italians in New York contributed more to the tax rolls in Italy than some of the poor provinces of Sicily and Calabria (Foner 2000).

Many of the sentiments that motivated migrants' prolonged home-country attachments still motivate them today. Migrants felt deep loyalty to their countries of origin. They wanted to hedge their bets by remaining economically active in both societies. Since they hoped to remain in the United States only temporarily, they knew that their successful return depended on their continued integration into the social networks of their home villages and towns (Morawska 2001b). Some countries, like Italy, also recognized that migrants were an important social and economic resource (Foner 2000; Glick Schiller 1999). By 1925 the Italian government subsidized twenty-seven organizations based abroad to help immigrants; it worked particularly hard to prevent the mistreatment of Italian workers. It also passed a requirement that a certain number of free passages be allocated on all steamships serving Italian ports so that poor emigrants wishing to return home could do so (Wyman 1993).

Despite these similarities between contemporary and earlier migration experiences, there are also significant differences. First, in several instances, the proportion of the sending-country population that currently migrates far exceeds the numbers that migrated in the past. Table 2 (see Appendix A) offers comparative estimates for several of the most important immigrant-sending countries in 1920. Following Ireland, which sent nearly a quarter of its population (23.6%), Poland contributed barely 4 percent of its population. Only 4 percent of the population of Italy migrated to the United States (Nugent 1992; World Alamanac 1920). These figures stand in sharp contrast to the double-digit numbers leaving sending countries today.

Second, new communication and transportation technologies permit easier and more intimate connections. These heighten the immediacy and frequency of migrants' contact with their sending communities and allow them to be actively involved in everyday life there in fundamentally different ways than in the past.

Like their present-day counterparts, early-twentieth-century migrants also communicated frequently with their families. They were avid letter writers. They had access to the telegraph and to national postal services. They kept abreast of village gossip. And they knew that if they behaved badly in the United States, their family members in the village would soon hear about it. Travel was also relatively easy. In the early 1900s, bigger, faster, and safer steamships than were previously available crossed the Atlantic in little more than two weeks. Tickets were reasonably priced and could be paid for in installments. One observer of Italian immigration, foreshadowing comments often made about immigration today, described how new transportation technologies contributed to the "annihilation of time and space" and kept migrants close to their homelands (Foner 2000, 174).

Receiving a letter every two weeks, however, is not the same as being able to pick up the phone at any moment of the night or day. A closeness arises just from knowing that you can be in touch immediately if you so desire. It also gives migrants the ability to be involved in the day-to-day decisions of the households they leave behind.

Transatlantic phone service was not available until 1927 and was prohibitively expensive. Even as recently as 1965, it cost $10.59 for a three-minute call to the Dominican Republic; today it costs less than $2 (Sontag 1998). In Miraflores, as more households get phone service and more business owners in Jamaica Plain offer low-cost phone service to the island, telephone calls are no longer special occasions but a normal part of everyday life. Mothers who send their children back to school on the island can check regularly on their progress. They can easily ask the next person traveling to Boston to bring back home remedies, medicines, or foods not available in the United States.

Video and television also shrink distance. Mirafloreños in Boston have instant access to news about the Dominican Republic on the Spanish-language stations serving the city. The availability of Spanish-language Cable News Network (CNN) in Boston and on the island means that migrants and nonmigrants easily get news about Latin America and the Caribbean and that they often watch the same programs. They can even watch the same *telenovelas* (soap operas), which is no small feat.

Watching *novelas* is a major pastime in Miraflores for both men and women. At certain times of the day, you hear the same program coming from each open window and door as you walk down the street. Visitors know, for example, not to drop by for a visit between 12:30 and 2 unless they plan to watch too. The ability to watch these programs in Boston, even if the sequence of episodes differs, allows migrants to be part of a shared conversation. That family members can talk to one another about a particular heroine or predict how a *novela* will end makes them feel as if they are living the same experience in a way not possible in the past.

Home-video technology plays a similar role. In addition to the televisions and compact-disc players that are now standard features of Mirafloreño households, video cameras are also quite common. These are used to record important events such as baptisms, birthday parties, and weddings so family members who are not present can also "attend." This ability to share life's important occasions also keeps people connected to one another in unprecedented ways and reinforces their ties to one another. Furthermore, it allows migrants and nonmigrants to see how the other lives. For migrants, this means getting a glimpse of the new funeral home and baseball field funded by their donations. For those who have never migrated, watching videotapes provides material from which to script an imagined life in Boston. They incorporate the abbreviated glimpses of the apartments or street corners captured on tape into their images of migrants' lives. This ability to visually move around in and explore the background of the scenes that earlier nonmigrants saw, if at all, in static photographs brings migrants and nonmigrants' worlds closer together in unparalleled ways.

Furthermore, since the introduction of airplane travel, physical movement is easier, faster, and more common. Returning to Miraflores when a parent becomes ill or passes away is not easy but, in most cases, not out of the question, either. Migrants can go back to the island for a long weekend without missing many days of work. Once they have visas, nonmigrants also come to Boston for extended stays. In several households, elderly parents now spend summers in Boston and return home to winter in Miraflores. Ease of transportation reduces the cost and time needed to maintain transnational ties.

The third difference between earlier and present-day migration experiences is that migrants today leave countries at a more advanced stage of economic development and nation building than in the past. In the late nineteenth century, most eastern and southern European migrants left without a clear sense of belonging to a particular nation-state. They moved from countries that were either colonized territories, such as Ireland or Poland, or states in the process of consolidation, such as Italy (Guarnizo 1998). Most migrants did not feel a strong sense of identification with or responsibility toward their countries of origin. When the kingdom of Poland was divided among Russia, Austria-Hungary, and Prussia in 1795, Poland disappeared as a nation. The ethnic Poles who left migrated from Austrian Galicia, Russian Lithuania, Belorussia, and the Ukraine; Poland did not become a nation again until 1919 (Nugent 1992). When the first parliament of the kingdom of Italy met after it had been united in 1861, the Italian leader Massimo d'Azeglio remarked, "We have made Italy; now we have to make Italians" (Hobsbawm 1992). At that time, fewer than 5 percent of the residents of Italy spoke Italian or knew the word *Italy* (Cinel 1991).

As a result, migrants often developed a strong sense of affiliation to a particular region or nation only after they arrived in the United States. They began to think of themselves as Italian or Polish after they were labeled that way in New York or when their sending states made claims on them based on these labels (Glazer 1954). Participation in home-country politics could also offer a welcome respite from the prejudice migrants encountered in the United States. Some, like the Irish, tried to counteract their low social status by embracing their ancestral lands through transnational activities (Ignatiev 1995).

Some states recognized that emigrants represented a potential economic resource that could aid them in their consolidation process. Politicians tried to strengthen migrants' attachments to their sending countries by incorporating them into national development strategies (Glick Schiller 1999). When these home-country governments reached out to emigrants, however, they generally hoped they would return home to live. The ultimate interest of the Italian government, for example, was "to preserve ever stronger the ties of the mother country with our emigrants in order to facilitate their return" (Carol 1976, 13, in Guarnizo 1998).

The character of contemporary states is very different. As production and governance are increasingly enacted on a global stage, states' authority is weaker and their scope more limited (Sassen 1996). Furthermore, sending states today often define emigrants and their descendants as equal partners whose permanent incorporation abroad poses no barrier to their participation as citizens in their ancestral homelands. They expect migrants not to come home and live but, instead, to continue to be active and contribute from their receiving-country base as long-distance nationalists (Glick Schiller 1999).

A fourth difference in the nature of present-day transnational relations is the economic and cultural conditions within which they develop. Migration today takes place in the context of heightened global economic interconnectedness. The spread of global media has brought the "core" to all the world's "peripheries." Many of today's migrants arrive already partially socialized into aspects of Western, if not North American, culture. They often identify strongly with U.S. values because they have been thoroughly exposed to them through the media and through their conversations with migrants. Morawska

(2001c) calls this phenomenon "pre-migration westernization," while Alarcón (1989) uses the term *nortenización* to describe this premigration transformation and value convergence among Mexicans.

The changing nature of the U.S. economy also means that migrants are incorporated into the labor market in different ways. In the early to mid-1900s, rapidly industrializing U.S. companies needed low-skilled labor for jobs that often did not require workers to speak English. In contrast, today's migrants enter a postindustrial economy that courts high-skilled workers but offers limited opportunities for the unskilled, non-English speaker. In 1950, for instance, one in every three workers in the Boston metropolitan area worked in manufacturing, while in 1990, only one in twenty workers did (Bluestone and Stevenson 1998). Many new migrants find work in the service sector, which pays less, offers fewer benefits, and affords more limited opportunities for advancement than the manufacturing sector.[17] Others find jobs in the informal sector, which isolates them even more from mainstream opportunities for integration and advancement.

The changing nature of the labor market encourages transnational practices to continue in several ways. Service-sector jobs attach employees in a much more fluid manner to the labor market. Though migrants may work for the same company for extended periods, they are subject to recurrent layoffs. Mirafloreños, for example, frequently had an informal understanding with their supervisors that they could take a month off at any time and generally expect to be rehired when they returned, provided work was available. Because contemporary migrants are often incorporated insecurely into the labor market, it is easier for them to maintain a transnational lifestyle than workers with steady employment. Because their jobs pay less and provide fewer benefits than the blue-collar jobs of the past, poor migrants today face more limited prospects, a condition that may also encourage long-term transnational ties.[18]

Finally, the kinds of homeland connections sustained by migrants today differ from those in the past because they are forged within a cultural context more tolerant of ethnic pluralism. At the turn of the twentieth century, and particularly during the period preceding World War I, migrants were under tremendous pressure to naturalize and become good Americans. Settlement-house workers and progressive reformers devoted themselves to teaching immigrants English, the principles of citizenship, and allegiance to American institutions.

Educators worked hard to weaken ethnic sentiments and ties to the home country because they believed doing so was an essential part of training immigrant children to become good American citizens. Native-born Americans viewed with suspicion foreigners who actively demonstrated continued home-country attachments. The government endorsed "100% Americanism" campaigns designed to suppress foreign cultural and political differences that might nurture anti-American sentiments (Gerstle 1997). Most Americans wholeheartedly supported President Woodrow Wilson's assertion that proper hyphenated Americans retain "ancient affections" but keep their hearts and thoughts "centered nowhere but in the emotions and the purposes and the policies of the USA."

In contrast, the United States of the early twenty-first century is more tolerant of ethnic diversity. The pressure to conform to some well-defined, standardized notion of what it means to be "American" has greatly decreased.[19] Contemporary migrants enjoy the protections of new anti-discrimination and affirmative-action legislation. Displays of continued ethnic pride are normal, celebrated parts of daily life. Similarly, most of the countries that send the largest number of immigrants to the United States today have completed the nation-building process. As a result, the loyalty claims they make of their members, their political discourse, and the ways in which they represent themselves culturally tend to be less exclusionary than their early-twentieth-century efforts (Morawska 2001a; Glick Schiller 1999).

A Road Map to the Book

Findings from this book are based on fieldwork conducted between 1992 and 1995. I spent more than eight months living with a family in Miraflores, during which time I conducted formal interviews; completed a household survey; and attended meetings, celebrations, and religious observances. I also spent a good deal of time accompanying friends and neighbors in their daily routines. I tried my hand at Dominican cooking and at dancing the merengue. I looked forward to watching *novelas* each afternoon and evening. I sought relief from the afternoon heat alongside my neighbors, drinking coffee under the wide shade trees. When I was not in the Dominican Republic, I spent many hours talking with people in the homes, stores, and parks of Jamaica Plain. I attended dozens of meetings and rallies organized by the Partido Revolucionario Dominicano (Dominican Revolutionary Party). I also went to the weekly meetings of the Miraflores Development Committee and helped organize a dinner-dance fund-raiser attended by nearly 500 residents. A more detailed description of the study methodology is included in Appendix B.

This book is organized into three parts. I begin, in the following chapter, with a historical overview of the Dominican Republic, its migration patterns, and the Latino community in Boston. In Chapter 2, I introduce the concept of social remittances. Part Two describes how migration transforms daily life in ways that encourage transnational-community continuity. Chapter 3 examines changes in work, family, and school life. Chapter 4 describes the value transformations underlying these changes. Part Three analyzes the political, religious, and community organizational forms that create and are created by these relationships and their consequences for social and political life. I examine the Partido Revolucionario Dominicano, the Catholic Church, and the Miraflores Development Committee. The conclusion includes a summary of my findings and a discussion of their implications for our thinking about incorporation, participation, and citizenship.[20]

Part One

Chapter One

The Historical Context

Though large-scale migration from the Dominican Republic is relatively recent, its causes are deeply rooted in Dominican economic and political development. The U.S. government has dominated Dominican politics since the late 1800s. During much of the 1900s, as the Dominican state grew more and more indebted to its U.S. creditors, the United States actually took control of the country's government or managed its affairs from afar. Much of the country's land and commercial agricultural activities came under U.S. jurisdiction. U.S. economic, political, and cultural quasi-colonization of the republic throughout its history and the patterns of land tenure, commercial agriculture, and industrial development that ensued sowed the seeds of large-scale migration long before it began.

The Historical Roots of Migration

Christopher Columbus knew he had found gold when he arrived on the island of Hispaniola because of the beautiful ornaments the Tiano Indians who greeted him wore. Most of the island's indigenous inhabitants soon died after being forced by Columbus and his men to work in the gold mines. By 1508 only 60,000 survived out of an estimated population of 400,000 (Moya Pons 1995). By 1519, following a smallpox epidemic, the population had declined even further. Depleted gold deposits sent many earlier colonists back to Spain or on to Mex-

For a more in-depth account of Dominican history see Moya Pons (1995), Hoetink (1982), Wiarda and Kryzanek (1982), Black (1986), Betances and Spalding (1996), Betances (1995), and Torres-Saillant and Hernández (1998).

ico in search of silver. The remaining settlers dedicated themselves to sugarcane production and raising cattle. In 1520 they began importing African slaves to help them, replacing the decimated indigenous labor force.

Though the island's economy initially flourished, Spain's preference for Havana as a trading port and the restrictions it placed on commerce reversed these early gains. In addition, Protestant ideas from Holland and England "infiltrated" the island due to rampant piracy throughout the Caribbean. To reassert their control and to "protect" the primarily Catholic colonists from heresy, the Spanish forced those living in the northern and western regions of the island to move to Santo Domingo. These *devastaciones* greatly impoverished many settlers because they lost their livelihoods when their cattle died along the way. They also left the northwestern part of Hispaniola severely underpopulated and vulnerable to outside attack.

When hostilities over colonial territories between Spain and Holland erupted in 1621, the French and English sided with the Dutch. This weakened Spain's position, making it unable to prevent English and French adventurers from landing on the island's northern coast. Thus began a two-century-long struggle between the French and Spanish for control over Hispaniola. Both Spanish and French colonists lived poorly during this period. Most traders avoided Santo Domingo because of danger from Dutch sailors during the Thirty Years' War (1618–48). Cuba and Puerto Rico replaced the island as strategic points in Spain's Caribbean defense. Hispaniola's poor shipping facilities also discouraged production. Conditions improved in 1679 when France and Spain made peace. Trade expanded, as did the number of French settlers. By 1681 the French greatly outnumbered the fifteen hundred Spanish families on the island and had plans to continue their expansion (Moya Pons 1995). In fact, in 1680, French colonial governors requested that a boundary be established between the two territories. The Peace of Ryswick, signed in 1697, created a formal partition dividing Hispaniola into two distinct colonial spheres.

The French, however, remained unsatisfied. To prevent further expansion and to repopulate the island, the Spanish encouraged Canary Islanders to migrate to Hispaniola. They founded the Hato de Santa Ana, later renamed Miraflores, in 1730. In 1762, a second group, numbering 292 immigrants, arrived at Sabana de Baní, where they established the town of Baní the following year. People from the western part of the island near St. Michel de L'Attalaya also settled in the area (Franjul 1991). These first inhabitants traded salt, *resina del guayacán*, and precious woods, such as cedar and *caoba*, to the lower Netherland Antilles.

In 1804, when the French colony Saint Domingue became the newly independent Haiti, the Spanish still controlled Santo Domingo. Its residents faced rampant poverty and severe population declines. To help them defend themselves against the French, who wanted to reclaim their former territories, the new Haitian leaders were determined to unify the island. Some groups in Santo Domingo supported unification with Haiti. Others were more interested in gaining independence from Spain. In 1821 these pro-independence groups came together under the leadership of Licenciado Núñez de Cáceres, who proclaimed El Estado Independiente del Haití Español. Cáceres planned eventually to unite the newly independent state with Simón Bolívar's proposed South American union.

Despite his initial support for the new Dominican state, Haitian President Boyer had other intentions. He wrote to Núñez de Cáceres, arguing it was impossible to have two separate countries on the same small island. A unified Haitian Republic was the only way to preserve independence. Núñez de Cáceres knew he could not win. Boyer had won the support of large numbers of mulattos in Santo Domingo by promising to give them land and to abolish taxes. The ruling class also opposed Núñez de Cáceres because he had deposed the Spanish. He wrote to Boyer in 1822, accepting the protection of the Republic of Haiti and recommending to residents of Haití Español that the new Haitian rulers be received peacefully.

Despite promises of friendship, President Boyer arrived in Santo Domingo with 12,000 troops. Problems arose quickly. The Dominicans resented changes in land-ownership laws imposed upon them by the Haitians. They also resented being forced to cultivate cacao, sugarcane, and cotton commercially. Most Dominicans wanted to continue as subsistence farmers or to pursue more profitable activities such as ranching or tobacco farming. Religious leaders also opposed the occupation because Haitian leaders had confiscated church lands. The Haitians soon maintained power only by sheer force. In 1838 a group of Dominicans established a secret society called La Trinitaria to create a new, separate country on the eastern part of the island. They proclaimed their independence on February 27, 1844, soon after President Boyer's overthrow.

The ways in which Dominican leaders countered Haitian opposition to their independence set the tone for the new republic. The liberal faction of the Trinitarios wanted to go on the offensive against a possible Haitian occupation, while the conservative faction thought they should seek support from France to avoid such an invasion. A major rift split the group, with the conservatives eventually gaining control of the presidency and the army. General Santana was elected president of the new republic on November 13, 1844. The new country's constitution established a democratic government but also allowed its president to "freely organize the army and navy, mobilize the national troops, and consequently be able to give all orders, decisions, and decrees which are fitting, without being subject to any responsibility" (Moya Pons 1995, 163). This marriage between partial democracy and authoritarianism, which was consummated at the republic's birth, has remained strong throughout its history.

A second key factor defining Dominican nationhood is that it emerged from a rebellion against a harsh Haitian occupation, leaving Dominicans with an enduring sense of hatred and distrust toward their neighbors. The Dominican national identity that evolved is, in many ways, an anti-identity. It arose in such strong opposition to Haitianness that even today many Dominicans define themselves as what Haitians are not (Cassá et al. 1986). Though the majority of Dominicans have mixed African and Spanish blood, they strongly reject a black racial identity. This is particularly true among Banilejos.[1] Because the Canary Islanders who originally settled the area resisted intermarriage with their black neighbors for generations, Banilejos tend to be lighter-skinned than Dominicans in other parts of the country. Mirafloreños are generally quite proud of this and have fought to preserve their "whiteness" by pressuring villagers not to marry those who are darker-skinned.

A third element shaping the kind of country the Dominican Republic became was its leaders' strong commitment to making sure that history did not repeat itself. Almost immediately following independence, the Dominican government sought protection from foreign powers to ensure that a second Haitian occupation did not occur. Dominican post-independence history is, in large part, a search for a foreign guardian. When the United States assumed this role in the early 1900s, migration's roots were established.

The new country faced an uphill economic battle. The economy in the northern part of the country revolved around tobacco production. The economy in the south was based on lumber exports. The two regions functioned like separate countries because there were no roads connecting them. Because there were so few funds in the public treasury for such improvements, President Santana began printing money, though it had little value. By 1859, the government had issued money at least 33 times (Moya Pons 1995). Santana's economic troubles led to political unrest. In 1857 northern growers and dealers revolted against an economic devaluation they felt was particularly biased against them.

Though Santana was able to restore order, the overwhelming difficulties he faced prompted him to seek foreign aid. A former French consul informed him that if he failed to accept unification with Haiti, the United States would annex the country or Haiti would occupy the republic by force. Santana knew that the U.S. adventurer William Walker had already seized control of Nicaragua.[2] He became even more fearful when a group of U.S. explorers landed on a part of the island rich in guano deposits and claimed it for their nation. Though Santana reestablished sovereignty, he realized that the United States coveted much of his territory. He asked Spain to establish a political and military protectorate over the country to preserve Dominican independence.

Tensions arose almost immediately following the Spanish annexation in 1861. The Spanish did not redeem the Dominican currency as they had promised. They required Dominican planters to "lend" their mules and oxen to the Spanish military. They tried to limit foreign trade in ways that benefited Spain. Anti-Spanish sentiment among merchants, *campesinos*, landowners, and the military eventually led to the Restoration War of 1863, which reestablished Dominican independence. Sovereignty and economic self-sufficiency, however, would always prove elusive, as would political unity. Politics had basically become a contest between two factions. The large landowners, who raised cattle and cut wood in the south, supported General Buenaventura Báez, a rich property owner and mahogany exporter from Azúa. The cultivators and merchants in the north, who favored industrial development and trade, supported General Santana. In 1879, after more than 50 uprisings and 20 changes in government, Báez took power (Moya Pons 1995).

The enormous debt Báez faced when he took office immediately crippled his government. To alleviate this, he negotiated with the United States to sell Samaná Bay, strategically located on the country's northern coast. When it became clear that an immediate agreement would not be forthcoming, Báez arranged for an interim loan with a European speculator. He accepted such a high rate of interest that he literally mortgaged the country to a British firm. These monies enabled him to run the government while he waited for the U.S. Congress to approve what had now become a plan to annex the entire republic.

Both Dominican and U.S. groups opposed this. Though Báez eventually won support from the Dominican people, the U.S. Senate rejected the proposal in 1871. Nevertheless, the country's continued indebtedness, fears for its sovereignty, and dependence on external resources for economic growth set the stage for foreign investors' long-term dominance over Dominican economic affairs. Sugar planters from Cuba were among the earliest arrivals (Georges 1990). Soon European, Puerto Ricans, and U.S. financiers arrived in search of new investment opportunities, establishing large-scale enterprises aimed at the world market. In the south, foreigners acquired huge tracts of land for sugar cultivation. The peasants they displaced supplied what became an increasingly proletarianized labor force, whose members worked alongside migrants from the British territories in the Caribbean and Haiti. A new local elite emerged as land values and world sugar prices rose (Hoetink 1982; Georges 1990).

U.S. interests quickly dominated. At the end of the nineteenth century, large portions of major economic sectors had been sold or leased to U.S. companies to alleviate the debt burden. Under Ulises Heureaux, a dictator in power between 1886 and 1899, a group of U.S. investors called the Santo Domingo Improvement Company lent the Dominican government $1.25 million (Moya Pons 1995). By 1893, the country owed 17 million pesos, which was several times its national budget. Heureaux also allowed the Clyde Steam Lines Company to establish a monopoly over freight and passenger transport between Santo Domingo and New York.

By 1904 the Dominican government was under increasing pressure from European creditors to make debt payments it could not meet. At the same time, U.S. president Theodore Roosevelt wanted to prevent European expansion in the region. In September of that year, the U.S. secretary of state persuaded the Dominican government to allow the United States to take charge of its customs agency and to assume control of the collection and distribution of all customs receipts. Dominican leaders also agreed they would not alter their customs duty rates without U.S. government consent. By sanctioning this arrangement, Dominican leaders granted the United States unprecedented power over the country's financial and administrative affairs, a role that only continued to grow. Under Juan Isidro Jiménez, who took office in 1914, the State Department requested that a U.S. comptroller be formally appointed. When the Dominican Congress refused, the United States imposed one by force. In 1916, when his critics threatened to remove him through impeachment, U.S. leaders, who considered this a coup d'état, landed the marines in Santo Domingo and quickly sent troops throughout the country.

The eight-year U.S. occupation that followed irrevocably incorporated the republic into the system of global economic relations. When capitalist economic relations penetrate less-developed countries, they initiate social processes that encourage people to move (Portes and Walton 1981; Sassen 1991; Castells 1989). As commercial crops are substituted for subsistence production, the resulting economic and social consolidation weakens traditional land tenure systems. Mechanized production diminishes the need for manual labor and creates a mobile labor force. The insecticides, fertilizers, and machines that produce higher yields at lower costs push smaller, noncapitalist farmers out of the market. The substitution of cash crops for staples means that farmers are no longer producing for their own consumption and thus become dependent upon imported food stuffs. And the introduction of material and cultural goods from more advanced societies whets the appetite of consumers, who feel they need more money to satisfy these desires (Massey et al. 1993).

The U.S. occupation set all these processes in motion. Land consolidation begun earlier in the century advanced considerably, creating large numbers of landless peasants. The Land Registration Act of 1920 consolidated U.S. control of commercial agriculture, particularly in sugar production (Calder 1984; Del Castillo and Cordero 1980). By 1924 sugar companies controlled almost a quarter of the country's agricultural land; 80 percent of these were controlled by U.S. interests

(Gleijeses 1978). This accelerated the expansion of a plantation economy that was dangerously dependent on the world sugar market. Restrictions imposed on European investment also increased dependence on the United States, which became the principal supplier of industrial and food imports. This hurt local producers, who could not compete with products imported into the country virtually duty-free. Moya Pons (1995) estimates that incipient industrialization begun before 1916 was set back twenty years as a result. The occupation also marked the rise of U.S. cultural influences. From then on, English words penetrated the language, baseball replaced cockfighting as the national sport, and U.S. music became a sign of good taste among the urban elite.

Major public works projects supported by the U.S. government brought formerly disconnected parts of the country into communication with one another. Rural producers could now sell their goods more easily in urban areas. Miraflores had always been something of a way station on the shipping route between Baní and Santo Domingo. Farmers sending crops to the capital had to pass through Miraflores on their way to the harbor. Goods from the city, sent back on the boats that returned, went through the village on their way to Baní. The highway constructed between Baní and Santo Domingo during the U.S. occupation irrevocably connected Miraflores to urban commercial life. Mail service and sanitation improved. Education became a government priority. These efforts dampened the power of local political bosses and paved the way for a more centralized politics (Black 1986).

The Dominican Republic remained a U.S. protectorate even after the United States withdrew its forces in 1924. Though Dominican officials regained control of the administration of their own citizens, the U.S. government still reserved the right to control customs and authorize increases in the public debt. As Moya Pons writes, "From this time on, the exercise of sovereignty would be understood by Dominican leaders as always conditioned by U.S. foreign policy" (1995, 339).

In 1930, Rafael Leónidas Trujillo, a young general who had risen to commander in chief of the Dominican Army, took control of the Dominican presidency by force and began an oppressive, dictatorial rule that lasted for the next 31 years. Trujillo successfully transformed the Dominican economy from one primarily dependent on subsistence agriculture to one based on industrial growth. He also accumulated tremendous personal wealth in the process.

Trujillo pursued industrialization through import substitution, using indigenous raw materials to produce goods for the domestic market and decrease the country's reliance on imports. To reduce foreign economic domination, he built his own sugar mills and used state and personal funds to buy back most of the foreign mills operating in the country. He also created new industries or took control of existing ones. These enterprises flourished because they were protected from foreign competition and labor unrest and because they received special concessions and tax exemptions from the government. Trujillo also instilled a strong sense of national identity and pride among the Dominican people. By standing up to foreign interests and demonstrating that Dominican companies could succeed on their own, he made Dominicans feel that their country could "sit at the table of nations" for the first time (Derby 1994).

Trujillo presented himself to the Dominican public as the restorer of economic autonomy. In 1941 he finally regained control over the Dominican Customs Office, though all monies collected still had to be deposited in the National City Bank of New York. By 1947 the government had paid off its creditors in full. Though Trujillo succeeded in diminishing the country's economic dependence on the United States, he still relied heavily on its leaders for political backing. U.S. politicians were well aware that Trujillo used repression and force to remain in power, but they generally turned a blind eye, as evidenced by President Franklin Roosevelt's statement, "Trujillo is an S.O.B. but he is our S.O.B." (Eric Williams as cited in Bosch 1983, 7).

The root causes of migration were firmly established during the Trujillo era. Dependency theorists highlight the role of external factors, such as foreign capital and unequal terms of trade between developed and developing societies, in precipitating migration flows (Cassá 1982; Vincens 1982). But external dependency encourages rather than causes migration. Internal, institutional factors, such as the ways in which government policy favored a select group of industrialists and the economic development strategies that emerged from these class-state alliances, also accounted for migration in the Dominican case (Grasmuck and Pessar 1991).

According to Grasmuck and Pessar (1991), migration began in response to social and economic changes brought about by the reorganization of the sugar industry under Trujillo. During the U.S. occupation of 1916–24, the government expropriated considerable tracts of

land and devoted them to sugar production. Output increased significantly and was used almost entirely for export. The intensified concentration of land holdings weakened local subsistence agriculture and
created a mobile labor force that depended on the sugar *centrales*, or
mills, for seasonal income and employment. The government dedicated most of its resources toward modernizing production in its export sectors while agricultural production generally remained ineffi-
cient and undercapitalized.

Trujillo used his position and power to capture control of large sectors of the sugar industry. He personally controlled nearly two-thirds
of all sugar production by the time he was assassinated in 1961. He
also established a monopoly on the commercialization of cacao and
coffee. Export earnings from these crops also increased during the
1940s and 1950s, benefiting an expanding agro-export sector and a rural petty bourgeoisie (Sharpe 1977). Landholdings devoted to these
export crops also expanded in response to rising export prices.

The high proportion of rural land devoted to sugar and other export
crops negatively affected other kinds of agricultural production. One
percent of the farm owners controlled more than half of the total
farmland in 1960 (Clausner 1973). Land scarcities and limited access
to credit meant that production of important food crops declined during the 1950s. Since the labor required for export-crop production
was less than that needed to grow ordinary food crops, the agrarian labor surplus increased.

Under Trujillo, the Dominican economy gradually evolved from
one based primarily on agriculture to one based on low-level industrialization. Because there was little competition, most of the enterprises that developed were monopolistic, poorly run, and unproduc-
tive. Industrialization was also accomplished without participation by
a national bourgeoisie. Trujillo applied tariffs, tax exemptions, and
government subsidies to benefit a select group of friends. The scope
of his control was astounding. Almost 35 percent of all cultivated land,
more than 25 percent of all livestock, most of the rice production, and
12 out of 17 sugar refineries belonged to Trujillo (Bosch 1983). At the
time of his death, he controlled nearly 80 percent of the country's industrial production and his firms employed 45 percent of the country's active labor force (Moya Pons 1995). Dominicans could not obtain food, shoes, clothing, or shelter without in some way benefiting
either Trujillo or one of his family members.

Under Trujillo, Baní's economy revolved around coffee production in the hills to the north of the city and sugar and short-cycle *frutos menores,* such as tomatoes, plantains, bananas, papaya, and peppers, in the coastal plains near Miraflores. These crops had become the economic mainstays of the village in the early 1900s, when irrigation techniques were first introduced. Onions and *cebollines* brought to the area by the French in the mid-1800s were particularly important.[3] Since plantains, *bacalao,* and *cebollines* were staples of the Dominican diet, market demand was high. The largest privately owned farm in the area, El Carbonal, produced for the commercial market. There were also four or five smaller landowning families in Miraflores who constituted the local elite. Most Mirafloreños, however, owned no land. They worked as either sharecroppers or day laborers for this landowning group or they were employed by the *intermediarios,* or middlemen, who bought up local production to sell on the national market.

By the late 1950s the Dominican economic miracle began to fade. Declining sugar prices hurt the economy, which still revolved around sugar production. Because Trujillo kept wages low, Dominicans had only so much disposable income. Their limited purchasing power constrained domestic market growth (Cassá 1979). There was also increasing opposition to the almost daily torture and killing of political prisoners. As economic conditions deteriorated and the regime's critics grew more vocal, U.S. leaders feared that a Communist takeover, similar to that in Cuba, was imminent. By 1960, when President Kennedy took office, the U.S. government withdrew its support from Trujillo. He was assassinated in 1961.

A period of political turmoil followed. A U.S.-backed provisional government was organized to hold presidential elections. A progressive leader, Professor Juan Bosch, was elected in 1963, and a democratic constitution was ratified. Seven months later, a group of military officers ousted Bosch from office and formed an unstable alliance with large landowners, industrialists, and international trade merchants to replace him. In April 1965, a military faction called the *Constitucionalistas* broke from the alliance and tried to reinstate Bosch. Their rebellion quickly escalated into a popular uprising. Four days later, 40,000 U.S. marines landed in Santo Domingo to prevent an "almost certain" Communist revolution.

Prior to the 1960s, few people migrated from the Dominican Republic. Trujillo severely restricted movement out of the country, fearing his opponents would organize against him from abroad. He also sought to restrict the flow of information entering the country from places like Venezuela or Cuba, where authoritarian regimes had been deposed (Georges 1990). Those individuals who did migrate tended to be well off and from the northern Cibao region. During the first part of the 1960s, migration to the United States increased from a yearly average of almost 1,000 persons during the 1950s to nearly 10,000 persons per year (INS 1970). The first migrants left fearing President Bosch's left-leaning policies, while later migrants feared the instability that plagued the country after his defeat.

The overthrow of the Bosch government, the civil unrest that followed, and the subsequent U.S. intervention created a pool of potentially volatile antigovernment opponents. To prevent these individuals from further increasing instability, the U.S. government allowed more people to enter the United States. Migration was intended to act as a political safety valve that would weaken opposition and stabilize the Dominican political scene (Castro 1985; Mitchell 1992). Most of these individuals went to New York City.

The first significant wave to migrate to the United States were political refugees. Once migration began, though, it was further encouraged by the economic development strategies pursued by the two governments that followed. Both failed to modernize agriculture and continued to exclude labor from the benefits of increased industrialization, creating a growing but frustrated middle class. Migration provided a needed complement to the Dominican government's policies, because without it, a great deal of unrest might have occurred (Grasmuck and Pessar 1991).

Elections sponsored by the United States in 1966 installed Joaquín Balaguer, Trujillo's former presidential secretary. His rule, which lasted from 1966 to 1978, has been called "Trujillismo without Trujillo" because of the strong continuities between the two regimes (Black 1986). Like Trujillo, Balaguer enjoyed strong support from the military, the civil bureaucracy, and a small group of emerging industrialists, and he maintained power through repression and fear. He also pursued economic development through import substitution (Espinal 1994). He introduced protectionist measures, tariffs, tax exemptions, and eased access to credit to promote industrial development. In addition, he encouraged growth by increasing public-sector employment, by launching large public works projects such as highway and public housing construction, and by securing international loans.

At first, high prices for export commodities, strong foreign investment, and increased government spending resulted in high rates of economic growth. The gross domestic product (GDP) grew an average of 11 percent per year between 1969 and 1974 (Guarnizo 1992). These measures, however, did not translate into long-term job creation. Overall efficiency declined between 1970 and 1977 (Vedovato 1986). Most foreign investment went toward industries requiring more capital than labor. Inflation rose while wages remained stagnant. Balaguer strongly repressed those who challenged his approach.

Though nearly half of the Dominican labor force still worked in rural areas in 1970, Balaguer pursued policies that favored urban workers. The price controls he imposed on agricultural products, and the terms of exchange he established, hurt rural producers (Lozano 1985). Agriculture's contribution to the GDP declined from 26 percent to 12 percent between 1965 and 1978 (Vincens 1982). The concentration of landownership also increased. By 1971, 14 percent of the country's landholders owned 79 percent of all lands, while 70 percent of the population occupied 12 percent of the arable land (Boin and Serullé 1980). Since population growth rates were high, the sons of these small landowners inherited plots of land that were not large enough to support their families. These factors triggered a rural exodus to the cities. Between 1965 and 1984, the rural population decreased from 65 to 45 percent of the total population (World Bank 1986). Rural employment also decreased from about 46 percent of the population in 1970 to 24 percent by 1981. At the same time, an urban middle class was emerging as a result of increased professionalism and the growth of certain service-sector jobs. These individuals had consumption aspirations and expectations about their future social mobility that social and economic conditions would prevent them from realizing (Grasmuck and Pessar 1991).

Import-substitution-led development is often accompanied by high unemployment rates and income inequalities. The Dominican case was no exception. Because most of the industrial growth occurred in sectors requiring more capital than labor, there were too few jobs for those who migrated to the city. An estimated 20 percent of Santo Domingo's labor force was unemployed in 1973. A mismatch between employment supply and demand ensued. Even educated individuals who found jobs earned salaries barely higher than those earned by manual laborers. Real wages for laborers also decreased.

Dominican migration grew steadily during this period. It rose from 9,250 in 1968 (after an initial high of 16,503 in 1966) to 13,858 in 1973 (INS 1980). This sustained exodus complemented the capital-intensive industrialization strategy that Balaguer pursued, relieving some of the pressure that large numbers of unemployed workers would have put on the system had they stayed behind (Grasmuck and Pessar 1991). Rapid urbanization threatened to weaken Balaguer's political base, since much of his electoral support came from rural areas. By allowing relatively high rates of migration, particularly from urban areas, the government exported potential sources of political opposition and was able to remain in power for twelve years (Mitchell 1992).

In 1978, tired of Balaguer's repressive policies and their diminishing economic gains, the Dominican public elected the Partido Revolucionario Dominicano (PRD) candidate, Antonio Guzmán, in what most consider to be the country's first democratic election. During his first two years in office, Guzmán introduced a number of economic and political reforms. He liberalized the political climate, allowing a number of new labor organizations and unions to be established. He raised the minimum salary. He also created numerous public-sector jobs to decrease unemployment and stimulate consumption. Between 1979 and 1982 the number of government employees grew by 72,000 (Espinal 1987).

Despite these efforts, the PRD's first term coincided with the Dominican Republic's worst economic crisis in years. Balaguer's strategy of financing industrial growth with export earnings proved untenable for the PRD because of declining sugar prices, increasing debt obligations, and rising oil prices and interest rates in the early 1980s (Torres-Saillant and Hernández 1998). By 1982, conditions had deteriorated to such an extent that the International Monetary Fund (IMF) imposed an austerity plan to decrease government spending as a condition for providing assistance. The structural adjustment policies put in place were designed to curtail imports and reorient the country's traditional base toward tourism, service-sector employment, and export processing zones, where goods are manufactured duty-free for sale outside the country.

These strategies narrowed Dominicans' employment opportunities even further. The gross domestic product declined to an average of 1.6 percent between 1980 and 1988. During the PRD's second administration, under President Jorge Blanco, real salaries declined by 22 percent (IDB 1987). Official unemployment rose from 24 percent in 1970 to 30 percent in 1988. According to some estimates, 45 to 60 percent of the workforce in the 1980s was employed in domestic service work or in the informal sector, which is made up of micro-enterprises or small-scale manufacturing firms operating outside legal and regulatory review (Kleinekathoefer 1987). Though international export prices continued to decline, and the government received repeated warnings to diversify its export base, the PRD made little effort to implement such policies. The state sugar bureaucracy had provided too many powerful people with too many benefits. Thus, under President Blanco, the state continued to rely on the sugar industry as its principal engine of economic growth and to allow continuous increases in food imports (Grasmuck and Pessar 1991).

The government's financial policies also stimulated migration. While exports continued to be priced according to the dollar, imports were priced according to a "parallel market" that fluctuated but was normally higher. This meant that Dominican real wages declined considerably, particularly in relation to the value of the dollar. According to Grasmuck and Pessar (1991), by 1987 the minimum monthly salary for a full-time job in the United States was six times higher than what one could earn in the Dominican Republic.

Further frustration and economic strain prompted the Dominican public to reelect Balaguer in 1986. Under his leadership the government finally moved the economy away from its dependence on traditional exports. During the 1990s, export processing zones (EPZs) and tourism became two of its most important industries. Revenues from tourism increased from $368.2 million in 1985 to roughly $1.1 billion in 1992. Between 1980 and 1988, firms in the EPZs drove up the country's exports from $117 million to $517 million. These gains are fragile and continue to be driven by forces located outside the republic. Sixty-three percent of the EPZ industries are owned by U.S. companies who do not pay taxes (Betances 1995). In 1993, more than 60 percent of the workers were women who received an average hourly wage of 50 cents. Though export earnings increased, the Dominican economy remained stagnant at an average growth rate of 1.1 percent (Safa 1995).

When President Leonel Fernández took office in 1996, he introduced a bold reform package aimed at creating a market-oriented economy that could compete internationally. He proposed a devaluation of the peso, income tax cuts, a 50 percent increase in the sales tax, and a reduction in import tariffs. Though many of these reforms stalled in the legislature, the economy grew vigorously between 1997 and 1998. The estimated GDP real growth rate for 1998 was 7 percent. The service sector accounted for 56 percent of the GDP (as estimated in 1996), followed by industry (25%), and agriculture (19%). Following tourism, sugar processing, ferronickel and gold mining, textiles, cement, and tobacco constituted the country's strongest industries (www.cia.gov).

Migrants have become a key force in the Dominican economy. The $796 million in remittances migrants sent in 1995 surpassed all industries, except for tourism, as sources of foreign exchange (*Migration News* 1998). The $1.4 billion migrants remitted in 1999 was more than half the government's operating budget (Hart 2000). These figures do not include the significant sums of money that migrants send back through informal channels or personally carry back to the island. They also do not reflect the money migrants spend on vacation trips, consumer goods, houses, lands, and businesses, nor how they stimulate growth in particular economic sectors, such as the construction industry, when they return to live on the island. According to Carlos Dore, a close adviser to former President Fernández, migrants "are the sine qua non for Dominican macro-economic stability, including monetary exchange rates, the balance of trade, international monetary reserves, and the national balance of payment" (Guarnizo 1997, 7). The country's political and economic fortunes still depend primarily on events in the United States. As one Mirafloreño put it, "When the U.S. sneezes, we catch a cold," a relationship unlikely to change under new PRD President Hipólito Mejía.

A Profile of Migrant Miraflores and the Context That Receives Them

Migration from the Dominican Republic grew rapidly during the 1970s and 1980s.[4] Because anthropologists who were studying rural areas conducted much of the earliest research, it was assumed that migrants were small-to-medium-sized landholding peasants or rural proletarians (Sassen-Koob 1978).[5] Ugalde, Bean, and Cárdenas (1979) first challenged this view when their analysis of the 1974 Diagnos National Study revealed that although 53 percent of the Dominican population resided in rural areas, only 24 percent of international migrants left from rural parts of the country (Georges 1990). A number of subsequent studies confirmed that most Dominican migrants come from urban areas.[6]

Once begun, migration broadened to include a wide cross section of Dominican society. While relatively educated, middle-class individuals left during the 1960s and 1970s, during the two decades that followed, less-skilled workers and highly skilled professionals also migrated. A 1991 national survey revealed that nearly 21 percent of urban households had migrant members, compared to 11 percent from rural areas. Migrants tended to come from better-off families and from better-off regions of the country. Households with incomes of more than 3,000 pesos per month had two times more migrants than those with lower incomes. Better-educated groups also tended to migrate more. Forty-eight percent of the households with migrants had household heads who had secondary or university education, while only 11.5 percent had heads with no education or who had not completed primary school (Profamilia 1992).

Nonmigrants reported high levels of dependence on remittances. According to a 1992 survey conducted in the Dominican capital, 77 percent of the households had at least one relative in the United States; 27 percent received financial support once a month from a migrant family member (Lozano 1992). Return migration was also fairly common. Warren (1988) estimated that 24 percent of the Dominicans who went to the United States between 1960 and 1980 returned to live and work on the island. In 1991 the return rate was estimated at 29 percent; and more individuals returned to cities (33%) than to rural areas (17%) (Profamilia 1992).

Migration from Miraflores grew in response to the same economic and political factors that precipitated outflows throughout the country. Declines in the prices of sugar and coffee on the world market hurt the local economy. The demand for *cebollines* decreased as Dominican dietary patterns shifted toward other foods. In addition, a severe drought in 1975 and a hurricane in 1981 decimated crop yields and left some land uncultivable. Apart from farming, there were few other job opportunities in the area. As a result, in 1994, more than one-third (35%) of all households in Miraflores said they had no income-earning members. Among those who did work, 12 percent owned their own businesses,[7] while 17 percent worked in stores, offices, government, or in sales. Fewer than ten villagers found jobs at the canning factory or export processing zone located near Baní. Instead, the majority worked as agricultural day laborers or in land-rental/sharecropping arrangements (35%). Fewer than 20 percent of the households in the village owned their own land. Of these, most held small parcels, or *minifundios,* ranging from one to fifty hectares.[8]

Not surprisingly, more than 75 percent of the Mirafloreños who migrated said they did so for economic reasons. The first to leave were the more educated, better-off members of the community as Ernesto, a thirty-nine-year-old return migrant, described:

I went because I was married, I had a son, and I was eighteen years old. I was studying, but I didn't have a job. I thought, I know the Cárdenas are there, I can try it out, make some money, and come back in a few years to start a business. I knew it would be hard, but I thought they will help me and it's worth the risk. I went and came back after a year. I didn't like it there, but then I couldn't get used to living in Miraflores again. So when the World Series was coming up and I wanted to see it, I went back again, and this time I ended up staying eighteen years.

Social networks played an important role in migration's spread. Most Mirafloreños trace their journey back to one individual who they say is responsible for setting the network-building process in motion. Jaime Cárdenas first came to Baní when Trujillo was in power. In those days Trujillo controlled commercial shoe production on the island. To ensure a captive market, the dictator made it illegal to go barefoot and set the fine for doing so higher than the price of shoes. Don Jaime opened his own shoe factory in Baní to cater to the provincial market. Despite his success, he was ostracized by the city's elite. After his first marriage ended in scandal he moved to Miraflores, where he built a large home and began a new family. He became popular among his new neighbors, and among young people in particular, because he generously supported the village baseball team. When his factory eventually went bankrupt, he migrated to Boston with his children and encouraged some of the young men he knew to follow him there. Many of the first to go stayed at the Cárdenas' apartment when they arrived.

When I first got to Boston in the early 1970s, there were four or five other people there. The first night I got there I went to Cárdenas' house. He was not there, but his daughter, María del Carmen, said that I could stay there for a few days until I found a room. I did until I got a job packing oranges and I rented a basement room there on Mozart Street. Then María del Carmen was supervisor for a cleaning company and she got me a job cleaning buildings downtown. (Jorge, 41, return migrant, Miraflores)

As more village members settled and found work in Boston, a network of connections between Miraflores and Jamaica Plain deepened and spread. New migrants followed more easily. Early migrants helped those who came later to find work, as Jorge described:

Finally I got a job at a factory making shoulder pads. At first it was just me and the owner. Then eventually we grew and I became supervisor. Since there was a lot of work, every time someone came from Miraflores, I would bring them over there and give them a job. I was supervisor for thirteen years.

Since 1970, migration from Miraflores to Boston has grown steadily.[9] Unlike other country-of-origin groups, who move first to urban centers before migrating across borders, nearly all Mirafloreños traveled directly to the United States (96%). More than three-quarters went to Boston, while 12 percent went to New York.

Boston has always been an important point of entry for new immigrants, who have long been attracted to its manufacturing and commercial opportunities. Between the Civil War and World War II, most of the city's foreign-born came from Ireland, Canada, and Italy. The Boston Brahmins, or the well-established Protestant power elite, did not welcome them warmly. In one striking example, after the Irish community had begun to establish itself, the Catholic Archdiocese initiated construction of a new cathedral, which was to be as large as Westminster Abbey. The Protestant majority objected so strongly to this display of power by these Catholic "upstarts" that the city's leaders built an elevated subway line directly across from the completed structure (Shand-Tucci 1998). Subsequent migrants created their own economic niches and political organizations to circumvent the resistance they encountered. Their legacy of ethnic neighborhoods, and the residential segregation that characterized the city as a result, still persists.

The first Latinos to migrate to New England on a large scale were Puerto Ricans. In the 1940s, the Migration Division of the Department of Labor of the Commonwealth of Puerto Rico and the Massachusetts Department of Employment Security agreed to recruit farm laborers to work in the apple orchards, cranberry bogs, and vegetable farms to the south and west of Boston. Migration grew as individual farmers paid their employees $10 a head and plane fare to bring additional workers to Massachusetts. After the growing season ended, some relocated to the city in search of factory employment. Many settled in Boston's South End.

During the 1960s, urban renewal and subsequent gentrification pushed Latinos out of the South End into other neighborhoods. Newly arriving Dominicans found homes in Jamaica Plain, following on the coattails of the Cubans who had already settled in that area. Jamaica Plain had traditionally been home to the city's Irish immigrants. Those who flourished lived in the large mansions along the edge of Jamaica Pond. Their working-class counterparts settled in the triple-decker-lined streets closer to the elevated subway line.

In 1999, an estimated 921,883 persons of Dominican ancestry resided in the United States, up from 521,151 in 1990. Table 3 compares their basic demographic characteristics with those of other major racial and ethnic groups in the United States between 1996 and 1999 (see Appendix A for all tables). Dominicans are slightly younger. Along with African Americans, they are less likely to be married. Table 4 reveals that nearly 60 percent of all the Dominicans in the United States were foreign-born. Slightly less than 20 percent had become U.S. citizens, while 40 percent had not naturalized. The majority were recent arrivals; more than two-thirds came between 1980 and 1999. As of 1999, the Dominican Republic ranked twelfth among those countries sending the largest numbers of immigrants to the United States. Dominicans were also among the most residentially concentrated groups. Nearly 70 percent (68.9%) migrated to New York State, with 65 percent settling in New York City (U.S. Census 1992). As table 5 shows, between 1996 and 1999, more than 80 percent lived in the mid-Atlantic region. The next-largest concentrations of Dominicans resided in the South Atlantic region, particularly Miami (10%), and in the New England region (5%) (CPS 1996–99). Few Dominicans owned their homes, as table 6 reveals. During the 1996–99 period, over three-quarters rented their places of residence.

Three major changes have swept the greater Boston metropolitan area since Mirafloreños first arrived. The first is demographic. In 1950 minority residents constituted only 5.3 percent of the city's population. By 1990 41 percent of the city's 574,283 residents were racial minorities, including 11 percent Hispanics.[10] Puerto Ricans were the largest Latino group (42%) while Dominicans made up 13% of the city's Latino population.

Despite this heightened ethnic diversity, racial and ethnic relations remain strained.[11] Residential segregation has been stubbornly persistent. Boston is the fourteenth most residentially segregated city in the country. Both black-white and Hispanic-white residential segregation continues at levels at or above those of other major American cities (Bluestone and Stevenson 1998).

The spatial reorganization of production is the second major change that has occurred in the region. Much of Boston's population and many of its economic enterprises relocated outside the city's boundaries between 1950 and 1990. The overall population declined from 800,000 to 560,000. Much of Boston's manufacturing base also moved to the suburbs or left the region altogether. Retailers followed their customers. As a result, the urban core lost jobs and experienced declines in wholesale and retail trade while these activities increased in the areas surrounding the city. City officials also dedicated significant resources toward creating a "new Boston" that physically reflected the modern, streamlined character of the new high-tech activities spearheading the city's economic growth. New hotels and office buildings replaced much of the low-cost housing formerly available downtown. Even Boston's Combat Zone, the last bastion of adult entertainment and urban decay, has been slowly eradicated. As a result, there are fewer jobs and affordable housing for newly arriving immigrants.

The most dramatic change in the past three decades has been the economic shift from manufacturing to high-tech and service industries. This story, though familiar throughout the country, was particularly dramatic in Boston. The proportion of those employed nationally in nondurable manufacturing, such as textiles and apparel, declined from 14 to 7 percent between 1950 and 1990, while in the greater Boston metropolitan area, these numbers decreased by 16 percent. The 1970s recession also reduced the manufacturing sector considerably. About one-fifth of jobs lost involved unskilled labor (Harrison 1988). Suffolk County lost 50 percent of its manufacturing jobs between 1965 and 1987[12] (Falcón 1993).

The high-tech industrial growth that later propelled the state toward the "Massachusetts Miracle" of the 1980s sidestepped many Latinos (Osterman 1990). While Boston gained 80,000 jobs for workers with at least some college education between 1970 and 1980, jobs for workers with only a high school diploma or less declined by 125,000 (Kasarda 1989). Mirafloreños, and Dominicans in general, did not have the education or the skills to succeed in this new economy. As table 7 highlights, only 5 percent of all Dominicans had graduated from college between 1996 and 1999, compared to 16 and 24 percent among whites and Asians, respectively. In 1990 fairly high numbers of Dominicans (52%) classified themselves as speaking English "not well" or "not at all" (U.S. Census 1992).

As a consequence, most Dominicans faced significant barriers to entry in the labor force. They could not get well-paying, stable jobs. In general, as table 8 indicates, they fared somewhat less well than African Americans, Native Americans, and non-Dominican Hispanics, and poorly compared to whites and Asians. Dominicans were less likely to find full-time employment and were less likely to be self-employed than these other groups. The majority of Dominicans were employed in service-sector jobs (28 percent) or in manufacturing (30 percent), as shown in table 9 (for tables, see Appendix A). Table 10, which shows work experience by industry, reveals that relatively large numbers of Dominicans were also employed in retail trade.

Because their occupational and language skills did not fit well with the current labor market, and because the kinds of jobs they got paid poorly and offered few opportunities for advancement, almost 40 percent of all Dominicans lived below the poverty level. As table 11 shows, 23 percent of all Dominican households received public assistance between 1996 and 1999.

This general profile holds true for Mirafloreños.[13] In 1994, nearly half held only part-time jobs. Slightly more than one-quarter worked in manufacturing, and more than a third worked in low-level jobs in the service sector. The majority cleaned office buildings at night. A small group worked in small businesses that were generally Dominican-owned.

Despite their incorporation into low-wage jobs, Mirafloreños assumed increasing responsibility for supporting their nonmigrant family members. Almost 60 percent of the households in Miraflores received some of their monthly income from those in the United States. For nearly 40 percent of those households, remittances constituted between 75 and 100 percent of their income. In contrast, only 31 percent of the households earned their money entirely in the Dominican Republic.

These high levels of economic dependence reinforce migrants' and nonmigrants' ties to one another. They remained in close touch. More than half of the villagers spoke by phone to their relatives in Boston at least once, if not twice, a month. Telephone contacts have risen considerably since 1994 because new phone cards now make calling much cheaper. Nearly three-quarters of those who migrated returned home to visit; more than half had been back to Miraflores between two and four times. In fact, few Mirafloreños indicated a desire to remain permanently in the United States. More than 80 percent left intending to return to the island. In nearly a quarter of the households, at least one person had returned to live; in 5 percent, two migrants had come back. Though the majority of the community entered the United States without the necessary visa, by 1994, 73 percent were legal residents; fewer than 1 percent had become U.S. citizens.

Mirafloreños' economic and social marginalization in the United States, nonmigrants' high levels of economic dependence on those who have migrated, and their frequent levels of contact with one another are just some of the factors creating this transnational village and making it likely to endure. The social remittances migrants introduce to those remaining behind also play a critical role in transnational-village creation and perpetuation. They are the focus of the next chapter.

Chapter Two

Social Remittances

How Global Culture Is Created Locally

Most Mirafloreños agree that Esther Báez is one of their community's most prominent residents. It is not that she is wealthy. She and her husband live in a modest, though very comfortable, home. He works for the Baní city government and she supplements the family's income by making cakes and sweets that she sells from her living room. Rather, what has earned Esther the Mirafloreños' respect is her community leadership. She is a pillar of the church. She is a secretary of the Miraflores Development Committee. And her neighbors consider her someone who is wise and fair and who knows a great deal about who they are.

During the course of our many conversations, after mass on Saturday evening or sipping a cool drink in the shade of her back patio, Esther slowly pieced together the puzzle of Miraflores's past and present. "Our lives are totally different now," she would begin,

and so much has to do with what we have learned from the United States. It's both good and bad. When Javier told us that he wouldn't stand being tricked by politicians anymore or having to wait on long lines at city hall because they are so unorganized there, these were good things that he taught us about his life in the United States. But when people come back saying that they care more about themselves than about our community or that you can make a lot of money by selling drugs and that is okay, then we would rather not learn what the U.S. has to offer.

Esther is describing the positive and negative ways in which social remittances transform village life. Social remittances are the ideas, behaviors, identities, and social capital that flow from host- to sending-country communities (Levitt 1999). They are like the social and cultural resources that migrants bring with them to the countries that receive them. The role these resources play in promoting immigrant entrepreneurship, community development, and political integration is widely acknowledged.[1] What is less understood is how these same ideas and practices are transformed in the host country and transmitted back to sending communities such that new cultural products emerge and challenge the lives of those who stay behind.

The process of global cultural diffusion is not very clear. Most sociological analyses focus on the ways in which social relations shape diffusion (Strang and Meyer 1994). Coleman, Katz, and Menzel (1973), for example, found that physicians with high levels of social contact were more likely to adopt new drugs than those with fewer relations. When the individual disseminator is a trusted, valued member of the community, others are more likely to respond favorably to the new ideas they introduce. Diffusion is also understood as a function of geographic distance. The farther away something is disseminated, the more diluted and changed it becomes in the process. The size and configuration of social networks also shape cultural diffusion. In relatively small groups, many weak ties can be more effective in "getting the word out" than a few strong ones (Granovetter 1973). Strang and Meyer (1994) argue that social elements flow better between units in a system when they are perceived to be similar to one another. Adoption is also more likely when the practices being diffused are seen as "modern" or "westernized."[2]

Much of the research on global cultural flows focuses on how macro-level institutions and regimes spread throughout the world's economic and political system. It emphasizes demand, as opposed to supply-side, factors that influence dissemination and adoption (Scott 1995). There is, however, a second way that global culture is diffused. Ordinary people, at the local level, are also cultural creators and carriers. Migrants send or bring back the values and practices they have been exposed to and add these social remittances to the repertoire, both expanding and transforming it. Later migrants bring this enhanced tool kit with them, thereby stimulating ongoing iterative rounds of local-level global culture creation.

From Social and Cultural Resources
to Social Remittances

Studies of evolutionary institutional change suggest useful approaches for understanding social remittance production. Evolutionary change is shaped by the structure of existing institutional arrangements. How things are already done both enables and constrains subsequent choices about how things will change in the future (Campbell 1995). These types of change processes are often called path-dependent. They are events that arise through a branching process such that once a particular choice is made, other routes are no longer possible (Scott 1995).

A similar design process occurs in social remittance evolution. Migrants interact to varying degrees with the host society. They make sense of their experiences using the interpretive frames they bring with them. Just as institutional actors' choices are shaped by the routines and norms already in place, so the new behaviors and views migrants adopt are also a function of how they did things at home. A number of blending scenarios result. In some cases, existing ideas and practices go unchallenged. In others, new elements are grafted onto existing ones. In still others, creolization occurs, whereby new social relations and cultural patterns are created by combining sending- and receiving-country forms.

The degree to which migrants' interpretative frames are altered is a function of how much they interact with the host society (Portes and Zhou 1993). This, in turn, depends upon their socioeconomic profile and the opportunity structures available to them. Mirafloreños who have enough money, education, and social capital to start their own businesses have much more contact with the broader community than those who work alone cleaning offices. When migrants interact more intensively with the host society, they receive more exposure to its features. They are more likely to make comparisons with their established ways of doing things and become more open to incorporating new routines. Those who remain firmly embedded in their ethnic community face more limited challenges to their long-standing practices and beliefs.

For heuristic purposes, I identify three broad patterns of interaction with the host society. Clearly, Mirafloreños do not fit precisely within these categories. I offer them as conceptual tools for clarifying how different levels of social contact influence social remittance emergence.

At one end of the spectrum are *recipient observers*. Most of these individuals do not work outside their homes or, when they do, they work in places where most of their co-workers are other Latinos. Recipient observers are more likely to be women than men. They generally shop and socialize with other Dominicans and report few social contacts with the Anglo community. They do not actively explore their new world because their lives are structured such that they do not come into close enough contact with it. Instead, they take in new ideas and practices by passively observing the world around them. They listen to how others describe it. Or they learn about it by reading the newspaper, listening to the radio, or watching TV.

Other Mirafloreños are more fully intregrated into life in the United States. Their interactions at work, on public transportation, or with medical or educational professionals force them to shift their reference frames. They need new skills to be able to get along. These *instrumental adapters* alter and add to their routines for pragmatic reasons. They adjust the way they interpret the world to equip themselves better to meet the challenges and constraints of migrant life.

Finally, some Mirafloreños are *purposeful innovators*. In contrast to recipient observers, they are sponges who aggressively seek out, select, and absorb new things. Unlike instrumental adapters, they want to get ahead rather than just get by. They do not change because they have to, but because they want to learn and benefit from the new world around them. They creatively add and combine what they observe with their existing ideas and practices, thereby expanding and extending their cultural repertoire.

Several patterns of social remittance evolution result. Each of these is most common among, though not restricted to, one of the three types of social actors I have described.

In some cases, migrants abandon some of the social and cultural tools they arrive with. Either they are not relevant in their new homes or the organization of immigrant life makes them too difficult to use. For instance, when her father died, Doña Gabriela did not organize a Hora Santa, a popular religious ceremony to honor the deceased, because it was too difficult to do so in Boston. She could never be sure that enough people would come because they were always so busy or because they did not want to go out at night when it was cold. Beliefs also weaken and behaviors become unfamiliar when they are not used regularly.

Another pattern of social remittance evolution leaves the social and cultural resources migrants bring unchanged. This occurs most frequently in the *recipient observer* group. Many of their norms and practices go unchallenged because they interact so infrequently with the host society. Their sending-country repertoire still works because their lives are very similar to those they led in Miraflores.

A third pattern of social remittance evolution occurs when migrants add new items to their tool kit that do not alter existing elements. They expand the range of practices they engage in without modifying their old habits or ideas. This occurs most often among *instrumental adapters,* such as Mirafloreña women newly entering the workplace. Since most of the women in the village did not work outside their homes before they came to the United States, they learned a new set of skills in the process of looking for a job alone.

When I got here, my sister tried to get me a job, but there was no work at the company she was working for. I had to go down and speak to the supervisors at the places people told me about. I wasn't used to talking to people I didn't know. We hardly ever met anyone new back home and when we did it was usually as a family. I had to use the telephone. In Miraflores, they had just gotten a phone at Carmen's house [her mother-in-law next door] and I wasn't used to talking to people that way. I had to find my way downtown on the subway. And I had hardly ever been to Santo Domingo by myself. (Gabriela, 38, migrant, Boston)

The new skills Gabriela learned during her job search do not challenge her old routines. She added to her repertoire of skills and understandings but did not transform it.

In a fourth scenario, which is most common among *purposeful innovators,* migrants' ideas and practices combine with host-country norms. In these instances, cross-pollination occurs, producing hybrid social forms.

Dress is a good example of this, though its impact is most apparent in Miraflores, where these remitted practices have taken hold. Mirafloreñas generally like to wear tight-fitting, brightly colored clothing. They continue to dress this way in Boston, albeit with some modifications, exchanging shorts for pants and sleeveless blouses for long-sleeved shirts. They also wear boots in the cold weather. Nonmigrants observe these styles when migrants come to visit. They also receive clothing as gifts. Because young women, in particular, want to emulate U.S. fashion, they combine elements of their own wardrobes with items from the United States, creating a new hybrid style. Women wear boots with shorts. They wear long-sleeved clothing in eighty-degree weather. Patterns of dress no longer reflect climate. Rather, current styles meld fashion statements from the island with those from the United States.

Whether expanded upon or hybridized, these social and cultural resources become the substance of social remittances. The following section describes the actual content of social remittance transfers and differentiates them from other kinds of cultural transmissions.

What Is Exchanged?

There are at least three types of social remittances — normative structures, systems of practice, and social capital.

Normative Structures

Normative structures are ideas, values, and beliefs. They include norms for behavior, notions about family responsibility, principles of neighborliness and community participation, and aspirations for social mobility. Normative structures also include values about how organizations should work, incorporating ideas about good government and good churches and about how politicians and clergy should behave.

Several prior studies have described normative structure–type social remittances without defining them as such. The changing values and social ties that Polish immigrants to the United States wrote about to their nonmigrant family members in the early part of the twentieth century were said to foster greater individuality at home (Thomas and Znaniecki 1927). The mutual aid societies formed by return migrants to the Italian *Mezzogiorno* eventually evolved into political organizations. According to Wyman (1993, 158), "Social progress of the people, extremely slow so far, begins to make headway, thanks to the *Americani*" (those who returned from America). Return migrants to the West Indies repatriated a vision of social reform they learned from the

Black Power movement in the United States (Patterson 1988). Mi-rafloreños also communicate the values and norms they observe to those at home.

When I go home, or speak to my family on the phone, I tell them everything about my life in the United States. What the rules and laws are like. What is prohibited here. I personally would like people in the Dominican Republic to behave the way people behave here. The first time I went back to the Dominican Republic after nine years away, I arrived at the airport. I saw the floor was filthy and that the smokers threw their cigarette butts everywhere. And I said wait a minute. I even said it to the police who were there. How can this be? The gateway to our country is the airport. It should be clean and neat and people should be polite. When people put out their cigarettes they should use an ashtray. Tourists will get a bad impression when they see this mess. So when I smoked, I used an ashtray. It's not just saying things but do-ing them to provide a good example. When I'm in Miraflores, when I see people throwing garbage on the ground, I don't go and pick it up, because that would be too much, but I get up and throw my own garbage away and everyone sees me do it. And those that have a little consciousness, without me saying anything, the next time they have to throw something out, they'll probably remember that they saw this, and it's the right thing to do, and they'll do it. These things and many more, the good habits I've acquired here, I want to show people at home. (Pepe, 35, migrant, Boston)

Host societies offer both positive and negative role models, and migrants are equally adept at emulating both. A common complaint among the adults in Miraflores is that the community's youth "don't want to work hard anymore." They are used to receiving without hav-ing to work for it, these adults say, and they have never known what it is like to have to do without.

Life in the U.S. teaches them many good things, but they also learn some bad things as well. People come back more individualistic, more materialis-tic. They think that "things" are everything rather than service, respect, or duty. They are more committed to themselves than they are to the commu-nity. They just don't want to be active in trying to make the community bet-ter anymore. Some learned to make it the easy way and they are destroying our traditional values of hard work and respect for the family. (Javier, 56, nonmigrant, Miraflores)

Migrants' sense of themselves also changes in the United States because they do things they have not done before. Their social stand-ing improves, particularly with respect to nonmigrants. These transformed identities expose nonmigrants to a more ample range of self-concepts from which to choose.

In Miraflores, there have been particularly strong challenges to gender identity. Migrant womens' ideas about what women should do and how they should behave changed in response to their more active participation in the workforce and to their contacts with schools, health clinics, and social welfare agencies. They transmitted these new ideas about identity back to Miraflores, where nonmigrant women used these social remittances to construct new versions of womanhood. Some came to believe that women in Miraflores should also work outside their homes. Others became convinced that husbands and wives should make decisions together and that that they should share household chores. While their ideas were often romanticized, they still represented a marked change in thinking about gender relations.

I don't want anything to do with the men from here anymore. They are too *macho.* They just want a woman to be waiting around to fulfill their every need. I see the way the couples act when they come back to visit. The men have changed. Couples do things together. The man doesn't just leave his wife at home and go out to enjoy himself with his friends or with his girlfriend. He takes her with him and shows her respect. They make decisions together. When I start my own family, I want it to be like that. (Adriana, 19, nonmigrant, Miraflores)

Systems of Practice

Systems of practice are the actions shaped by normative structures. These include how individuals delegate household tasks, the kinds of religious rituals they engage in, and the extent to which they participate in political and civic groups. They also include organizational practices such as recruiting and socializing new members, goal setting and strategizing, establishing leadership styles, and forming interagency ties.

In Miraflores, these types of social remittances have far-reaching effects. They challenge long-standing patterns of social interaction and political participation. For instance, Mirafloreños used to spend most of their days outdoors because of the heat. Families passed many afternoons watching village life unfold in front of them from their ringside seats on their front *galerías,* or porches. They socialized constantly with their neighbors while at work and at leisure and conducted much of their private lives in public view.

Mirafloreños in Boston live much more isolated lives. Several respondents told how they lived in the same building for years without ever meeting their neighbors. While this made some quite lonely, it instilled in others a greater sense of independence, which they enjoyed. They liked living without everyone having something to say about their affairs. When they returned to Miraflores, they wanted to preserve their privacy, and this motivated them to build different style houses. Some eliminated the front *galería* and built a more private patio in the back, which redirected the focus of daily life away from public view. Others built homes surrounded by high walls that discouraged the spontaneous, frequent visiting that had been such an important part of a typical day.

Social Capital

Both the values and norms on which social capital is based, and social capital itself, are socially remitted.[3] Basch (1992) found this among Vincentian and Grenadian immigrant leaders and activists who were able to use the prestige and status they acquired in the United States to further their political platforms on the islands they came from. This also occurred in Miraflores. Those who worked toward the betterment of the community in Boston could use their social capital in Miraflores. They could get things done on the island using the goodwill they generated and the favors they stored up working for the community in Boston. The social capital they acquired was transferable. Nonmigrant family members also benefited from the obligations incurred and respect earned by those in Boston. For instance, when the nonmigrant sister of the president of the Miraflores Development Committee (MDC) in Boston became ill, her family asked the doctors at the health clinic to make a home visit. When they refused to do so, her relatives reminded the physicians that she was related to the president and that it was the MDC that had just paid for the renovations to the clinic. When the doctors heard this, they suddenly became available. The president's family in Miraflores harnessed the social capital he had accumulated in Boston to help a family member who remained behind.

When social capital declines, this also registers in Miraflores. When someone is seen as not helping the community as much as they are perceived to be able to, their social capital diminishes. Their nonmigrant family members also feel their ostracization. It used to be, for example, that Enrique's family participated actively in organizing and supporting many of the sports activities around Miraflores. But when Enrique had a falling out with some of the important migrant leaders about not pulling his weight, his family in Miraflores was also marginalized. According to Javier, his brother: "Last year, when they had the meeting to organize the committee that supports the baseball team, no one came to invite my father. It was like what Enrique did over there really put us in a bad position over here."

Mechanisms of Transmission

Social remittance exchanges occur when migrants return to live in or visit their communities of origin; when nonmigrants visit those in the receiving country; or through exchanges of letters, videos, cassettes, e-mails, and telephone calls. The mechanisms of social remittance transmission differ from other types of global cultural dissemination in several ways.

First, while it is often difficult to distinguish how world-level institutions and global culture emerge and are disseminated, it is possible to specify how social remittances flow. Social remittances travel through identifiable pathways; their source and destination are clear. Migrants and nonmigrants can state how they learned of a particular idea or practice and why they decided to adopt it.

A second feature that distinguishes social remittances from other kinds of global cultural flows is that they are transmitted systematically and intentionally. A social remittance occurs when migrants speak directly to their family members about a different kind of politics and encourage them to pursue reforms. In cases such as these, ideas are communicated intentionally to a specific recipient or group. Villagers know when and why they changed their mind about something or began to act in a different way. Nonmigrants also change their behaviors in response to catalysts that are not social remittances. They may begin to think about holding their politicians more accountable when they hear on the radio that the president of the United States is being investigated for his extramarital affairs. But the radio report is not a social remittance because it is not a specific message directed at a particular individual.

A third distinguishing aspect of social remittance transmission is that these remittances are usually transferred between individuals who know one another personally or who are connected to one another by mutual social ties. Social remittances are delivered by a familiar messenger who comes "with references." The personalized character of this kind of communication stands in contrast to the faceless, mass-produced nature of global cultural diffusion. Several studies have already highlighted the interpersonal nature of idea transmission among elites. In this work, idea carriers were able to convince others to adopt the technical expertise and skills they introduced because of their influential social positions.[4] The Miraflores case underscores that ordinary individuals are also social-remittance carriers. The ideas and practices they introduce function as the local-level, change-from-below counterpart of elite idea carriers' influence on national affairs.

A fourth characteristic differentiating social remittances from global cultural flows is the timing with which they are communicated. In many cases, a staged process occurs, whereby macro-level global flows precede and ease the way for social remittance transmission. Since many nonmigrants were already eager to emulate the patterns of consumption they observed in the U.S. media, they were more receptive to the new political and religious styles migrants brought back to the village. Calls for greater political and economic participation by women met with greater acceptance because they came on the heels of an already familiar global discourse about women's rights. Social remittance flows do not arise out of the blue. They are part and parcel of an ongoing process of cultural diffusion. Gradual transmission sets the stage for future remittance transfers that then seem to make more sense.

Determinants of Impact

A variety of factors determine the nature and magnitude of social remittance impact.

The Nature of the Remittance Itself

Social remittance impact is in part a function of how easy it is to transmit a particular remittance. Some remittances are difficult to package. They do not translate easily into neat data packets. Instead, they are slippery, unstable, and unwieldy to send. They are sometimes so complex that it is difficult to "theorize" or communicate them (Strang and Meyer 1994); or, they have to be broken down into smaller parts to be transmissible, a process that increases the potential for misinformation and confusion. In contrast, other types of remittances are fairly straightforward. They are easy to articulate and travel cleanly through transmission channels, after which they are either adopted or ignored.

In the case of Miraflores, social remittances, such as membership recruitment techniques or vote-winning strategies, were easily communicated. They were either appropriated as is, modified and adopted, or disregarded. In contrast, values and norms about gender relations and racial identity fluctuated more easily. Migrants constantly redefined and renegotiated them. Their unstable nature made them more difficult to simplify and express and therefore diminished their force.

Remittance impact is also stronger if, by adopting these new ideas and behaviors, individuals signal to others that they are better off, more "modern," or more "American." Since some Mirafloreños covet all things from the United States, they are more open to the new styles and practices that migrants introduce.

The Nature of the Transnational System

The features of the transnational organizations and the social networks through which remittances are communicated also influence their impact. Remittances flow more efficiently through tightly connected, dense systems because they consist of similar parts and use similar technologies. Transfers within more open, informal systems are sloppier, less efficient, and more prone to interference by other cultural exchanges. As in the child's game of "telephone," each time a message is recommunicated, it becomes increasingly distorted in the translation.

Transnational religious ties between Boston and the Dominican Republic, for instance, arose primarily out of personal relations between priests, parishioners, and seminarians. Communication tended to be unsystematic and leaky because these ties were based on personal, informal connections. In more structured settings, or in cases involving more tightly constructed social networks, remittances flow through more efficient transmission channels. The connections between the organizational parts or the members of the network are closer and more systematic, increasing remittance impact.

The open nature of the religious system also meant that social remittances were more vulnerable to interference by other global cultural flows. For example, Catholic religious messages competed with evangelical ones communicated outside the Church's purview. In contrast, since the Partido Revolucionario Dominicano established an organization in the United States that mirrored its Dominican structure, political social remittances traveled directly, and with some degree of protection, through these organized, secure channels. Since the technology used to transfer remittances and the organizational units that they flowed between were similar, remittances were more likely to have a stronger effect.

Finally, remittance impact also changes at different stages of organizational development. New organizations or organizations in flux are more malleable or amenable to change. After the PRD's 1986 electoral defeat, the party organization was overhauled. Return migrants who suggested new approaches felt that party leaders were more receptive to their ideas because so many aspects of party life were up for discussion during this period of organizational change.

The Characteristics of the Messenger

The strength of remittance impact is also influenced by the characteristics of their messenger. Individuals occupying higher status positions get listened to more. In Miraflores, these individuals are generally men, people with money, older community members, or established community leaders.

In some cases, these individuals can pressure others to listen to them because the person receiving the remittance relies upon them for economic support. Receptivity is higher because remittances are delivered with a golden glove. Doña Sara, for example, began saving to open a small business in her home because her brother in Boston thought it was a good idea for women to have some income of their own. Since he sends her money almost every month, she felt she had to do his bidding.

In other cases, villagers adopt remittances because they want to emulate their peers. Since everyone else in a certain strata is "doing it," they feel they must also "keep up with the Joneses." Young men and women who were never particularly interested in fashion now feel that they too must have the latest jeans or backpack from Boston in order to hold their own. Others adopt remittances because they want to become more like remittance transmitters. If they accept a particular practice or point of view, it signals to others that they have ascended to a higher-status social or economic group.

The Target Audience

Remittance impact also depends on the gender, class, and life-cycle stage of the receiver. Individuals with more resources and power, and who therefore control more aspects of their lives, have more freedom with which to accept or reject remittances. Women with some income of their own can adopt remittances more easily than those who are completely dependent upon their husbands. Families with some savings can experiment with different business schemes, while those on the economic margins cannot.

Similarly, younger, unmarried women have many choices ahead of them, while married women with children have already made important decisions that constrain their ability to adopt new ideas. Unlike Doña Sara, Sandra could not start her own small business. All the extra money she saved had to go toward paying her son's private school tuition.

Differences between Sending and Receiving Countries

Social remittance impact also depends on relative differences between sending and receiving countries. If the value structures and cognitive models migrants import are similar to host-country norms, then social remittances are likely to be assimilated more quickly. If the new patterns of social relations have elements in common with those already in place, then social remittances are also more likely to be adopted (DiMaggio 1988; Westney 1987). If the remittance is a completely new idea or behavior, then it will face greater barriers to acceptance. In this sense, remittance adoption, as well as evolution, is path-dependent, in that existing normative, cognitive, and structural constraints condition future choices.

Mirafloreños, for instance, adopted new religious practices from the United States more easily than they did political ones. Religious remittances were often stylistic variations of the Catholic practices that Dominican and Boston parishioners already shared. The modified version of a particular prayer or ritual looked enough like what villagers already did that it was easy to assimilate. In contrast, political remittances that promoted a more egalitarian leadership style went against the grain of "business as usual" and contradicted long-standing power hierarchies. These remittances represented a sharper departure from deeply entrenched political ideas and behaviors and were therefore a harder sell.

Features of the Transmission Process

Some remittances have a stronger effect because they travel with other remittances. When those that are introduced initially are accepted, receptivity is heightened to those that follow.

Remittances traveling through multiple pathways also have a more significant effect. Community leaders in Miraflores, for example, began managing contributions to community projects more carefully in response to demands from the Miraflores Development Committee (MDC) in Boston and from migrant community members in general. MDC members' calls for stronger financial controls coincided with social remittances introduced by migrant community members, who told nonmigrants about the management practices they observed while working in Boston.

Remittances reinforced by global cultural flows also heighten remittance impact. Nonmigrants begin demanding better social programs because they hear about the kinds of services their relatives receive in the United States and because they see such programs on the Cable News Network (CNN). The PRD decentralized decision-making, in part, because return migrants pressured them to do so and because an international pool of ideas that favored markets and democracy came into favor (Domínguez 1997). Young adults in Miraflores were open to new ideas about gender because they related these to the movie and magazine images they were already so familiar with.

Finally, the force of transmission affects remittance impact. If many remittances are transmitted consistently during a short time, their impact is greater than when they are transferred periodically. If there are many, simultaneous calls for men to share the housework, and numerous examples of this, nonmigrants are more likely to change their behavior than if they are exposed to only infrequent, isolated examples of these new social forms.

Part Two

Chapter Three

Reshaping the Stages
of the Life Cycle

When I asked the many Mirafloreños I spoke with to describe how migration had transformed their community, they generally began by pointing out the homes, school, and health center that were built and renovated with money from Boston. They proudly displayed their collections of nested Corningware baking dishes and Tupperware containers, which were used more often for decoration than for cooking or storage. They said that most people live better now, with enough money for food and clothing, though there are still families who wait anxiously for their remittances each month. Further discussion, though, revealed the hidden costs of these gains to their community. Material progress came at a high price.[1]

The story of Miraflores, and other transnational villages like it, is about trade-offs. The impact of migration is both positive and negative because its effects are contingent upon the context in which migration is embedded (Portes 1995; Portes and Sessenbrenner 1993). In the case of Miraflores, migration prompts calls for political and social reform at the same time that it introduces new ways of breaking the law. Though most villagers have more income and live better than they did before large-scale migration began, few have achieved this through their own labor. Instead, they have grown accustomed to greater comfort, and they covet even more, as their ability to accomplish this on their own grows weaker. They are more satisfied at the same time that they are more restless. They see their village becoming the place they always dreamed it should be and a place where they can no longer afford to stay. They cling to their old ways while they experiment with new ones, finding that neither works particularly well in the rapidly changing context in which they live.

In this chapter, I explore the ways in which migration and social remittances reshape the stages of the life cycle and in the process constitute and perpetuate transnational community. I focus on how migration alters family, school, and work life. Much of what I describe about migrants' experiences in the United States resonates with the experiences of other immigrant groups.[2] My goal in this chapter is to contribute to a deeper understanding of how changes in immigrant life in Boston challenge sending-country norms and practices and to provide concrete examples of how migrants and nonmigrants create global culture at the local level.

Childrearing

Twenty-year-old Elena cannot remember a time when she actually lived with her mother, Nuria. For as long as she can recall, Nuria lived and worked in Boston, while Elena and her two siblings remained behind in Miraflores to be raised by their grandparents. In fact, her grandparents' house is overflowing with children left behind by their migrant parents. There are two other cousins whose fathers also live in the United States. Recently, her Uncle Alberto brought back his three American-born children, who can barely speak Spanish, to live in Miraflores after he separated from his wife.

Elena's childhood memories are filled with vivid images of her mother's once-a-year visits. Every Christmas, Nuria would arrive home with a suitcase filled with new clothes and toys. For those three weeks, Elena was completely content. She remembers nearly bursting with pride as she showed off the gifts she received to her friends. Her mother always took everyone out for ice cream or for an afternoon outing to the swimming pool. In the evenings, the family would sit under the large tree in their yard and welcome the neighbors, who all came to greet Nuria, the returning hero. The pride Elena felt almost made up for how deeply she missed her mother during the year. After all, it was *her* mother who everyone respected for doing so well in Boston and who everyone appreciated for the seemingly boundless supply of presents she brought back.

Elena knew her mother was supporting the family. She overheard her grandparents talking about how they would never be able to manage without Nuria's help. Elena's uncles in Boston never seemed to be able to "make good." She felt proud that Nuria was the reliable, responsible one. But she often felt incredibly lonely. Why was she left to bring up herself, and her younger siblings, on her own? There were things Elena wanted to ask her grandmother, Amelia, but Amelia always seemed busy caring for the other members of her ever expanding household. Elena imagined that if her mother were there, she would know what to do, so she would save up all her questions for Nuria's next visit. But when Nuria finally arrived, there were always too many people around. When they did get some time alone together, Elena felt awkward. Her words did not come easily. She was suddenly shy after all those months of waiting and she could not make herself speak.

Elena's experience of being brought up across borders is increasingly common.[3] She was raised jointly by her mother in Boston and by relatives in Miraflores. By distributing the tasks of production and reproduction transnationally, Mirafloreños create and strengthen their transnational community. Migrant family members earn most of the household income, while nonmigrants remain behind to care for children. Transnational ties grow stronger as household members become more and more dependent on one another.

Sharing child-rearing responsibilities is not new in Miraflores. Extended families generally live close to one another in one "neighborhood" of the village. El Rincón de los Guerreros is the corner of Miraflores where most of the Guerrero family lives; most of the Quiroz family lives near the school. Three generations of the same family often live under the same roof or in the same compound or complex of houses. They spend most of their day working, caring for children, and relaxing together outdoors or in communal spaces like the kitchen, dining area, or patio. Privacy is minimal. In many homes, it is easy to hear what goes on in all corners of the household because walls extending just three-quarters of the way to the ceiling are the only things separating the bedrooms. Curtains substitute for doors. No one seems to have a particularly strong claim on any one room, or even bed, since sleeping arrangements change as members enter and exit the household.

Family boundaries have always been fluid in Miraflores as well. Common-law marriages have been the norm in the Dominican Republic since the seventeenth century. Most couples did not marry in the church because there were no priests around to marry them. Men often had mistresses or fathered children out of wedlock (Moya Pons 1995). Today, many couples still live in union. Even if they decide to marry legally, they are unlikely to do so within the church. A 1991 national survey found 33.3 percent of the population living in union while only 22.5 percent were officially married (Profamilia 1992). The informality of these unions, however, indicates little about their long-term future. They seem to be as brief or as long-lasting as legally sanctioned marriages.

Mirafloreño men also frequently form stable unions with a "second wife." They have a primary household, where they sleep, eat, and keep their belongings, and a secondary household that they also contribute money to, visit regularly, and feel a sense of commitment toward. These kinds of relationships are an integral part of community life. When Mirafloreños are asked how many brothers and sisters they have, a typical response is, "I have five brothers and sisters from my father and mother, and four from my father." This means that their father has a second long-term relationship with another woman with whom he also had children. In fact, it is not unusual for the two families to be in contact with one another. Pablo was born to his father's second wife but raised by his father's first wife. He spent nearly ten years living under her roof. When Toti's father passed away, his mother sent word to the children from his "other marriage" to come and meet their half-siblings. The two families have been visiting each other at holiday time ever since.

These fluid family arrangements mean that children in Miraflores have always been raised by multiple mothers. Grandmothers and aunts, along with parents, play a central role in their daily lives. That Elena was brought up by relatives, then, is not out of the ordinary. What is new is that family boundaries and shared child-rearing now regularly cross borders.

Raising children transnationally poses new challenges. These arrangements exacerbate conflicts within the community at the same time that they reinforce its cohesiveness. For one thing, separating parents and children for extended periods has clear emotional consequences. Though well loved and cared for, several respondents talked about how painful it was for them to miss out on that primary, maternal-child bond. When I asked Mariana, a twenty-eight-year-old return migrant who spent much of her childhood living with her grandparents, what she wanted for her own children, she responded:

I want so many things that I can't even say. I want them to have a profession that they want. I want them to be able to grow up with their mother and father so they can have our support. I grew up with my grandparents. My mother was always helping me but lived apart. When someone stays with their grandparents, especially in a big family, even though there is love, when the aunt and uncle come over, they make you feel the difference between a daughter and a granddaughter and you see that you are not really a daughter. I always felt that there was no one to care only about me.

Second, it is not always clear how decision-making and power-sharing should be managed when the roles of production and reproduction are separated from one another. Because absent parents can always be reached by phone or visit fairly regularly, no one person is totally in charge. Authority weakens when it is reallocated to a "generalized adult." This dramatically changes the relationship between young people and their elders.

For instance, though Nuria left Elena when she was five, there are several children whose parents left Miraflores when they were infants. Nancy got her visa when her baby, Germán, turned two months old. When she went to the U.S. consulate to get a visa for the baby, the consular officer advised her, "Either you go by yourself or the two of you stay here." Since she had already waited two years to join her husband, she left her son with her mother and sister. Though she tried to come back every four or five months, she missed his baptism, his first tooth, and his first steps.

Sometimes I feel he is not sure who his mother is. I would come back longing to hug him and he would cling to my sister. I could only coax him out of his shyness by giving him all the gifts I brought. As he got older, he got to know me better, but I felt that there was always something missing, like I had missed so many important parts of his childhood. We couldn't make it up. I would try to correct him or teach him to act in a certain way and he wouldn't listen. I didn't want to spend my whole visit arguing.

A great distance separates Nancy from Germán. As with Elena and Nuria, she cannot communicate easily with him. She cannot "make up for lost time" and develop a rapport easily during her short visits. She is the "party thrower," the special fairy godmother laden with gifts, instead of the day-to-day problem solver, confidante, and comforter. She has trouble commanding respect from her son, but she does not want to spend the little time they have together demanding it from him.

Elena's brother José has very different memories of his childhood.

Now that he is almost eighteen years old, he gets along well with his grandfather. But when he was growing up, he says, there were daily battles about going to school, when to be home, and whom he could go out with. His uncles, who were also living at home, would tell him one thing, his grandfather something else, and then they would call his mother in Boston, who would also tell him what to do. He felt he was always getting caught among several bosses, and he was never sure who he was ultimately accountable to.

I never knew who I should be listening to, who was in charge. My mother would tell me I had to keep going to school, my grandfather wanted me to help with the farmwork. My uncles stayed out all night but wouldn't let me go around with my friends. It was very confusing. My grandfather was always telling me that I was disrespectful and that I was heading for trouble, but it was really that I didn't know who I was supposed to take orders from.

In José's case, confusion over who he was accountable to, rather than loneliness, was the problem. His mother lacked authority because she lived so far away and because he did not really know her very well. When they did see one another, a sort of holiday-like, permissive mood prevailed. But it was not easy for the relatives Nuria left in charge to fill her shoes. They felt they lacked final decision-making power, offering disclaimers like, "We are not his real parents because his real parents are over there." Many grandparents expressed similar sentiments, claiming they were too tired for such battles after having struggled to raise their own children. Many said they lacked the strength to go through everything again, particularly widows and divorcées who often felt they needed a man to be the strict disciplinarian.

Cheap telephone rates and airplane fares make it easy to believe that parenting across borders is possible. Instead of acting when a problem first comes up, an aunt might call the United States for instructions. Her version of the 1950s aphorism "Wait until your father comes home" is, "Wait until I talk to your parents in Boston." When migrant parents admonish their children to change their behavior or order that they be punished, they are never sure if their instructions are carried out. Some children actively exploit this disparity between real and surrogate parental authority. They know their grandparents need the money their parents send. They use this as a bargaining chip, threatening to tell their parents if their grandparents do something they do not like.

So many kids are living with their grandparents. When their parents come back, their kids are so big, they can't control them anymore. The kids are just waiting, holding over the grandparents the envelope that comes every month. They have an attitude, a certain arrogance. You can't discipline them because it is their parents who are sending the money. They say, I will let my parents know what is happening here and they will stop sending so much money back to you. My sister sends $200 a month to support my nephew. When I was his age I was already working in the *conuco* (the fields) producing something. That kid does not do anything. He is a leech. (Javier, 48, nonmigrant, Miraflores)

Because grandparents need their migrant children's support, they are reluctant to assert their authority. Consequently, a whole generation of young people, many Mirafloreños fear, is being brought up without proper discipline or guidance.

This is particularly true when children, like Eduardo, are sent back and forth to live between Boston and Miraflores. Eduardo says he often feels unsure about where he belongs. His mother and father left him with his aunt and grandmother when he was less than a year old. By the time he joined them in Boston five years later, his parents had divorced. His mother soon remarried and started a new family. Since then, he has been back and forth between Boston and Miraflores, unable to feel completely comfortable in either place. When he has trouble in school in Boston, he is sent back to live with his grandmother in Miraflores. Things normally go well when he first arrives, but within months new problems always seem to crop up. A series of frantic phone calls to Boston about what should be done ensues.

Eduardo's grandmother says she is too old to take care of him, throwing her hands in the air to express how overwhelmed she feels. Because Eduardo disobeys her when she tells him to be home by midnight, she waits up half the night to make sure he comes back in one piece. His aunt, who was responsible for his day-to-day care when he was an infant, now has a son of her own. It pains her that she cannot reach Eduardo anymore since she was the one who changed his diapers and shared his bed when he was little. She tries to talk to him about doing well in school and about staying away from the *delincuentes* (delinquents) in town. Though he promises to change, the next day he is back at it again, doing the same things. This hurts her, she says, but she just cannot be responsible anymore.

In Boston, Eduardo's mother also feels that she is at her wits' end. Eduardo does not fit easily into the new family she has made with her second husband. She is tired of the constant phone calls she gets from his teachers at school. She now has a job and three other children to take care of, who all seem so well behaved. When she sends Eduardo back to Miraflores it is as if she is holding her breath, hoping that once her problem is out of sight, it will disappear. Meanwhile, Eduardo grows older, falls farther behind in school, and stays out later and later with a rough crowd in Miraflores.

Relations between migrant adults and children in Boston also have to be renegotiated because of the new demands of immigrant life. Parents have less control over their children because they have to work long hours away from home. Many parents only see their children briefly, when they come home to eat and bathe between their daytime and evening jobs.

These arrangements stand in stark contrast to Miraflores, where family members spend most of the day together. Even most of the men who farm come home to eat and relax for at least part of the afternoon. They can always be called home if a problem arises. Since there is a sharper separation between work and family life in Boston, and work schedules are more rigid, parents cannot move as seamlessly between these two worlds as they do at home.

Furthermore, in Miraflores, parents raise their children with help from the entire community. In Boston, they are on their own. Mayra, a thirty-two-year-old migrant, reported that in Miraflores, when her daughter walked home from school holding hands with a boy, she heard about it within an hour from four other mothers. In contrast, when her son Nicolás got into the habit of stealing candy from the grocery store on his way home from school in Boston, no one was watching.

Here you have to bring your kids up a little differently because there [in Miraflores], you know how it is. There, it's very small, everyone knows one another and where you live. If the kids go to the park, everyone knows they've gone to the park. It's more difficult in Boston because in Miraflores everyone brings up the kid and in Boston you have to be at the school at the moment they get out so that you make sure they don't get into trouble. If they want to go out after school, they have to ask permission. In Miraflores, the neighbor is watching. I've seen some families who try to bring up their kids in the same way they would in Miraflores. When they say to their kids, you have to be at a certain place at a certain time, the kid is not there. They ask where they were and the kid says that it's none of their business. "I was where I was." In Santo Domingo, this would never happen.[4]

Because they are working, most parents cannot watch their children as closely as they would like. Elisa has to leave the house at 5 A.M. to catch her ride to work. She thought her daughter and son were going to high school each day until she received a call from the truant officer telling her that her daughter had not been to school for weeks. Carmen has to hope that her kids make it the five blocks home each day because she cannot be home until an hour after school gets out and there is no one she can ask to help her.

I couldn't bring my kids up in the same way I would have in Miraflores. Our lives were so different. My husband left early to go to work. He didn't see the kids when he left in the morning because they were sleeping and he didn't see them when he came home at night because they were already in bed. We hardly knew our neighbors. When I had to go out in an emergency, I had no one I could ask to watch the children for me. They grew up quicker, but they were also more difficult to control. (Carmen, 35, return migrant, Miraflores)

Carmen liked how responsible her children became in Boston. She was pleased that her boys learned to cook and that they helped support the family. But these same gains made it more difficult for her to supervise them. She feels that kids in Boston just grow up too fast.

Two other factors, not unique to Miraflores, also tip the balance of power away from parents toward their children. As is the case of many immigrant families, language becomes an issue. As kids spend more time in Boston, they become less fluent in Spanish, while their parents, who have little time to study, acquire only minimal English skills. Parents and kids have a hard time communicating with one another. According to Ana María, a semi-transparent scrim seemed to separate her from the English-language world of her children.

I didn't know how to speak English, and the kids were not learning Spanish that well because they heard so much English on the television. They were turning into *brutos* because they spent all day watching ghosts and monsters. Little by little it was harder to communicate because we didn't speak English and they were mentally developing in this world of North American television. I felt I couldn't control them because they were partly living in a world whose rules I did not understand. (Ana María, 43, return migrant, Miraflores)

Parents often felt they could not make themselves understood. In Miraflores, kids looked up to their parents and believed they could solve any problem. In Boston, children could sense how insecure and confused their parents felt and how much their parents depended on them. It was Javier's daughter, not Javier, who translated the letter from the Medicaid officer and who told him that he had to meet the guidance counselor at school. In Miraflores, Javier would have been the uncontested head of the household. In Boston, it seemed, both he and his children had to take orders from teachers, welfare workers, and priests. As a result, parents felt, and were sometimes perceived by their children to be, less powerful and competent than they were in Miraflores.

Both parents and children also learn about the child-abuse laws in the United States. Several parents claimed they could not discipline their children as they would have liked because "spanking is illegal in the United States" and "parents get put in jail for teaching their children right from wrong." Some kids even threatened they would call "the DSS," or the Department of Social Services, if their parents touched them. These regulations become larger than life because the information Mirafloreños receive about them comes second- or third-hand. Here again, they feel disempowered and are perceived by their children as such.[5]

When we lived in Boston, everyone was always talking about the DSS, the government agency in charge of making sure that families are okay. All of us from Miraflores were confused because we heard that if you spanked your kids they would come and take them away. We didn't know what was really going on. But we were afraid that this would happen. I remember one time my son, Nelson, got in a fight at school. Normally my husband would have given him the belt, but we were afraid that the police would come. We stopped hitting him and, after a while, he stopped obeying us. (Gabriela, 45, return migrant, Miraflores)

When migrant children visit Miraflores, or when they call their friends and relatives who stay behind, they introduce new ideas about how parents and kids should act toward one another, thereby challenging the status quo. Nonmigrant youngsters like what they see and hear. To those who have not migrated, Boston begins to look like Mecca. They, too, want more say over what they do and when they do it. They want the independence their friends enjoy because they have jobs that put money in their pockets. Young women also want to be able to go out without a chaperon.

Social remittances and cross-border parenting have transformed parent-child relations in Miraflores. They have produced a new generation that no longer subscribes to deeply entrenched norms about respect and authority. According to Ramón, a fifty-two-year-old non-migrant, parents have to give in.

There is too much pressure to continue to do business as usual. We are in the middle of a lot of change. When high-school-age girls come back to visit and they are used to being able to go out with their friends and they don't have to tell their mother where they are going all the time, I can't continue to keep my own daughter at home under lock and key. I can't force kids to participate in the cultural events we used to organize if all they want to do is go to the discotheque. So we have to come up with a new way of being.

There are indications that this "new way of being" is already taking shape. Sandra reported that many of her friends no longer address their parents using *usted,* or the polite form of *you,* but prefer the more familiar, less hierarchical *tú* instead. Chacho claimed that children are less likely to greet their parents or a respected elder by asking for their *bendición,* or blessing, as they have always done.

Laura, a thirty-five-year-old return migrant, is unsettled by these changes. She asks, which rules should apply?

Look at Doña Mercedes. She has been bringing up her four grandchildren since they were infants. But how can she watch them the way their parents would? It is impossible for her to give them the kind of attention and guidance that their own parents would. Those children are bringing themselves up, and it shows. Those girls are not learning the proper respect, they are out in the street too much, always playing rather than learning how to help out at home. And they do not know what rules to play by. Are they supposed to act the way we did toward our parents, where what the father said was the rule of the land? They haven't lived with their father for years. Or do they act like little Americans, where kids are more equal to their parents, where they can question the rules and make up their own minds about what they want to do?

School

Community members in Boston have done much to improve the educational facilities in Miraflores. Monies raised in the United States purchased the land on which the community school was built. Migrant community members funded the reconstruction of the school after the cyclone of 1975. The Miraflores Development Committee renovated the school in 1992 and also pays for monthly maintenance costs.

Despite these physical improvements, however, migration has under-cut the value and importance of education for most of the commu-nity's younger members.

According to Doña Helena, the school principal, about 60 of 300 stu-dents circulate back and forth between schools in Boston and Mira-flores each year. Because these students lack full linguistic or cultural fluency in either setting, they often fall irrevocably behind. Just as they begin to catch up, she says, their parents move them again:

When children are taken away from a place they love, they stop growing. Take Juan, for example. He is exactly where he was when they first took him away from here when he was five years old. They took him out of a place where he liked being and put him someplace where he doesn't want to be. Now he doesn't know how to get along in either place because he never stays long enough to learn how. In school, it is a disaster. Kids like him, and there are increasing numbers of them, cause serious behavior problems.

The possibility of migration also increases dropout rates and dis-courages students from going on to secondary school.[6] Many kids say they do not have to do well in school because their parents take care of everything. They do not have to work hard or choose a career be-cause they get a check from Boston each month. Other kids feel that attending school in the Dominican Republic is not necessary because they will migrate as soon as their papers arrive. "Why should I study here?" Luz asked. "I'll be migrating as soon as I get my visa and I can go to school in Boston."

As a result, there are few incentives to pursue further education. According to Eduardo, a forty-seven-year-old community member,

These kids are growing up in an environment in which studying and working are far from their minds because they have all their needs taken care of. Their parents are irresponsible because they are not demanding that they study or work. [The kids] just wait for that check to come each month. They have more than we ever dreamed of. When I was their age, I had to get up at 5 o'clock in the morning, I worked in the fields, then I went to town to high school, and then back out to the fields when I got home. Everyone had to do this. It made us learn hard work in a way these kids don't know.

Approximately one in four eligible students finishes high school each year. There is less and less pressure from the community do so. While seven students graduated from college in the 1970s, not one student from Miraflores was enrolled in the university in 1992. The migration option was just too attractive. Parents who tried to force their children to remain in school, met with little success.

We tried to tell Roberto that he was making a big mistake. Even if he ends up migrating, he still needs an education. If he goes to Boston and he doesn't even have a high school diploma, he will get stuck in an awful job. But he looked at all his friends around him, the whole bunch of them that drive motorcycle taxis. He sees only the money in their pockets, not their empty futures. We argued with him. There were many fights. But finally, we just couldn't compete with this migration fever. (José Carlos, 49, nonmigrant, Miraflores)

Some kids do enroll in school when they get to Boston, but the majority of those who are over sixteen go directly to work. They say they plan to get a graduate equivalency diploma (GED) at some point, but they rarely do.

Migration also divides the student body between those with migrant parents and those without. The children with parents in Boston have better clothes, fancier bookbags, and a whole set of school supplies that have become "required fare." Kids without migrant relatives feel they cannot keep up. They cannot even afford the uniform or equipment that is required to play the game. According to Doña Helena,

The kids whose parents live in Boston tend to be better dressed and bring in all sorts of fancy pencil boxes and notebooks. They brag about it and compete with one another. They taunt those who don't have the tennis shoes or the jeans. The ones whose parents are here feel badly, like they can't keep up. We tried to limit it. The kids wear uniforms, but you can't tell them what to wear on their feet. With so many students with relatives in Boston, it gets out of hand.

Migration has a paradoxical effect on the educational system. Migrants' contributions ensure that bathrooms work, classrooms have doors, and teachers have the supplies they need. At the same time, migration lends credence to the notion that a Dominican education — and, in some cases, education in general — is superfluous. Because young adults reject one of the few ways to get ahead on the island, they ensure that migration and transnational practices will continue as integral parts of Mirafloreño life.

Earning a Living

Migration has similar contradictory effects on the world of work. Most Mirafloreños now live better and have more disposable income than they have ever had before. This higher living standard is only possible, though, because so many villagers have migrated. Those who remain behind have become dependent upon and, in some cases, addicted to a level of material comfort and consumption they cannot sustain on their own.

Mirafloreños traditionally took great pride in farming. Most hard-working men could make a comfortable living, and they were respected by their neighbors for doing so. But during the 1970s and 1980s, as crop prices declined, it became more difficult to support oneself by farming. At the same time, villagers saw migrants earn what had been unprecedented amounts with seemingly little effort. As Roberto explains, "They began to ask themselves, why should we kill ourselves working in the fields when we can go to Boston or let those in Boston support us?" They became accustomed to living better, but they could only do this because of the remittances they received.

These days the only people who farm in Miraflores are elderly men and Haitian immigrants. Young men simply will not go into farming anymore. "If I earn 50 pesos a day [about $4] working in the fields and it barely puts a roof over my head," says Gustavo, "why should I bother?"

It used to be that people taught their children how to work in agriculture and passed this on to them. They were proud to be farmers. This doesn't happen anymore. These kids say to themselves, why should I work eight hours beneath the hot sun if they send me $50 each month from Boston? I have enough to eat, so why am I going to work that hard? (Manuel, 34, nonmigrant, Miraflores)

That Haitian migrants do most of the farm labor that Mirafloreños reject discredits agriculture even further. Most Mirafloreños consider any job done by Haitians to be beneath them. As Haitians gain more of a foothold in this ethnic occupational niche, it becomes less and less likely that farming will recuperate its former status.

By exacerbating and solving the problem of limited employment in Miraflores, migration again makes transnational community a necessary part of everyday life. It shrinks the number of jobs available by diminishing farming's prestige and reclassifying it as an occupation of disrepute. It inflates material appetites and prices so much that many of the Mirafloreños who work on the island feel they cannot keep up. Some of the people who could work but receive remittances drop out of the labor force because they feel their efforts are futile. Their Dominican-size salaries cannot compete with those in Boston, especially as consumption patterns shift toward imported goods. For example, families increase their costs significantly when they substitute imported foods for standard Dominican fare. An imported box of corn-flakes, which has replaced yuca and plantains as the food of choice for breakfast, can cost two times its price in dollars in the United States and six times as much as traditional food (Torres-Saillant and Hernández 1998).

Migration offers the solution to the very problem it creates. As Eduardo, a thirty-nine-year-old return migrant, explains:

You cannot work in Miraflores anymore because the fields are filled with Haitians. You have to migrate, but this has generated a standard of living that surpasses the one we used to have. It is a false standard of living because it is not based on work we do here. Dominicans go to the United States to do the work that Americans won't do anymore. They do what is too denigrating to Americans. But now for the Banilejo it is too denigrating to work in the fields. There is so much work to do here, but people just won't do it anymore. They rely on those in Boston to make ends meet.

The depth of material appetites and the pressure to succeed in satisfying them cannot be underestimated. Whereas in the past, community members were admired for their hard work and community service, people now look up to those who have acquired the most things.

They place a lot of importance on the material aspects of life. They are so proud of all the material possessions they have acquired. They dress differently. They take a lot of pride in talking about their imported clothes and what they have brought from the U.S. The person who doesn't have these things feels terrible. It is like all the things we used to admire—being good to one's family, working hard for the community—don't matter anymore. It just matters if you have a big house or a lot of gold jewelry. (PRD leader, Santo Domingo)

Instead of saving or investing productively, Mirafloreños spend their money to display their heightened status.

They had to go through so many somersaults and so much risk to earn it, yet it goes up in smoke when they come back, burning it on houses, cars, gasoline, clothing, all the things you can see. Banilejos are known for showing off. We are also very ambitious. We like to make money. This is part of our culture. And this goes well with how Americans are. They also like to earn a lot of money and show it off. This tendency to brag grows even stronger when they are in the U.S. This is one of your social remittances. They come back and the idea of modesty or humility is out the window. (Gustavo, 40, nonmigrant, Miraflores)

In the past, Mirafloreños criticized ostentatiousness. Though everyone wanted to earn money, the community disdained those who were too pretentious about their success. As Charo, a thirty-six-year-old return migrant describes, a fundamental change has taken place in a very short period.

I know people whose parents couldn't afford a wagon and in two years, they have five jeeps and twenty cars. They feel an insatiable craving for luxury. Anyone who goes to college and gets a degree in this country will never be able to afford this. These people live surrounded by things that twenty years ago would have been inconceivable. But twenty years ago, society was much more moderate. There was less rivalry, and people didn't feel like their highest calling was a new TV. They were less ostentatious about it. Your biggest goal was not to show your neighbor that you have a VCR and he does not.

Luis, a thirty-four-year-old returnee, further described:

What you have in society now is two kids, one kid whose father buys him a bike and the other kid whose father cannot buy him a bike. So the other kid says, I'll lend it to you but you can't have it because it's my bike. So the other kid is always envying the other kid's bike and desire turns into want and then into need. They feel they need it. The people who migrate come back with this American dream of wealth and show it off to people who have never owned a pair of shoes. They tell them they are making a mistake. They must leave the island and they can come back and they can buy all the shoes they want. It's more and more out of control because so many families are envying each other.

A vicious circle has been set in motion. Initially, the gifts nonmigrants received from the United States awed them. They felt deeply indebted and grateful to their benefactors. Now, many take these monies and gifts for granted. They feel they cannot get by without the beauty supplies, clothing, or food they regularly receive. Migrants are considered failures if they arrive home without a suitcase full of gifts for everyone, yet many of them are tired of catering to this "spoiled child they have created."

I know my people, and I wish I was wrong, but what could be better than to sit in your house and have someone bring you everything—if someone comes to you and says, you stay here, I'll bring you everything you need, you just stay home, watch TV, take care of the kids. But if you don't have someone do that for you, you have to go out and work for a living. Unfortunately, we have gotten them used to the idea that we are a hen who lays the golden egg. . . . I am not saying that those of us here shouldn't send stuff. I think it is good that we send money to them, but they shouldn't just be sitting there waiting for it. This is not the way to get ahead. Do you know why? It's fine to get a present from someone from Boston every once in a while, but it is much better if you are not sitting around waiting for it. The person who gives it to you should know that you are also trying to work in agriculture or construction or whatever. (Javier, 34, migrant, Boston)

Those who have never migrated are unrealistic about what it takes to send home so much money and to bring home so many gifts. Many migrants have not told them what their lives in Boston are really like. They have never described how they save every dime or how they live in windowless basement rooms so they can save on rent. Once their full suitcases became commonplace and expected, it was too late to fill in the blanks. It would have diminished migrants' hero status in the eyes of those who stayed behind, which is often what sustained them between visits back to Miraflores. As a result, migrants reinforce non-migrants' skewed understanding of U.S. life and perpetuate their un-realistic expectations of migration's rewards.

Adult Family Life

Mirafloreños who stay behind are clearly the weaker partners in the interdependent relationship that arises between migrants and nonmi-grants. They need migrants for their economic support and to help them to migrate. Migrants need those who stay in Miraflores to raise their children, manage their affairs in the village, and to serve as the yardstick against which to measure their enhanced status.[7] By redis-tributing power, status, and decision making within the household, mi-grants and nonmigrants ensure their continued commitment to each other.

When a household's breadwinning function relocates offshore, so does its locus of control. Migrants' power increases as their family's economic dependence on them grows. Parents find themselves be-holden to children who go abroad, but the children often assume responsibility for decision making, even when their decisions go against their parents' better judgment.

The relationship between fathers and sons has been completely transformed. Before, the father defined and upheld the norms. Now, no. It is the son and it doesn't matter if he is the youngest in the family. If he goes to the States and he earns a bit of money, he is the one who is consulted and decides and imposes his view on the other family members. Before, for example, if the father knew that his son was involved in some sort of questionable business deal, he punished him. Now, it is the other way around. A lot of those who migrate make money fast and people know that they are dealing in drugs. But the parents justify this, and the kids become, in the family context and in the context of the community, not someone condemned, but a sort of hero. He goes and is successful and it doesn't matter how. (Folklorist, Baní)

These shifts in the power dynamics of the family are part and parcel of the emerging division of labor across borders, and they are constantly being renegotiated. But what do nonmigrants do to fulfill their part of the bargain?

Cecilia, a forty-year-old woman with three siblings in Boston, knows it is her responsibility to clean, wash, and cook for five extra people and treat them as royal guests when they come to visit, but she admits it is a strain. She wants to give something back to her brothers and sisters, but she is exhausted when they leave. She appreciates the money they send, but she hates having to wait for it and never being quite sure when it will arrive or how much there will be. Mirafloreños expressed a variety of sentiments about their relatives in Boston, ranging from "María is so good, she sends me something every month and I know I will be taken care of" to "I don't know what those children of mine are doing up in Boston. They haven't sent any money in weeks. We are in debt at the grocer's, the pharmacy; [we haven't paid] the telephone bill. I think they've forgotten about those they left behind." Migrant children are ranked according to how much money they send back and how reliable they are about doing so.

Migrants also struggle with how to manage these obligations. They may be financially strapped themselves, but they cannot say so because it would cause too much worry at home. They feel burdened by their responsibility and resent it when they feel their efforts are being taken for granted. They want to help out but not when it is at the expense of their own spouse and children.

Migrants also expressed a range of emotions about being treated like returning royalty. While many felt they had earned the right to such a reception, and described with pleasure how much they enjoyed being brought their paper and coffee each morning, others felt uncomfortable with such special treatment.

In Miraflores, the schedule is very rigid. You have to eat every meal. You can't skip lunch or dinner. You have to eat at 12 P.M. on the dot. It is cooking and cleaning all day long and then it's time to discuss what we should eat at the next meal. I try to help, but they won't let me. They say, what will the neighbors say if they see you cleaning the house or carrying water? They don't want you to do anything like that. They don't even think I would know how to clean if they let me. (Ana Cristina, 37, migrant, Boston)

Subtle bargaining maintains the peace. Javier, a fifty-four-year-old returnee, who owns one of the few successful businesses in Miraflores, talked about his own struggle to balance these conflicting pulls. He feels a strong sense of responsibility toward his family and, in particular, toward his widowed mother. At the same time, he is confused about his obligations toward his siblings and cousins. While living in the United States, he became more individualistic. He visited with his family much less frequently. Though he recognizes how difficult it is to make a living in Miraflores, he feels that nonmigrants should at least try to earn something on their own. In fact, he would feel more predisposed to help them if he sensed they were making an effort. When they fail to do so, he feels he is being taken advantage of, especially when he considers how hard he worked when he lived in the States. Since he kept at it and succeeded under difficult conditions, why can't they do so as well? He resents the claims being made on him but cannot ignore the social sanctions he would face if he turned his back on his family.

In the U.S. everyone has to work. It would be very difficult for you to have your brother living in your house for a year without contributing anything. Maybe for a week, but not for a year. Here it used to be different. If my brother isn't working and he doesn't have work, then I have to support him because I work. I have to do this because he is my family. In the U.S., there is always work if you want to work. They say there is a high rate of unemployment, but that is not an unemployment rate, that is an index of the people who want to live off the government because they don't want to work.
   In the U.S., your responsibility to your family changes. You don't have to feel obligated to support anyone who just doesn't feel like working. The same family hardly shares at all, although they are Dominicans, although they are

brothers. I had a brother who I hardly saw. You get more distant from your family. It's a question of work. I left for work every day at 5 A.M. When I got back, I bathed and at 6 P.M., I ate, watched TV, and then went to sleep. My brother was doing the same thing. He opened his market at 7 A.M. and he didn't get home until midnight. How am I going to invite him over? If I wanted to see him, I would go to his store.

But in Miraflores, what can I do? If he shows up at my house at lunchtime, what can I do? I must give him food, and if he needs to sleep, I must give him a roof. But I have to say, this is changing. When I was in the U.S. I couldn't bear the thought of my mother being hungry. I sent money to my mother, but since two of my brothers were living under her roof and my aunt came over all the time, there was a line of "beggars" always outside her door who were living off my check. I started to feel that they should work. One starts not wanting to sacrifice in the name of the *vieja* [the old lady], like we say around here. You think they should work even if they earn a little less. When I lived here before I went to the U.S., we used to send out four or five truckloads of products each week. Now we take in four or five truckloads of crops from other places to be able to survive. Producers have now become consumers, but where is the money coming from to be able to consume?

Despite these reservations, Javier continues to help his family members because, by doing so, he reasserts his position as family head. Those who remain behind accept less power and prestige in exchange for migrants' continued economic support. Since males, in particular, are often strongly affected by their diminished social position in the United States, they are especially keen to have their achievements acknowledged and respected in Miraflores. By granting migrants this status, nonmigrants encourage their continued commitment to the family and community, thereby making bounded solidarity and enforceable trust sustainable across borders.

The Feasibility of Return

Almost everyone who leaves Miraflores does so with the intention to return.[8] Most migrants, however, remain in the United States, and the longer they do so, the less likely it is that they will live in Miraflores during their working years. For those who do, the transition is difficult. I focus here on men's experiences, as I will focus on the experiences of women in the following chapter.

Returnees fall into three broad groups. The first is by far the most common. These migrants leave Miraflores poor, with little land and minimal education. In the United States, they are recipient observers or instrumental adapters who work in jobs where they learn little English and few skills they can use in Miraflores when they return. Though they come back able to buy a small home and some appliances, or even start a small business, they often find it difficult to put a long-term income-generating strategy into place. If their entire family returns, so that no more remittances are forthcoming, many of these families eventually find themselves in the same position they were in before they left. They are better off at first, but their ability to sustain these improvements is questionable.[9]

Pepe and Juanita's experiences exemplify this pattern. They live in the part of Miraflores known as Las Casitas. Shortly before he was assassinated, Trujillo planned to convert Miraflores into a sugar production colony. Though he never realized his plan, he did build a group of modest wooden homes at the southern part of the village, where sugar workers would have lived. Pepe and Juanita owned and lived in one of these houses before they migrated. Pepe worked as a truck driver, while Juanita took care of their home.

Many of the houses in Las Casitas still have no running water or indoor plumbing. They are so narrow, it is difficult to walk through comfortably when there are visitors seated on both sides of the living room. Though Pepe and Juanita now have a television and small refrigerator, not much else has changed since their return. They still live crowded together with their teenage son and their daughter, who now has a baby of her own.

Pepe and Juanita lived in Boston for eight years. They left their three younger children behind with their eldest daughter and her husband. Pepe worked as a janitor at the University of Massachusetts and Juanita worked at a factory. Eventually they saved $11,000 and decided to return home. Their plan was that Pepe would buy his own truck and work for himself. They described their experience as follows:

So before you went to Boston, how did you consider yourself compared to other people in Miraflores? Did you think you were poor, medium, or well off?

P: Poor.

And now that you've come back, how do you see yourself?

P: I think I'm as poor as ever.

So your economic situation didn't improve at all?

P: The only thing that changed is that when we came back my wife said to me that we should buy that cabinet, that refrigerator, and the stove. We fixed up some of the furniture in the house.

J: We came back and my husband wanted to buy a truck, but the man said that we didn't have enough money to buy it. So we decided to mortgage the house. And now, look, we've lost it and I don't know where we are going to live. We're going to have to rent something, but we don't have anything now.

The trucking business didn't go well?

J: It went well at first, but then Pepe got involved with a woman and she took away all the money. So now here we are—we lost the house and the truck. Now he only works every once in a while, when Antonio [his old boss] needs him to drive.

What do you think about all of this?

P: That I am sick with worry because I don't know where we are going to live.

The second group of returnees are what most Dominicans would call "Dominicanyork." This broad label refers to those who go to the United States empty-handed but who soon return with jewelry, cars, and lots of money most assume they made illegally in the drug trade. No one knows how many Mirafloreños are actually involved in drug trafficking, though several community members are suspected of this. None has returned permanently to live in Miraflores. Instead, they circulate back and forth, spending several months in Boston followed by several months on the island. No one is ever sure what they do in either place.

Most community members try to keep these individuals at bay. Doña Graciela and her family, for example, treated one young man who often stopped by to visit with a cautious sense of humor. They were always gracious. They found his brazenness mildly entertaining and begrudgingly admired his nerve. They let him get away with what would have been considered very bad manners for someone else. But they welcomed him only conditionally into their household, sensing he belonged to a place they did not want to go. Many afternoons he would come speeding through Miraflores in his new blue convertible, looking for "someone to play with," but even the cash in his pocket could not convince most people to pretend that they were not home.

Dominicanyork who return are often accepted only begrudgingly back into Banilejo society. The local economy needs them and yet they are socially ostracized.

It's easy to tell who made their money honestly and who has been into something illegal. In Baní, the business community looks to these return migrants because they are the only ones with capital to support new business growth. Everyone else is struggling. But invite them to join the Baní Country Club? Never. The old elite needs them but won't let them sit at the same table. (Claudia, 42, nonmigrant, Baní)

A third, smaller group is more successful at returning. They leave Miraflores with more education and resources, and these advantages make them more successful in Boston. They are purposeful innovators who are more likely to become supervisors or managers. They pick up more English, interact more with Anglos, and acquire new skills that they can use when they return. They tend to come back with more money to families who were relatively well off to begin with. If anyone has a chance to mount a successful return, it is this group.

Even with this head start, however, many are unable to do so. "I am just not sure," says José, a forty-eight-year-old returnee, "about what one can really do. I mean, how many *colmados* [grocery stores] can a small place like Miraflores support?" Some members of this group become gentlemen farmers, managing their family's land and making improvements to it. Others become money changers who convert dollars into pesos for a small fee. Others start small businesses aimed at migrants, like the garage Ernesto built to house the cars of those who are away. Or they try living off their savings and investment income. Most combine several pursuits, saying:

We come back with money and ideas, but it's not as if the economy here has changed that much. There just isn't that much to do. I thought I would come back and open a bakery or an ice cream store and then I realized that people still don't have enough money to buy bread every day. They are still wedded to the old idea that you have to have rice at every meal, not bread. Then when I thought about doing something in Baní, there already are three bakeries.

So I'm just going to bide my time and make a decision slowly because there just aren't that many things you can really do." (Rodrigo, 39, return migrant, Miraflores)

Finding a social niche is also a problem. The social hierarchy in Miraflores is more complex than it was in the past. Before migration began, Miraflores was basically a two-class society, consisting of a small landed or business-owning elite and a large class of landless farm laborers. Now many additional rungs have been added to the ladder. Negotiating a new place, particularly at a higher status, is difficult. Even if returnees try to pick up old relationships where they left off, their neighbors often assume they want something different, as Octavio, a thirty-nine-year-old returnee, described:

One comes back and one has to once again readjust to the system of life in this country. Twenty-three years in the U.S. is a long time. One loses the habit. I am not going to say that one loses friendships. But people from the *campo* [village] don't see me as one of theirs anymore. Now they look at me as something different because I worked there, I earned money, I can live well. I haven't felt good here at least during these first few months. I think with time . . . I think they must think that I am a different sort of person now. I have never thought about it this way because I like to deal with people, the less they have the better. I have always liked to help those who are the least well off. I think with time we can get to know our neighbors better again.

As we have seen, migration transforms family, work, and schooling in Miraflores in ways that heighten divisions and reinforce community at the same time. As the tasks of production and reproduction are distributed across borders, the seeds of migrants' and nonmigrants' interdependence and differentiation are sown. Nonmigrants need migrants' economic support, particularly as migration weakens the economic base and the educational system in Miraflores further. Migrants need those who remain behind to raise their children, manage their affairs, and show them the respect they are denied in Boston. Both parties accept changes in the balance of status and power, and negotiate new ways to define these, partly out of love and commitment to one another and partly because they have little choice. Heightened class and generational divisions are part and parcel of increasing social and economic interconnectedness across borders, making this strong but conflict-ridden community likely to endure.

Chapter Four

Making Values from
Two Worlds Fit

Chapter 3 described the tensions that have emerged in Miraflores over such things as the importance of material possessions, the distribution of power between young people and their elders, and the ways in which individuals have tried to balance their responsibilities to themselves and to their families. In this chapter, I further chronicle how Mirafloreños manage these contradictory pulls by creating new cultural forms and making values from two worlds fit. I focus, in particular, on values related to gender, race, and the law.

Gender

At first glance, women in Miraflores appear to have little power. Many depend entirely on their husbands for economic support and seem to have little say over household decisions. The first time they work outside their homes and earn their own money is in Boston. It is also the first time they are in regular contact with schools, medical institutions, and government agencies. Because their lives in the United States and on the island are so different from one another, we might expect women to be transformed by the immigrant experience and to introduce social remittances that would strongly challenge existing gender relations.

The truth, of course, is far more nuanced.[1] Mirafloreñas are not as powerless or as dependent as they first seem. Many have carved out powerful positions for themselves within the context of their economic dependency. In addition, not all women want to be independent. Some are happy to return to Miraflores from the United States, quit their jobs, and be cared for by their husbands. The returnees who want to do things differently, and the nonmigrants who have been captivated by these travelers' tales, have to find ways to achieve change within the context of existing expectations and constraints.

Socializing boys and girls differently, and assigning them to separate physical spaces, begins at an early age in Miraflores. Little girls are dressed in party dresses, lace socks, and patent-leather shoes and brought to the Sunday-evening dance for their first instruction in merengue soon after they learn to walk. Their mothers cultivate their sense of rhythm and style from the time they are toddlers. Once they enter school, mothers also begin teaching their daughters to care for younger children and to help with household chores. Though boys are also taught to help their fathers, they are generally kept out of the kitchen. According to Alfredo, a thirty-seven-year-old return migrant, "I never had the opportunity to wash or cook a plantain before I migrated. The women didn't allow you in the kitchen. My father used to take me to the fields, but more often than not I spent my childhood running around Miraflores with the other boys."

In this way, men and women are taught from an early age that they belong to distinct social spaces with distinct social rules. Daily life is organized around small, single-sex groups, made up of family members and close neighbors who are generally at the same life-cycle stage. Groups of boys and girls walk separately to school and play separately when school is over. When they reach adolescence, these same groups of friends and family accompany one another to their first coed events. Socializing always occurs collectively; the group chaperons itself because boys and girls are not supposed to be alone with one another.

Our mothers used to say that we couldn't go out alone. People are always talking because they are always into each other's affairs. They have something to say about everything you do—how you act, how you dress. Since I am the oldest, I have to protect them [the rest of the girls in the group]. People think if we go out alone, we might go off with some man alone or a man might try to take advantage of us. Our mothers feel better about letting us go out because I am in charge. (Teresa, 22, nonmigrant Miraflores)

When talking about their relations with men, the young women in Miraflores expressed a sense of adversariness combined with feelings of magnetic attraction. Men were irresistible but untrustworthy. Women should build lives that include men but do not revolve around them because men cannot be depended on. Apart from their sexual relations with them, many women viewed men as a kind of necessary evil that had to be patiently tolerated and humored but that did not figure large in their daily lives.

While young women had to protect their reputations, young men were expected to "sow their wild oats." Most Mirafloreños assumed that even once they were married, men would have extramarital affairs. They needed to do this, and the community expected them to, though they were also expected to "settle down" when they reached middle age. According to Alberto, recently married for the second time with two children, "I will go out and I will see a young lady and if I see she is promiscuous, I will engage and I will see how far I can take her. I don't think of her as someone I would like to spend the rest of my life with, but [I] like a challenge to see how far I can go." The men who don't "go out looking," as Mirafloreños referred to it, find that their manhood is called into question. They are considered somehow deviant, as Ana María and Leonel describe:

You know Montse and her husband. He is always home at night with her and the children. He never goes out. He doesn't go around with other women. And people look at him and say, what's wrong with him? He's not worth anything. (Ana María, 34, nonmigrant, Miraflores)

A lot of my friends think I am crazy. I work. I go home. I stay there with my family. I have nothing to do. Married guys don't do that. They go home. They eat, they take a bath, and they go out. I have American habits. (Leonel, 40, return migrant, Miraflores)

In fact, most women held the cheating man's wife somehow responsible for his roaming. Mariela, a twenty-one-year-old nonmigrant, characterizes the situation as follows:

Men continue to take lovers. There are many marriages in which their wives don't give them what they get with their lovers. . . . I just know what they tell me. There are many marriages in which the wife doesn't like to go out, she is kind of cold with her husband. He decides that if he goes out he can find someone different. I think this is okay because his wife is the one that's guilty because she doesn't give him what he wants.

Would you accept this?

Well, it's difficult. I don't think I would stand for it, but if he comes home to me every night I would. What most women say is, what does it matter to me who he is with as long as he sleeps with me?

As a result, men and women build very separate lives. The community expects men to stay out working and socializing. *Mujeres serias*, or good, serious women, are expected to stay close to home once they are married.

Within these boundaries, however, women are more powerful than it outwardly appears. Even those who depend entirely on men for money reclaim some autonomy by building lives in which men are only supporting actors. Women expect men to be *machistas* (chauvinists) and they move on from there. They build their own support systems with other women. The adolescent girls who go to their first dances together later become married women who feed, clothe, and bring up their children together. In many cases, they do so with minimal help from their husbands. These coping strategies do not negate the fact that women still need men for economic support, but they do endow women with some maneuvering room and bargaining power.

For example, Doris knows she can count on her neighbors when she is down to just a few pesos because her husband has not given her any money in weeks. In fact, she usually gives some of what she cooks each day to her next-door neighbor, who also regularly sends her plates of rice, beans, and plantains. She knows she can borrow clothing if she needs something special to wear. She also knows that when Ana Claudia's husband drinks and tries to beat her, it is her responsibility, along with her other neighbors, to take Ana Claudia in. Doris is not lonely because she spends all day conversing with her neighbors as she washes, cooks, and cleans. In the afternoon, these same women gather to *tomar fresco*, or sit in the shade together, and in the evenings they watch the nightly *novelas* together in Doña Mercedes's living room.

Most men around here are *sinvergüenzas* [without shame]. They cannot be relied upon. They go for days just coming home to eat, bathe, and then go out again. How are we going to depend upon them for anything? So, we know that. The women who live around here help each other. We give each other food. We lend each other money. We can survive on our own. We don't need the men to help us. (Julita, 39, nonmigrant, Miraflores)

"Men," says Rosa, "have to be made to feel like they are the ones in charge, even if we are really running things." By consciously acting as if men make the rules, and convincing men that this is true, women gain greater independence and power at home.

Clarisa, a thirty-one-year-old return migrant, told how she purposefully made her husband feel he was "the boss," though she knew very well that she was the one making the decisions.

It was his idea at first [to open a store] but when we finally did it, it was all my responsibility. I was in charge. He didn't know how to run it. I had never done that either, but I learned quickly. He got scared of having to talk to the customers. He never learned the price of anything. He would say to the customer, come back when the *señora* is here so she can tell you the price. And there we were, losing a sale. He also got confused about how you move money from one account to the other. I was the one who said, okay, today we'll do this and tomorrow we'll do that. . . . Sometimes I thought he must feel bad because I was telling him what to do. I would tell him, look, we spent this on this and we need this to be able to do this. I would think that I was pressuring him a lot. So I would say to him, you know, we need to pay for this, do you think that this week we can? You are the one who should decide because you know best. Or I would say, let's see if this week we can't pay for that. I protected his ego, so if he wants to buy something, he buys it. I made him feel as if he is the one giving orders, but it was really me who was running things. That way he is happy.

What happens, then, when Mirafloreños migrate? How do these dynamics change, and what are the consequences of these changes back in Miraflores?

Almost three-quarters of the women who migrated found paid employment in Boston; none of these women had ever worked outside of their homes before. Each family found its own way to manage their household once there were two income earners. About 40 percent of the women gave their paychecks to their husbands, who then gave them spending money for expenses. Another 40 percent said they put their salary into a jointly managed account. The rest of the women kept their own check and either paid for household expenses themselves or received some additional money from their partners.

Ana Paula, a twenty-nine-year-old return migrant, told of the following arrangement with her husband:

When you lived in Boston and you were earning a salary, how did you manage the money? Did you each keep your own earnings, or did you combine them?

When I got there, I was earning my own money and he would take my checks from me and I just signed them and he cashed them.

So who paid for the housekeeping?

He would give me money for shopping and laundry.

What about housecleaning?

Well, some days, he would cook and I could find the food already made. I would get home at 3:30 and there would be food waiting. He would leave the pots, and when I got home from my other job at 10 P.M., I would clean up.

And here does he help with anything?

No, nothing.

María del Carmen said that on Fridays, she and her husband would both cash their checks and decide together how to spend the money: "On Saturdays we would do the shopping together. If there was anything extra we had to buy, we would decide, we'll save this much and put this much aside so we can buy that new chair in a few months. It felt wonderful to me to be able to plan for myself."

Regardless of the kind of deal they negotiated with their husbands, most women felt fundamentally changed by their experiences in Boston.

I felt that my mind was more open after I went to Boston. I felt that I could count on myself. One sees things, one works, one manages one's own money and isn't dependent on anyone. I sent money back to my kids and I went to stores. The woman that migrates develops in many ways. She has to learn how to live alone, to do everything, and not to ask for anything. It might be that she can ask her neighbor how to get to the doctor but she also has to be able to get there alone. In Boston, it's very rare that anyone will do anything for you. (Gloria, 48, return migrant, Miraflores)

Many said their family life in Boston also changed. Men spent less time with other women and more time at home. It was too cold for them to be out on the street during most of the year. It was too expensive to drink beer in the Irish bar on the corner (where they were not welcome anyway). And because women worked, men normally helped out with some of the cleaning and child care. Several couples said they developed a greater sense of partnership while living in the United States.

"We were closer in Boston," said Eloísa, a twenty-eight-year-old return migrant. "We would come home from work and cook together. In the summer, Alfredo might go down and spend time on the street with other people from Miraflores. But when it got cold, he stayed home with us. We would sit around together and watch TV. I didn't have to worry about him and other women." Word of these changing household dynamics reaches all corners of Miraflores. When I asked those who had never migrated about their images of family life in Boston, they almost always described a scenario in which both men and women were working and men helped out with household chores.

In the U.S., I think the fact that she works makes her have more rights because she doesn't depend on him. If she sees a blouse or some jeans in a store, she can buy it for herself. If she isn't working, she always has to be asking him, and he will say, "How can you want pants when we have so many expenses in the house?" I think the fact that she works makes her more independent. (Roberta, 28, nonmigrant, Miraflores)

Those who remained behind were of different minds about their response to these new dynamics. Some men and women clearly felt that men should continue to tell women what to do. Julia, a thirty-two-year-old returnee, said she felt her husband still knew best and that she wanted to continue taking orders from him.

Sometimes I would say to him, "Should I buy this?" and he would say to me that I was the one who should decide. He would push me to make my own decisions because I was always too anxious to know what he thought I should do. To a certain extent, I liked that. I saw other women who resolved their lives on their own. They would buy things and they didn't need anyone. So, on the one hand, I wanted to depend only on myself, but on the other hand, I felt better, more protected, when he told me to buy a certain dress.

Though her economic situation has improved, the life she returned to in Miraflores is very similar to the life she led before she left. She is happy to stay at home again, taking care of her family and having her husband make decisions for her. Forty-four-year-old Mariana was also glad to stop working when she returned, saying, "I couldn't wait to come home and live a life of leisure. It was good working there, but now I am happy to live calmly back in Miraflores." In Mariana's case, her husband ordered her to stop working when they got back to indicate to the rest of the community that they had achieved the middle-class status they had gone searching for. She agreed, saying, "Who wants to work if your husband can support you?"

Increasing numbers of those who return, or those whose views have been changed by the new ideas and practices migrants introduce, however, do not want gender relations to remain as they are. Young men and women who have many life choices before them are particularly well represented among this group, though older, already married Mirafloreños also share their views. These individuals believe that women should earn their own money and have an equal say in household decisions. They believe men should help out around the house more. They want to be like the couples they see returning to Miraflores who, as they see it, face life as equals and are happier as a result.

To some extent, these individuals are all dressed up with no place to go. Women want to find outside employment, but there are few jobs for men in Miraflores, let alone for women. Even when someone wants to work outside her home, their job prospects are grim. Several women tried starting their own small businesses. Esmeralda buys appliances and furniture in Santo Domingo that she raffles off in Miraflores for a small profit. Magdalena goes from house to house doing manicures and pedicures. Jovita sells cosmetics and costume jewelry from a display case in her living room. Though these women earn nowhere near enough to support themselves, they do gain some small measure of financial independence that enhances their position within their households.

Changing gender relations is also difficult because deeply rooted community norms work against it. Male community leaders still believe that women should not be in charge of certain social events or fill certain leadership positions. Women seen as going out too much or as challenging their husbands publicly are still ostracized for being "uppity." Even though nonmigrants and migrants change their ideas about how men and women should relate to one another, there are still strong social norms preventing them from putting these ideas into practice. Javier, for example, talked about how hard it was for him to find a more independent mate.

It's hard to have a relationship with someone who is so attached to you. It becomes less like a marriage and more like a parent thing. I want a partner. I want someone who can give me their opinion. It doesn't mean I will do what they tell me. I just want to see some intelligence coming out of them. That's what I got from living in the U.S. (Javier, 36, return migrant, Miraflores)

Javier knows that the road to independence is not easy. He wants a partner to be his equal, but he knows how elusive this can be, based on his own mother's experience.

In the majority of cases I can think of, women have to depend on men for money. There are some women who sell some dresses or jewelry in their homes or make some sweets to sell, but this is pocket money. It's enough to give you a cushion but not enough to pay the bills. You still have to put up with your man. My father has had another woman for the last ten years. My mother accepts this because she does not have any alternative. She didn't do anything for herself. She allowed her husband to be the deciding factor in everything. If she decided to break up with him, it would be too hard for her to get on her feet, to get her own place to live, to get everything she needed. Her excuse was the kids. She always said that we were too young, that we needed our father, and that she couldn't make it on her own without him.

In fact a number of women believed they would only find greater satisfaction by marrying someone who had migrated. They said those who stay behind *no valen nada* (are not worth anything), while those who go to the United States can solve everything, including providing a "ticket out." According to Arcides, a thirty-four-year-old returnee,

For most women, there are two kinds of Dominican men. [The first is] the Dominican man who is a struggler, who hasn't left the island and is trying to survive by doing what he can. He is considered undesirable. And then there are those who went to the States and came back again and they are not the same anymore. They find themselves on totally unfamiliar ground. They are considered a ticket to freedom. Most women are under the false impression that they can live a better life with someone who has migrated and who they think can bring them economic stability. A friend of mine came back from the States. He has nice clothes and he wears a lot of jewelry. He borrowed his brother's car and women were flocking to him. He said to himself, "This is the life. I am John Travolta now. Before no one would look at me and now everyone is paying attention." And I said, "That is what you are looking for? That is your fulfillment in life?"

Older men and women who were already married with children also sensed that times were changing, but their previous choices prevented them from altering their circumstances in any significant way.

Even couples who returned to Miraflores wanting to live as they did in Boston had difficulty doing so, as Roberto reports:

I was never really *machista,* but maybe I have changed a little, yes. Maybe I thought that my wife shouldn't work or that she shouldn't go out alone anywhere and that I was the one who said what goes around here. But now I would say that one should share ideas equally and not just say, this is like this and this is like that. And if I get home, I should make the coffee or cook the food so when she gets home it is ready, or if I have to help her with the kids, I should help her.

What would your friends think if they saw you washing clothes here?

Can you imagine that? They would say, "Oh, well, look at that homosexual" is what they would say here, or they would say, "Look at how his wife controls him." They would see me as if I were not a man.

Did you feel a lot of pressure to go back to doing the same old thing then? Can you keep washing clothes or do you have to stop?

There is a way you live in Boston that you will never see in our country because the one thing we can't get away from is *machismo.*

Roberto's solution was to do chores inside the house where no one could see him. He washed the dishes, he said, but he would never be caught hanging up the laundry. He would go shopping, because that was okay for a man to do, but he would never let anyone see him mopping the floor.

In sum, gender relations in Miraflores are not as unequal as they first seem, nor does everyone want to change them. Migration introduces new possibilities into the mix. Migrant women are transformed by their experiences at work, at home, and in the street. Some of those who stay behind are not attracted to these new role models, while others want new kinds of relationships. Their desire to change, however, is frustrated by the lack of economic opportunities. Mirafloreños manage the dissonance between their new ideas and being unable to put them into practice by making incremental changes. Women start small businesses and men do dishes behind closed doors to ease the tension between promise and reality.

Race

Values and practices around race were even more resistant to change than those around gender. Though Mirafloreños' notions about their racial identity did not hold water in Boston, and a number of migrants experienced discrimination and prejudice for the first time, they did not bring or send back ideas or behaviors that seriously challenged the racial hierarchy.

I've now been a victim of racism and I've also been its cause. I went to a country where I was less important and now I am here and I am more important. I feel that I deserve it, I'm supposed to be treated as somebody. So I have a tendency to look down on certain people. And certain people accept me and that makes me important. Once you have traveled and you come back, you are no longer the same person. Now you are someone who has strived, who has had certain experiences, who has been farther away than many of these people will ever be . . . but even so, I still have the tendency to do the same thing. I was a victim of prejudice and I don't quite understand the prejudice here but I find myself submitting to the pressure of Dominican culture that I just can't resist. At work is where it starts. I can't bring a Haitian home with me, though I wish I could. The other workers would give me grief because they are so prejudiced against Haitians. (Felipe, 32, return migrant, Miraflores)

Perceptions about race in the United States differ considerably from its construction in the Dominican Republic. While individuals in the United States are considered black when they have even a single drop of African blood, to be any part white in the Dominican Republic is to be non-black. Furthermore, race in the United States is a relatively fixed label, while in the Dominican Republic, it fluctuates with status. Lighter-skinned individuals usually do better. Individuals come to be viewed as whiter as they move up the socioeconomic ladder (Wade 1997).

Anti-black sentiment in the Dominican Republic is extremely powerful. Though blacks and mulattos make up nearly 90 percent of the Dominican population, race has never been an issue around which Dominicans united to pursue change. In fact, according to Torres-Saillant (1995a), many Dominicans deny their blackness. Dominican identity, he claims, is based on how Dominicans see themselves, how they try to distinguish themselves from their black Haitian neighbors, and how they are seen by the powerful nations that have dominated their country since its creation.

The Dominican government tried actively to *blanquear la raza,* or whiten the race, at several points in the country's history. Trujillo was one of the only Latin American leaders to accept Jewish refugees during World War II, in part to further this goal. Though few Dominicans trace their roots back to the Tiano Indians, their national passport includes two categories, *Indio Claro* and *Indio Oscuro* (Light Indian and Dark Indian), so that no one has to choose *Negro,* or Black. As recently as 1994, former president Balaguer defeated presidential candidate José Francisco Peña Gómez, in part by emphasizing Peña Gómez's dark skin color, by calling attention to his family's connections to Haiti, and by accusing him of secretly planning to reunite the island. In 1996 the government accused dark-skinned Dominicans of being foreigners (or Haitians) who had registered illegally to vote in order to support Peña Gómez's candidacy (Torres-Saillant and Hernández 1998).

Many people didn't like Peña Gómez because they had the fear put in them that if Peña was elected he would reunite the country with Haiti. Since he is black he must care more about his black Haitian brothers than he does about us. The people must know that he is Dominican like everyone else and that even if he weren't, we still have an army that defends the sovereignty of the country. But even though he was a really popular candidate, they just couldn't get themselves to vote for a black man. (Carlos Eduardo, 37, return migrant, Miraflores)

Mirafloreños take racial distinctions seriously. They are proud of their ancestral ties to the Canary Islands. They admire those with "good" hair and "good" skin—people with the physical characteristics associated with whiteness. Banilejos, in general, are known throughout the country for their feelings of racial superiority. What a shock it is for Mirafloreños to go to the United States, thinking of themselves as white, only to realize that they are considered people of color. From the point of view of most Bostonians, they belong to the very racial category they reject so adamantly at home.

We Dominicans can assimilate someone from Czechoslovakia easier than we can someone from Haiti. The Banilejo is very racist. The same white-skinned Dominican is not treated as badly as a darker-skinned Dominican. So, when they arrive in the U.S. and they go to a restaurant or a medical appointment they don't expect to be treated badly. It is a big surprise when they are. They feel like saying, hey, don't you realize that I am white, too? (Juline, 54, return migrant, Miraflores)

The first strategy Mirafloreños used to navigate race relations in the United States was to differentiate themselves clearly from African Americans. They perceived it was in their best interest to affiliate themselves with Latinos rather than with blacks. As proof, almost twice as many Dominicans in Massachusetts classified themselves as "Other" than as "Black" on the 1990 Census (U.S. Census 1992). As table 12 shows, more than 80 percent of all Dominicans classified themselves as white between 1996 and 1999.

Mirafloreños also reported they had few social contacts with African Americans. Because many found jobs through immigrant social networks, they had few black coworkers. Instead, they observed African Americans from a distance, when they went out shopping or to one of the neighborhood parks. If it was difficult for them to understand the white world, it was even harder for them to understand black people's lives. Language differences sharpened the notions of racial social distance they brought with them. Because they had few actual interactions with blacks, they took in little additional data with which to construct a more informed view.

Carmencita, a twenty-eight-year-old returnee, equated African Americans in the United States with Haitians on the island, though U.S. blacks seemed less threatening because she had such little contact with them.

I wasn't afraid of them [black people]. Sometimes when I went to do the wash, they would be there and I would watch how they acted but I wasn't afraid. Haitians, yes, I am afraid of them because people say so many things about them that it makes me afraid. They say that they put spells on people. That if they want to harm you they can do it, that they would go back to Haiti and if they want someone to be killed they will do it.

Jesús, a fifty-four-year-old return migrant, formulated his impressions of African Americans by watching them in the neighborhood. It was as if he were viewing a movie with the sound track turned off because, though he spent lots of time observing blacks, he had actually talked to very few. He wanted to, feeling fascinated and fearful at the same time, but he could not figure out how.

When I worked in the *colmado* [grocery store], I would watch them walking down the street. They would be laughing and joking around. I wanted to know more, but I was kind of afraid because you know what we think about blacks here. They would come into the store and I would help them with what they needed, but it never got beyond "here is your bread" or "it's cold out today." There was no way for us to come together because there was no place to start the conversation.

Some Mirafloreños said they coped with race relations in Boston by "knowing their place." In situations where they encountered whites, they tried to draw as little attention to themselves as possible. This caused few problems for recipient observers and instrumental adapters since they lived much of their lives within the Latino community. Purposeful innovators, who interacted more with Anglos, faced greater difficulties. Chacho, a thirty-four-year-old returnee, described this experience, which echoed the stories told by many Mirafloreños:

The States are more racist than the Dominican Republic, only because they are more open. I was a victim of racism there. I worked for seven years for a catalog company. After seven years, I was only a production photographer. I saw a lot of people work with me who got promoted to higher positions than I was able to achieve. Even people whom I had trained. I said fine, I accept it, as long as I get paid, I'm satisfied. One time I ran into a coworker at the bank. We were both waiting in line to get our checks cashed. He had brown hair, blue eyes. And I looked at his check and then I looked at my check and then I looked back at his. I lost my job because I went straight to the boss and said after I had trained him, why is he making $100 more than me? And they looked at me and said, *you* are not the right color. And I said, then I'm not the right man for the job.

Marco, forty-six, coped by making himself into a chameleon:

I had to travel to work in South Boston every day.[2] But I never had any problems because I knew how to get along and live with people. Sometimes there were problems because, you know, South Boston is a difficult place. And there are some Latinos who go around in their cars with the music really loud or they ride with the top down in the summer and it would cause problems. I always drove with the windows up and the radio down really low and I would always put on American music. I never put on Latin music in South Boston.

Wealthier, better-educated community members railed against the discrimination they encountered. They understood what was happening to them, and it offended their sense of justice. They were not blinded by the idea that "racial prejudice could never happen in a place like the United States." Less-educated individuals, who had had fewer contacts outside of Miraflores before they migrated, were often unsure what was going on. They did not have the life experience or cultural capital to help them decode how they had been treated. They were reluctant to admit they had been tricked or excluded in the United States, where they truly believed there was little racism.

These experiences reinforced migrants' transnational attachments. They wanted to continue to belong in Miraflores because they realized they would never be allowed to achieve full membership in the United States. Enduring sending-community membership was like an insurance policy that guaranteed belonging in a place where they would always be respected, welcomed, and admired.

I will always be a minority in Boston. No matter how much money I make, I will never be considered a full-fledged American. People will always treat me as an outsider, as someone to keep out of the club. I did not know this before I came here. I was so naïve. I thought I could work hard, keep my head down, and make this my home. I don't want to be American anymore. I am tired of fighting. In Miraflores, I will always belong. I will always be accepted. (Alfredo, 42, return migrant, Miraflores)

Mirafloreños also want to stay connected to Miraflores because they can reclaim their whiteness there. Just as immigrant men want to return to the island to recoup their privileged male status, so Mirafloreños want to maintain their membership in the Miraflores community, where they are recognized for "who they truly are."

Rather than making them more sympathetic to minorities, their encounters with racism in the United States prompted some Mirafloreños to assert their racial superiority even more adamantly than before.

We are not colored, even if Americans think we are. I did not like that my boss put me in the same category as a black man. Couldn't he see that we are totally different? I am glad to be back here where people know that we are lighter-skinned. Everyone knows that there are boys in El Llano [a neighboring village] who have blue eyes and blond hair. (Leonardo, 55, return migrant, Miraflores)

Instead of easing relations with the Haitians who worked among them, migration caused the anti-black feelings expressed by so many Mirafloreños to go from bad to worse.

It is a funny thing. Sad, really. I went to the U.S. I never thought about being anything other than white. After a while, I learned I had to be careful in certain neighborhoods. I could never go into the bar down the street because I really wasn't welcome there. And when I came back, I talked to my neighbors about it. I said, you know, for white people in the U.S., we are just the same as black people. It doesn't matter where you are from. Dark skin is dark skin for the *gringos*. You would think that it would change things here a little. That we might get along better with the Haitians. But it hasn't. We just pretend that all those Haitians that are living in *bohios* [traditional thatched huts] way back in the fields aren't there. We don't see them when they come to buy something at the store. And we certainly wouldn't invite them to sit down and have a beer. (Manuel, 53, return migrant, Miraflores)

Maribel, a thirty-six-year-old migrant, echoes his sentiment:

These beliefs stay the same. I don't feel this way personally but there are people from Santo Domingo who live in Boston and don't want to know anything about Haitians or African Americans. They don't want to look at them. They say, those blacks who live there over a Paya [a neighboring village that is residentially segregated by race] or wherever it is, why don't they wash? And these attitudes have not changed. And now people feel this even more strongly because of all the Haitians that are working in agriculture and many people in Miraflores don't have any work. They say that the Haitians are taking away our jobs. But those people don't have any work because of what I just told you. They just got comfortable waiting for those in the U.S. to send them money. The Haitians are just taking advantage of the work there is available. They are not responsible for this. Everyone has to work to earn money.

Right and Wrong

Migration also calls into question ideas about right and wrong and the appropriate uses and abuses of the law. The result is again somewhat paradoxical. Calls for reform and greater accountability grow stronger at the same time that new ways to circumvent and take advantage of the legal system are introduced.

Ewick and Silbey (1998) define *legality* as the meanings, sources of authority, and cultural practices that we think of as legal, no matter who uses them or what their goals may be. Legality reveals itself in a variety of places, not limited to those formally associated with the law. To uncover when and where the law is present and what impact it has, we need to understand how legality is experienced by ordinary citizens. This is the study of legal consciousness, of which there are three types: conformity before the law, engagement with the law, and resistance against the law.[3]

When individuals perceive themselves as being before the law, they envision a legal system that is separate from ordinary life yet, at the same time, authoritative and predictable. The law involves a hierarchical system of known rules and procedures that is formally ordered and rational. Those who stand before the law believe in the appropriateness and justness that formal legal procedures are based on, though not necessarily in the fairness of their outcomes.

Those who view themselves as against the law have a "sense of being caught within the law."

They make do, using whatever situation presents itself to fashion solutions they would not be able to achieve within conventionally recognized schema and resources. People exploit the interstices of conventional social practices to forge moments of respite from the power of the law. Foot dragging, omissions, ploys, small deceits, humor, and making scenes are typical forms of resistance for those up against the law. (Ewick and Silbey 1998, 10)

When Mirafloreños migrate, they move from a context where they generally feel they are against the law to one in which a before-the-law stance predominates. Thus, while migration does little to change ideas about race, and has only a limited impact on gender relations, it transforms notions about legality in much more fundamental ways. The social institutions in which legality is constituted are more malleable at their margins than those where gender and race are constructed. In other words, though laws are inflexible with respect to major offenses, they can be supple and manipulatable with respect to slight infractions in ways that the socioeconomic structures where gender and race are enacted are not.

Elderly community members nostalgically recall a Miraflores that was virtually crime-free during the Trujillo era. They claim you could sleep in the street and not get robbed. They remember an educational system that worked better because schools were run more strictly. All students wore uniforms, and when a child was absent a truant officer came to their home to make sure that he or she returned to school the next day. Many also remember that when their family's sack of rice grew dangerously low, some government official always seemed to come to their rescue. "When Trujillo died," said forty-seven-year-old Marcelo, "even I cried because it was as if my own father had passed away." His generation grew up with the notion of government as benevolent dictator. They feared it and tried to avoid it, but they also valued the security and order that the state guaranteed.

This dictatorial legacy still plagues the Dominican judicial system.

Though Trujillo and Balaguer went through the motions of support-ing the rule of law, they frequently undermined it to satisfy their per-sonal whims (Espinal 1996). The president still controls much of the judicial system. Inadequate funding, corruption, and poor training are just a few factors contributing to judicial inefficiency.[4] "Here there is no justice, and without justice, there is no real democracy," said a judicial reform NGO director in Santo Domingo, "nor can there be real devel-opment. The institutions are weak and there is no equality between the powers of the state. The executive branch does what it feels like."

As a result, many migrants leave Miraflores perceiving themselves as against the law. The law serves a class of people they do not belong to. Poor, humble people like themselves have to avoid and outsmart the law rather than seek its protection. They must search for strategic cracks in the system where they can bend the rules to get ahead. They rely on informal authority to ensure social order and resolve disputes. They have unofficial, mutually understood ways of sanctioning, mak-ing restitution, and problem solving that meet these needs without re-lying on formal legal structures.

Both migrants and nonmigrants claimed that what really rules is "the law of the peso," which privileges and protects those who have money and arbitrarily demands things from those who do not. Though they tried to stay clear of the police, most community members never felt completely immune from law enforcement's caprice and brutality, as Javier, a thirty-five-year-old return migrant, described:

The other day, some of the people who work for me would have been ar-rested for no reason if I hadn't been there. It was 10:30, about eight of them were in a bar drinking. The police arrived, and since they were in a group, they looked suspicious, so they were searched, some of them were robbed, and they were going to be taken to jail. When they asked why, the policeman told them, "We'll solve that when we get over to the jail." I walked in and I said: "I am somebody here, this is my business, and these people work for me. If you take them in, you can take me in too. I want to see the lieutenant in charge." So one of them called me over and he said, "Take it easy, we are just doing our job. We have to pick up people in the way. What if they get them-selves drunk and cause a problem? Do you have something for me?" I gave him twenty pesos and that was enough to satisfy him and then they said, "Okay, let's get out of here."

Javier could solve this problem because he is a relatively well-off busi-ness owner who commands respect. Those with less money and power are more vulnerable. They have to keep the law at bay by paying deference to its gatekeepers. Mirafloreños regularly give gifts, cook food, or perform small chores for the officers at the local police station. They want to make sure they have sufficient social capital if a problem arises. Doña Elena, for example, makes *arepas* (a traditional Dominican dish) for the police every week. When her son got thrown in jail for being involved in a street brawl, he was released the next day by the officers she had been feeding.

Another way Mirafloreños get their needs met is to form relationships with one of the community's *patrones* (benefactors). These high-status individuals solve problems or offer protection in exchange for labor, services, or demonstrations of respect. Eduardo, for example, is known to have an *enllave* (keyholder or contact) at the local police station.

Eduardo can resolve problems when people get put in jail. He has many contacts. He makes contributions to the police and the military. There are many people who have a friend in the military or the government. They go and speak to them—whatever the problem, they can resolve it. In the U.S. people resolve problems with lawyers. Here, you don't need lawyers because any friend can resolve your problem, no matter how big it is. (Nicolás, 39, return migrant, Miraflores)

If most people view the official legal system with such disdain, what constitutes the social glue? First, Mirafloreños define wrongful behavior with a good deal of lenience. Most community members describe a normative world colored by shades of gray rather than clear-cut tones of black and white. Even when a person had acted wrong, his or her behavior could always be explained or excused. While a U.S. law enforcement officer referred to this as the "flexible way in which Dominicans interpret the law," a lawyer from Baní called the U.S. legal system a "legal dictatorship." He felt that the "who" and "under what circumstances" should be taken into account when deciding what was right or wrong.

This more "open to interpretation" stance toward morality came through in a number of scenarios respondents described. Though judges are not supposed to work as lawyers during their tenure on the bench, Don Geraldo, a judge in Baní, saw no problem in continuing to practice law. He simply arranged that a colleague would sign all the official paperwork he did for his clients while he was in office. Judges are also barred from participating in party politics, but since another judge in town was active in the Reformista Party, Geraldo felt it was also within his right to run for the senate, which he did in 1994. A prominent Mirafloreño who worked as a coyote, or person who helps people enter the United States illegally, saw nothing wrong with charging fellow community members exorbitant prices for his services. He thought of himself as providing a humanitarian service, claiming that because "not everyone can get a visa, the person who helps people to migrate is helping mankind."

Mirafloreños' flexible understanding of right and wrong also revealed itself in their notions of accountability. Traditional patterns of patron-client relationships partially explain this. Community members find it difficult to hold individuals they somehow feel indebted to accountable for their actions. For example, hardly anyone would hold President Balaguer accountable for the country's problems, though they believed his government was corrupt and they had suffered as a result. It was not the president but his advisers who were at fault, Gonzálo, a fifty-nine-year-old returnee, argued:

It is not Balaguer's fault. It is those around him. Our leader is blind, the poor guy, and aging. He is only aware of what they tell him about, not what he can see. I believe it is the people he has working for him who are doing him harm. Because he doesn't need much money, he doesn't have children, the sisters that he had are now dying of old age. What he does he does for the Dominican people. Since he is going blind, the people who work for him are taking advantage of his goodness. They realize that if he doesn't win this election [in May 1994], they are out of a job.

It did not occur to Gonzalo that Balaguer is ultimately responsible for what his advisers do since he chooses them. In fact, Gonzalo, like many other villagers, was reluctant to criticize the former president because he felt such a strong sense of personal, almost familial attachment to him. He also argued that all elderly people deserve respect and should be judged with lenience.

This kind of legal consciousness shies away from assigning responsibility to an individual because it assumes there is always a reasonable explanation for poor performance or rule breaking. It acknowledges human imperfection and allows good intentions to compensate for poor outcomes. This grows partially out of the prevailing sense that, as one lawyer expressed, "Honesty is a luxury in the Dominican Republic that only a few can afford." Since times are hard and possibilities few, one has to take advantage of the legal and not-so-legal opportunities that present themselves. This is the only way to keep up or get ahead. There is no harm done, then, when a customer takes a little more than the pound of rice he paid for or if the shopkeeper slightly overcharges for her goods. One has to overcharge, shirk, or overmeasure to get by. And one is a fool not to take advantage of lucky breaks when they present themselves. One has to do this to survive in a country that favors the rich so disproportionately, as the Baní district attorney commented:

I am single, I don't have a sick husband, so I can afford the luxury of being honest . . . but when you are in a position like mine with a lot of pressure and little job security and you go home and you have to pay for your house and the telephone, for the servant, for your kid's school, and one day comes and you don't have anything left and someone comes along and offers you a bribe . . .

Accepting such gifts is encouraged, she said, adding:

No one wants to see themselves on the bottom. So your friends start to tell you, you are being a fool, everyone who has held your post has taken money. You are in a very precarious position because you could be out of a job if the government changes. The cost of living has gone up, so people have to do anything they can to be able to buy a house or a car. So people become vulnerable and their friends say, don't be a fool.

Most people believe that soliciting bribes is a necessary part of daily life. Low-level employees need these "supplemental gifts" to make ends meet. While many Mirafloreños deeply resent it when they are asked for a "voluntary contribution," they also understand that this is the poor man's way of fighting back. According to one journalist: "The police in this country are the worst-paid public employees. In 1990, Balaguer said publicly that the *mordisco* in Mexico [the bribe demanded by public officials] was permitted here. . . . He said it to justify not raising public salaries."

A second factor that informally reinforces the social order is that Mirafloreños choose very consciously with whom they engage in relations of reciprocal exchange. They show a remarkable sense of solidarity toward one another, but this does not apply uniformly across the board. Instead, it is highly selective. Community members pragmatically enter into exchange relationships with some villagers and not others. They also may only expect reciprocity with respect to a particular task. The same neighbors who exchange food regularly never borrow money from each other because they know that the level of *confianza* (trust) they share will not sustain such interchanges. Households entered into relationships with those they defined as within their "circle of trustworthiness." These often included only family members, though family lines were sometimes conceived broadly, by evoking real or fictitious kinship ties. In this way, certain households almost merged with one another while they had only minimal contact with other neighbors next door.

Such strong, yet highly selective, ties to fellow community members arise because they are accompanied by a high degree of skepticism. They are based on *mistrustful solidarity*. Mirafloreños pledge their undying commitment to the community, claiming time and again they are the sons and daughters of Miraflores. At the same time, they are often wary of many of their fellow community members. "Here, people, I don't know why, but they are almost always trying to trick you," one man said in what was a widely expressed sentiment. "Not everyone— there are many friendships outside the family that are real—but you often trust someone and they abuse that confidence."

A third factor reinforcing social cohesion is the way in which Mirafloreños regulate their own behavior in anticipation of *qué dirán* or "what others will say." Villagers exercise some degree of self-censorship in anticipation of public sanction and gossip. Because Miraflores is such a tight-knit community, with so much of private life conducted in public view, community members cannot afford to alienate or offend their neighbors. They are too dependent upon one another to risk social isolation or a tainted reputation because there is no other community they can belong to.

Single women who go out for the evening, for example, think twice about coming home too late. They know their neighbors will be watching through the shutters to see what time they return. The neighbor who is renting a house from someone who has gone to Boston takes good care of the property because he knows his landlord will find out about it if he does not.

Dominican society has created its own mechanism for controlling its citizens. Since I was young, my community taught me how to behave. If my neighbor saw me doing something bad, they would say, "No, Roberto, you are not that kind of person." It was as if I had ten mothers, not just one. One becomes afraid to break out of that kind of pattern. The feeling of rejection would be too much. (Roberto, 26, nonmigrant lawyer, Baní)

The notions about law and justice that migrants bring with them to Boston developed in response to the corruption and ineffectiveness of the Dominican legal system. Most Mirafloreños avoid the law rather than seek its protection. They devise strategies for escaping its capriciousness. They give bribes when asked. They form relationships with powerful individuals who can intervene on their behalf. They exploit openings when they present themselves in order to get ahead. Alternative problem-solving arrangements, rather than the formal legal system, reinforce the social order.

If Mirafloreños see themselves as against the law in the Dominican Republic, and as constructing legality outside the legal system, their legal consciousness shifts once they arrive in the United States. In Boston they occupy multiple positions vis-à-vis the law, depending on which social group they are interacting with. In Anglo-dominated settings, Mirafloreños are generally "before the law"—that is, at some workplaces, schools, or health clinics, community members assume they are dealing with institutions that are just and predictable, and that the law will protect them. In other, more Dominican-dominated settings, like the streets, stores, and parks of the neighborhood, their home-country legal consciousness predominates. Different kinds of law and different kinds of legal consciousness define their Anglo and Dominican worlds. As a result, Mirafloreños feel protected by what they perceived as a more objective, better-functioning legal system at the same time that they devise new ways to profit from it.

Most migrants noted striking differences between the U.S. and Dominican legal systems. As Santiago, a twenty-eight-year-old migrant in Boston, observed:

In the United States, there is some corruption. It is not a perfect society. But there are some minimum standards that you can't break because you will be criticized by the press or by the church and civic organizations. Though there is some flexibility and latitude, you can't surpass certain limits or you will be penalized by the society.

Guillermina, a thirty-seven-year-old return migrant, commented:

In the U.S., when you go to university you know you were accepted because of merit. There is financial aid, but you know you don't have to bribe the official so they put you on the list. You know that your boss will pay you for the hours you worked. He might not pay a lot, he might not want to know anything about you because he is prejudiced, but he will pay you for what you worked, and he won't try to trick you. It is not like here, where salaries are based on dishonesty.

Both of these individuals expressed a sense that, though not perfect, the law in the United States is generally more efficient and impartial than that in the Dominican Republic. There are clear rules that apply to everyone, regardless of class. These laws touch Mirafloreños' lives each time they apply for public assistance, pay their taxes, or obey the traffic rules. Community members also feel the law's power when they read about its application each day in the newspaper. They begin to think of the law as a resource. In their dealings with the public, Anglo-dominated sphere, many Mirafloreños shift to a before-the-law stance.

Do you know that police in the Dominican Republic always pull you over for nothing? They make up any excuse and then charge you twenty pesos to get away. I liked that I could go out in my car and know that I would not be pulled over unless I did something wrong. I like to know that the police are there to help, though I'm certainly not going to ask for it if I don't need it. But in Santo Domingo, when I see a policeman, I think I should walk the other way. (Juan, 44-year-old return migrant, Miraflores)

At the same time, since so many migrants live their lives within the Miraflores they re-create in Jamaica Plain, they continue to employ many of the same economic strategies and problem-solving techniques they bring with them from the island. They still seek out spaces and push boundaries to gain ground. They maintain their against-the-law posture as they exploit opportunities and manipulate the rules just as they do at home.

Some community members, for example, set up small-scale illegal businesses. A dentist cared for her clients in their homes, though she was not licensed to practice in the United States. Other villagers sold Dominican lottery tickets on the sly. One return migrant claimed he made more money running domino games out of his apartment each weekend, where he also sold food and beer, than he did working two part-time jobs.

Some migrants did not realize that these "ways of getting by" were against U.S. law. Those who did made a distinction between the laws governing how they acted in the Dominican world and the laws governing their dealings with Anglos. They continued to see these minor infractions as rule-bending, not rule-breaking, and as necessary for their daily survival.

Small-business owners adopt similar strategies (Levitt 1995). They sell single cigarettes or half-packages of food to customers who can not afford to buy the whole box. They sell homemade cakes, puddings, and candies that would not pass muster with a health inspector. They sell drugs available over the counter on the island but that require a prescription in the United States. They illegally access phone lines to lower the cost of long-distance phone service. In some cases, these are clearly illicit moneymaking schemes mounted by entrepreneurs who see an opportunity for profit. In others, store owners are simply massaging the rules to make certain goods more affordable to those who need them.

This against-the-law stance is buoyed by the small but highly visible number of Dominicans who succeed at the drug trade. Since these "Dominican Horatio Algers" leave the island poor and return rich, their example sends a clear message to other Dominicans that exploiting the system is a smart way to get ahead. Young people listen particularly closely.

Most migrants balance these before- and against-the-law stances without dissonance. Either they feel there is little incompatibility between these two positions or they find ways to mentally accommodate the two. The widely known practice of feigning accidents at work to collect disability insurance provides a good example of this.

I was working in a job where it was very easy to fake a *caso*.[5] My friend said to me, "Let's pretend to have an accident so we can collect disability insurance, and then we can work under another name in another place and still receive insurance money." I told him I would do it but one never knows what one can do in life; there are many things that I have never thought of doing. I remember that we were cleaning the floor with a machine and he said to me, "You are going to throw yourself over there and then throw the machine over there so they know that it was an accident," and I told him "Let's go ahead," but then I didn't have the courage, and I didn't do it. I know that many Dominicans go to the U.S. to do these things, but I do not agree with it. (Marino, 48, return migrant, Miraflores)

Another return migrant observed:

There were lawyers who would tell you how to do these things because, as they say, there are Mafiosos everywhere. This opened people's eyes here. There are people who have mounted three or four disability cases. Imagine it. Many of the houses in Miraflores were built with this money because working honestly in the U.S., one can live more or less well, but I don't think that working in a factory or working for a cleaning company for a short time one can achieve these things. I don't agree with these Dominicans, or for me, these Dominicans are not Dominicans. (Edgar, 37, return migrant, Miraflores)

Orchestrating an accident at work to collect disability insurance clearly reflects Mirafloreños' multiple stances with respect to the law. Migrants outwit the law to get ahead, but they have faith that it will function effectively enough to reward their insurance claims.

The impact of the social remittances migrants send back to Miraflores mirrors these two stances. Calls for legal reform and an increasing number of Mirafloreños seeking the law's protection and support go hand-and-hand with the introduction of new, creative ways of getting around it. The vast majority of return migrants and nonmigrants favor legal reform. They have heard migrants' descriptions of the courts and the police in the United States.

Return migrants say to us that if I go to get a form in the U.S. I don't have to pay a cent because it is the state's obligation to give it to me. If I pay my taxes, I have the right to this, this, and this. If I don't consume two thousand pesos worth of electricity, I don't pay a two-thousand-peso electricity bill. Although they have menial jobs, they acquire a certain discipline that they didn't acquire here because here there weren't any jobs for these people. . . . These are the things that are transmitted in the process of resocialization. This is a benefit that these people bring back to our society. (PRD leader, Santo Domingo)

In response, some community members claimed they were tired of accepting discriminatory law enforcement and that they would not tolerate it anymore. Don Felipe said he finally complained to the mayor when his son was unfairly arrested during an arbitrary police sweep.[6]

Before, I would have just shrugged my shoulders and accepted this. I would have thought, what can one do? This is how things work around here and we have to go along with it. But when this last thing happened, I thought, I have had enough. I know that it is different in other places. People tell us all the time that things work differently in Boston. Why can't it be different here, too?

Other Mirafloreños said they were more likely to ask the police to help solve problems. After weeks of asking a local grocery store/bar owner to turn down his music after 11 P.M., a group of neighbors finally went to the authorities. "It's not as if we'll start running to the police all the time," said Doña Nelcida, "but at least we gave it a try."

Other social remittances counteract these positive changes by offering new models of law breaking. Individual migrants who win false disability cases or who make money selling drugs in the United States undermine reforms by introducing salient examples of the rewards of bucking the system.

Most community members make a clear distinction between the Dominicano Ausente (the absent Dominican) who worked hard and saved honestly in the United States, and the Dominicanyork. The prospect of making money fast by whatever means, however, is often too tempting to those who stay behind.

There is so much money around here because of the narco-traffickers who live in the U.S. They are in the U.S. for a year, they buy three houses, two jeeps, they have a million dollars in the bank. I have a brother in the U.S. who doesn't have $100 in the bank and he has been there for 10 years. He is working, and those who work don't have anything. Breaking the law is smart. (Mercedes, 34, return migrant, Miraflores)

The ways in which migration transforms the social fabric in Miraflores reinforces these negative impacts. As the community becomes more stratified and some families do better than others, new ideas about what is an acceptable way to achieve mobility take hold. As a result, more crime, and a grudging respect for those who commit them, go hand in hand with calls for a more law-abiding society. Community leaders claim there are a growing number of individuals willing to abandon *lo correcto* (what is right) to achieve material gain.

When so many houses are built with insurance money, there seem to be more and more people who cannot resist the temptation. People who before were *serio* [serious or morally upright] just fall into this trap, and it is breaking down the moral fabric of our community. I worry about these young men who just sit around all day. Any person who comes along and says they can make money by selling marijuana or something . . . they just jump at the chance. Everyone knows this, but they are afraid to speak out. (Don Pedro, 62, nonmigrant, Miraflores)

In sum, prior to migration, most Mirafloreños saw themselves as against the law. They devised strategies to circumvent a legal system they felt was so corrupt and poorly functioning, they had to avoid it or manipulate it to get by. The migration experience positions Mirafloreños both before and against the law. Migrants' lives are structured such that they cannot avoid contact with the legal system the way they can in Miraflores.

Their actions reflect a dual legal consciousness. They respect and seek refuge in the law's protective capacities and objective authority. At the same time, they creolize that absoluteness, using its predictability and fairness as a base from which they continue to creatively shift and outwit the law. This transformed legal consciousness, and the rewards and costs it entails, is socially remitted back to Miraflores with contradictory effects. Calls for reform accompany the introduction of new, admired ways to circumvent the system. Social remittances contribute to and impede change.

Part Three

Chapter Five

When Domestic Politics Becomes Transnational

Though basketball is not particularly popular in the Dominican Republic, during his 1996 campaign for the presidency, Leonel Fernández appeared in several television campaign ads "shooting hoops." In doing so, he wanted to remind the Dominican public that he had grown up on the Upper West Side of Manhattan, that he admires U.S. culture and practices, and that, if elected, he would put his international experience and style to work. He also wanted to acknowledge to the migrant community that he recognized their continuing involvement in Dominican politics and that he hoped they would remain active in the future. "It matters little," said a July 1997 *Boston Globe* article, "that Fernández picked up so many American habits in New York that his best friends admit the handsome lawyer falls short when it comes to that hallmark of Dominican culture: dancing the merengue." Fernández's strategy worked—he was sworn into office in August 1996.

Former President Fernández was not alone in his assessment of the Dominican political scene. In fact, all three of the principal political parties on the island, the Partido Reformista Social Cristiano (PRSC), the Partido de la Liberación Dominicana (PLD), and the Partido Revolucionario Dominicano (PRD), have recognized, to varying degrees, that political life is increasingly enacted across borders. In this chapter I analyze the political elements in the transnational field connecting the Dominican Republic and the United States. I show how local-level political linkages within the transnational village help form and are integrated into this multilayered cross-border arena.

Focusing on the Partido Revolucionario Dominicano, I argue that although many aspects of political party life became transnational, the

results of these efforts were primarily one-way. Transnational practices do not automatically produce transnational results. Though the
PRD and, to some extent, other political groups set transnational goals
and encouraged Mirafloreños to integrate politically in Boston, this has
not occurred to any significant degree. The party's cross-border activities have had a much greater impact on local-level Dominican politics
than they have had on achieving local-level political integration in Boston. This does not mean, however, that Mirafloreños gained little from
their experiences with U.S. politics. Even those who participated only
peripherally in the U.S. political system modified their political ideas
and practices as a result. They communicated their new views and
modeled new behaviors to those at home. Their attempts at reform
met with limited success, however, because there were few true organizational arenas where they could put their ideas into practice.[1]

Mirafloreño Political Culture

Long periods of authoritarian rule punctuated by short democratic
openings characterize much of Dominican political history. Since the
late 1960s the country has moved fairly steadily toward a more enduring democracy. During his first twelve years in office (1966–78),
President Balaguer allowed some democratic expression and organization, within the limits of his authoritarian regime. When the PRD
was elected in 1978, in what many consider to be the country's first
democratic contest, it furthered democratic consolidation by curbing
the power of the military, instituting human rights protections, and
implementing rule by constitution (Espinal 1986).

Throughout the last two decades, democracy has gained momentum, though it is still fragile and underinstitutionalized.[2] Hartlyn
(1998) argues that the republic's limited democratic experience cannot be attributed simply to its authoritarian heritage (Wiarda 1979),
dependent status, and history of foreign occupations (Gleijeses 1978).
Instead, he claims that "structural and cultural factors have interacted
with each other within the context of neopatrimonial political institutions, with all three mutually reinforcing each other amidst complex international constraints and occasional opportunities" (1998, 7).[3]
Neopatrimonialism limits the quality of the country's democracy and
its consolidation by inhibiting the emergence of a strong, workable
civil society and state and by creating weak and undemocratic politi-

cal institutions and parties. This, combined with international economic and political change, has weakened democratic practice.

President Fernández's election in 1996 raised some hopes that neopatrimonial politics would decline. Urbanization and migration, the ever increasing role of international influences over the Dominican economy and society, and an expanding civil society would all strengthen democratic practice. In fact Fernández's public pledge to respect democratic and constitutional norms, and the fact that his party, the Partido de la Liberación Dominicana (PLD), did not control the Dominican Congress, has substantially reduced informal abuses of presidential power. Furthermore, since the PRD, the PRSC, and the PLD are all undergoing generational succession, whereby longtime leaders are finally ceding control to younger party members, more internal democratization within each party is likely to occur. In short, Hartlyn (1998) concludes modest changes in political patterns and trajectories are likely to continue, though these are not guaranteed.

Political reform, however, matters little to many Mirafloreños. They deeply distrust politicians and the political process. From their perspective, good politicians build roads and bridges. It does not matter what their political ideas are or whether all Dominicans benefit equally from their projects as long as Miraflores gets its fair share. It makes little sense to become active in politics, they say, because politicians never keep their promises. In fact, political participation can only lead to trouble if one "roots for the wrong team." Many do as María Altagracia does, by "supporting all of the parties and none of them." That way, she is friend to all possible victors and not clearly associated with one particular loser.

Other villagers, even those who are skeptical about politics, live and breathe it. Politics figures large in their daily conversations because they see political activism as a way to get ahead. Some families blindly support one party, though this may have little to do with what the party actually stands for or how it differs from other groups. Instead, they simply have a tradition of supporting one party over generations. As Javier, a sixty-one-year-old nonmigrant, put it:

My grandfather was an ardent PRD supporter, so I am too. It's like I have the PRD in my genes. I like him [Peña Gómez] because I'm used to him. I've been a PRD supporter since I was a kid. It's a habit. I feel something sentimental toward him. He always fought bravely against Trujillo. And he's been able to go so far even though he was born in a place where they didn't even have any running water.

Javier and others like him really do believe their party would be better for the country. They feel an intense personal commitment to their leaders. The party is like a family to them. It is their social safety net because they know they can always get a loan or a sack of rice from party leaders if money is tight. And just as families have strong household heads who make decisions, so party members expect their leaders to tell them what to do. They are more comfortable taking orders than participating in a deliberative democratic process. They also expect to be rewarded for their loyalty with a low-level government job if and when their party is elected.

The Dominican Republic has a long tradition of clientelism, of *caudillismo*, of a tendency to centralize power and control. We tend to personalize the electoral campaigns rather than learn about the proposed policies of the government. We concentrate on candidates' personal qualities rather than their leadership abilities. It's almost natural that the country would be this way. The people have so many problems and for so long we have had these paternalistic governments, they believe that only the president, not even other lawmakers, can resolve them. There was an elephant in the old zoo and because there were no more animals there anymore the elephant was dying of hunger and sadness. The president had to intervene to get that elephant moved to the new zoo because no one had enough guts to make that decision on their own. And there it was on the front page of all the newspapers, that Balaguer had moved "Mami" the elephant to the new zoo. . . . And although one doesn't like to admit it, the Dominican people ask for it. If the person in power does not act like he is God, people think he is not a good leader. There is a sense that we must get past this, but it takes time because there is a Balaguer at every level of Dominican society—in every institution, there is a little Balaguer who makes all the decisions, who doesn't share them and keeps whatever decision he has made like a state secret. (PRD national vice president, Santo Domingo)

Other Mirafloreños are attracted to politics as spectacle. In a town where little breaks up the rhythm of the days, the motorcades that pass through every weekend for months prior to an election and the nightly block parties (at which candidates' speeches are really just the warm-up act for the live music that follows) are a pleasant distraction.

Let me tell you that Santo Domingo is one of the countries where they talk the most about politics. It is a country that is so politicized that you can't get any work done. The problem is that this has never been serious. There is no substance to it. The people enjoy politics. They like motorcades. They like flags. It is something that was restricted for many years. For many years, they did not have the right to fall in love so now, they fall in love with whoever comes along. (Nicolás, 40, migrant)[4]

The PRD's Transnational Political System

Long before migration became an important social force, the PRD established a tradition of expatriate political organization in the United States. Juan Bosch created the party in Cuba while in exile from Trujillo in 1939 and chapters soon formed in cities where there were significant concentrations of Dominicans (Sagás 1999). Throughout Trujillo's reign, the PRD used its ties with U.S. political leaders to mobilize public opinion against him.[5] During Balaguer's first twelve-year rule, migrant PRD members continued to pressure for change in the Dominican Republic from their beachhead in New York. They organized public demonstrations, published open letters in the U.S. press, and enlisted the support of U.S. political leaders to protest human rights abuses on the island.[6] When the party gained power in 1978, leaders shifted their attention to fund-raising. According to one former leader, migrants sent as much as $40,000 back to Santo Domingo each month. They also began to think about their own political advancement in the United States, which set the stage for later conflicts over the party's financial dependence on migrants and its political platform, which did not address the social and political realities migrants faced.

The 1986 election, which returned Balaguer to power, left the PRD in disarray. Bitter internal disputes discredited the party in the eyes of the Dominican public. To restore unity, and to regain and extend its base of support, the PRD underwent a major structural overhaul in 1990. Under the leadership of Dr. José Francisco Peña Gómez, it decentralized decision-making and instituted more democratic procedures. Party leaders introduced these reforms in part as a response to the growing recognition that migrants played a critical role in party life. Migrants made major contributions to the party budget and often dictated how their nonmigrant family members voted:

In addition to their economic clout, they also influence social and political decisions. Be it the father, mother, brother, or sister who migrates, a relationship of dependence is created because the person here needs the money that is sent. When their migrant relatives tell them how to vote, they listen. We went to Boston so that when people write to their relatives here they would tell them to support PRD candidates. (PRD leader, Baní)

PRD leaders also believed migrants could create a strong lobby that could advocate for Dominican national interests. As a result, they made various aspects of party life transnational in a much more systematic way than ever before.

Two factors further encouraged the transnationalization of Dominican politics. The PRD belongs to the Socialist International Party (SIP), a coalition of democratic socialist parties throughout the world.[7] As a result, the party regularly receives funding, technical assistance, and training from other SIP affiliates. In exchange, it has to modify its policies and procedures to conform to SIP directives. For example, in response to the SIP's campaign to integrate women more fully into its activities, the PRD accepted the SIP's worldwide goal that 25 percent of all party leaders and 25 percent of all its candidates would be women. It also underwent a process of modernization and implemented more technology-driven vote-winning strategies, similar to other SIP affiliates around the world. Its membership in the SIP meant that, at some levels, the PRD already acted across borders. The party's prior experience with assimilating strategies and techniques via long distance made it easier to begin acting transnationally at other levels of its operation.

The PRD also received major support from foreign-government foundations and aid agencies promoting democratic consolidation. The Freidrich Ebert Foundation of Germany, for example, funded the establishment of *escuelas políticas* (political training schools) to teach political skills and civic capabilities to PRD members. The U.S. Endowment for Democracy, a foundation with ties to the Democratic Party, supported members' visits to the Democratic Convention and to observe presidential elections. "They invited us," observed one PRD national vice president, "because we have friendly relations with them and they want us to support their views. . . . When you go and witness the actual election, one sees the democratic process unfold, and it is undoubtedly extraordinary." As a result, when the PRD articulated an agenda to address migrants' needs, it did so based on hands-on experience with the U.S. political system, a fact that made its transnational efforts more likely to succeed.

Throughout the 1990s several aspects of the PRD's activities became transnational. The first is structure. The PRD replicated and expanded its organization to include all migrants in the United States. Party leaders created base-level committees, comparable to those on the island, that were aggregated into municipal zones and then grouped into regional sections in New England, New Jersey, Florida, Puerto Rico, and Washington. In 1992 it also approved the creation of base-level committees for Dominicans who became naturalized U.S. citizens and for second-generation Dominican Americans. Four U.S.-section members represent the migrant community on the party's National Executive Committee in Santo Domingo. The party also appointed a coordinator for all U.S. party activities. His job is to facilitate cooperation between party members at all levels on the island and in the United States.

These ties were both horizontally and vertically transnational, thereby generating intricate and powerful organizational connections between the United States and the island. I call organizations *horizontally transnational* when there are ties between comparable, local-level chapters, such as parishes or local-level political groups, in the sending and receiving countries. In the case of Miraflores, the Catholic Church is horizontally transnational because there are connections between the local church in Miraflores and two local parishes in Jamaica Plain. Horizontal ties also connected the chapter of the Miraflores Development Committee in Miraflores with its sister chapter in Boston. Horizontal ties can form at higher levels of an organization as well. For example, the PRD's municipal committee in Baní was connected to the municipal committee in Boston. Likewise, there were relations between the archdioceses in Baní and in Boston.

Organizations are *vertically transnational* when these horizontal ties form part of a hierarchically integrated organizational system—that is, when the ties that horizontally connect local, municipal, and national levels of a political party are also part of a vertically coordinated transnational ladder. Since national cross-border activities are organized in conjunction with and intersect municipal and local-level ones, they are likely to be stronger and longer lasting.

A third distinction must be made between home-country organizations that become transnational by creating franchises or chapters in the receiving country and those that become transnational by actually joining forces with an established host-country organization. The PRD and the PLD created U.S.-based organizations, but neither party established formal or informal ties to a U.S. political group. In contrast, religious transnational connections were forged within the context of a single, worldwide church organization. Dominican clergy work under the auspices of the U.S. church and U.S. clergy in Santo Domingo work through the Dominican church. When transnational organizations are constituted by actually joining sending- and receiving-country groups together, their efforts are more likely to have an impact in both places.

Particularly strong local, horizontal ties emerged between Boston and Baní for several reasons. Jaime Benabarre, who founded the PRD in Boston, is from Baní. He was elected head of the PRD's municipal committee when he returned to live in Baní in the late 1980s. Carlos Alarcón, elected mayor of Baní in 1994, had a son living in Boston who was also active in the party. As a result, when PRD candidates came to Boston to campaign, they sought support for municipal and pro-vincial candidates as well as for presidential contenders.

The PRD also began articulating a discourse that was more trans-national in tone. As the party's financial dependence on migrant con-tributions increased and migrant members made their conditions for remaining active in the PRD clear, the party proposed new ideas about its relationship to its U.S. constituency. Party leaders recognized they needed to articulate a dual political agenda that simultaneously addressed the needs of migrants while furthering Dominican national interests.

"We began to understand," said a national vice president,

that the party had to be more realistic about capturing supporters in the U.S. We realized that they were living in a situation that is a little unusual—a dual lifestyle. They live in the U.S., but they don't have representation with re-spect to the government there. They feel Dominican and they want to be po-litically active. So the party developed new structures and is putting into place a strategy that is more realistic and more aggressive with respect to the Dominican community in the U.S. Our policy is to stimulate Dominican par-ticipación in political life in the U.S. but to also help them remain active in Dominican politics.

Several leaders mentioned the example of the Jewish American community as the model they wished to emulate. Just as the Jewish American lobby favorably influenced U.S. policies toward Israel, so the Dominican migrant community could generate support for favor-able sugar quotas, terms of trade, and development assistance.

The PRD's concern for migrants was evident at all levels of party activity. At a meeting to introduce the 1994 provincial and municipal candidates in Baní, five of the six men running for office mentioned the Dominicanos Ausentes (migrants) in their remarks. One candidate spoke compellingly about the party's feelings for its many "sons" who had migrated:

Each day it hurts us more and more that so many Dominican men and women must leave the country because they feel they cannot support their families here. It is our job to create the conditions that allow them to come back, but it is also our job to make sure that they know we still support them while they are in the U.S. The PRD will not abandon you. (PRD Senate candidate, Baní)

A third way the party became more transnational was with respect to policy. The PRD cultivated migrants' long-term loyalty by demonstrating its responsiveness to their concerns. Migrants wanted to be able to bring back cars, personal effects, and industrial equipment into the country without paying exorbitant taxes. They wanted to be treated decently by customs officials. The PRD responded with relevant policy proposals.

For example, a Dominican resident in the U.S. who decides to invest in this country would have certain financial incentives. They would not have to pay taxes on the income from the investments they made. Many people complain that the rules of the game are not clear in the Dominican Republic. When they come back, everything is a problem. Everything is difficult, The bureaucracy makes them run in circles. There is no information. No one knows anything and they are often tricked. Who would want to come back under these conditions? But if the government gives them clear information and guarantees, they are willing to come back and establish themselves here. We believed that by doing this, migrants would support the party and we could get them to consider coming back, especially those with resources who could stimulate economic development. (PRD leader, Santo Domingo)

The PRD also began to execute many of its activities across borders. The party's campaign strategies exemplify this approach. Election campaigns are notoriously lengthy in the Dominican Republic, where the next campaign is said to start the day after the last election. Dr. Peña Gómez visited the New England area three times prior to the 1994 election. Five other high-ranking party officials, including a former vice-presidential candidate and a member of the Executive Committee, also visited the region to campaign on his behalf. Accordingly, party leaders adopted new strategies and refashioned old ones to work across borders.

We are trying to be mindful of their [migrants'] needs as well and to put mechanisms into place that can help them in a number of ways. From a political point of view, by doing this we can only win. It is not only a question of taking from them but of giving to them as well. If we can do a series of things for the Dominican in Boston, seven or eight things for him, although this person is not initially in the PRD they could become a member. I would say a higher percentage would end up belonging to this party because it is the institution that helped them, that gave them a hand, that has resolved their problems where no other institutions, political or otherwise, have worried about them. The political goal of all of this, then, is that those that are able to vote for us will, [and] others will influence their relatives or friends who can vote and will send us more resources. (PRD Executive Committee member, Santo Domingo)

Leaders in Baní often use nonpolitical arenas to pursue political goals. Women organize religious groups and literacy classes to increase the party's visibility and legitimacy. Participants form a positive association with the PRD because most of the organizers are known to be party activists, though they never discuss politics directly during these meetings. Party leaders win new supporters by energetically fostering these links between politics and community service.

PRD members in Boston used this same tactic. They formed the Altagracianos, a church-based group that organized celebrations for the Día de la Virgen de Altagracia, the patron saint day of the Dominican Republic. They also formed a Dominican social club that sponsored social and educational events. Neither organization explicitly articulated political goals, nor were their most prominent organizers PRD leaders, but many of their behind-the-scenes board members were. Because of this clear association among the Altagracianos, social club directors, and the PRD, these groups also functioned like nonpolitical forums at which party goals were espoused. Again, since migrants strongly associated the party with the church and the *patria* (homeland), they were more likely to support the PRD.

Party leaders also created new forms of party affiliation. Many Dominicans shy away from formally joining political parties because if their group loses they will be ineligible for a public-sector job. The

PRD created new types of affiliation, enabling migrants and nonmigrants to support the party without this "official membership" liability. Mirafloreños could enlist as *simpatizantes* (sympathizers) or they could work for a group created specifically to support the party during election campaigns.

PRD leaders also expanded their notion of their catchment area. They encouraged members to organize *círculos de influencia,* or influence circles, of family members and close friends on the island and in the United States whom they could call upon to make donations or attend rallies. Some leaders envisioned these as encompassing transnational constituencies.

We have a special plan within the party. We have decided to expand the party, but this expansion is not based on predetermined geographic areas. We want to expand based on the areas of influence of our activists and leaders. You might live in Gazcue, but your area of influence could be very widespread. We have asked each leader to reach out based on their own area of influence. They can form groups of people in the U.S. and on the island. This means that there are people who are not Dominican citizens who are with the party. (PRD Executive Committee member, Santo Domingo)

Migration necessitated changes in new membership recruitment. In the Dominican Republic, leaders attracted new supporters through *cara a caras,* face-to-face home visits during which they personally invite individuals to join the PRD. Colder weather, less leisure time, and greater distances meant that the party needed different tactics in Boston. Though *comisiones* (work groups) still made home visits, they had to schedule them in advance. Leaders did not know, as they would have on the island, that José was always home after 5 P.M. or that he played dominoes at the corner grocery every Thursday evening so they could always visit him there.

Another way to recruit new members in Baní was to curry favor with opposition party leadership. If the tactic was successful, the leader's supporters (i.e., the members of his base committee) were likely to defect with him. Leaders in Boston also tried to appropriate members from one another. Since some individuals circulated back and forth or returned to live on the island, they often needed to be courted transnationally. It took PRD leaders three years to convince Alejandro to leave the PRSC for the PRD, but when they did, most of Alejandro's supporters in Boston and Miraflores switched parties as well.

The day-to-day life of the party had to be fine-tuned to function smoothly in Boston. An unofficial six-man team formed the party's principal leadership in Baní. Each member had his own *equipo de trabajo*, or group of close supporters, whom he met with every day. Dr. Feliciano's group, for example, got together for coffee and politics each morning in his garden before work; they could often be found at the end of the day doing the same. In Boston, these *equipos de trabajo* met less frequently in what tended to be stores or other public places. Party members from as far away as Providence could be found at La Rubia's Fashion, a clothing store owned by a party leader in Boston that became his faction's unofficial meeting spot.

Finally, party leaders appealed to migrants' localized identities to further their agenda in Boston. One individual, for example, organized an opposition slate for control of the New England section consisting only of candidates from Baní. He tried winning members' support by convincing them that the old guard in Boston did not adequately represent their interests because they were not from the same town.

The fifth dimension along which the PRD became transnational was leadership. Some leaders actually carried out their responsibilities across borders.

There are leaders who maintain their positions via remote control from the U.S. In Villa Altagracia [the city next to Baní], the president of the party has a business in the U.S. He is here some of the time and there the other part of the time. In Mao it is the same thing. One of the principal leaders lives in New York. One lives in Providence. He wants to become senator. People tolerate this because he comes home very often and he has friends and relatives that work for him. This isn't a majority, but it is significant. (PRD national vice president, Santo Domingo)

Many of the patron-client relationships Mirafloreños had established persisted across borders. These bonds continued to shape political outcomes in Boston as well as on the island. The Avila family was benefactor to several families in Miraflores; their bonds of mutual obligation remained strong even when several Avila family members migrated to the United States. When presidential candidate Peña Gómez visited Boston, PRD leaders asked David Avila to send *su gente,* or "his people," to attend the rally they were organizing. When he agreed, his brother in Miraflores also came on board. If David had decided against supporting the PRD, the family's clients on the island would probably have followed suit.

The final dimension of party life that became transnational was financing. The party leadership in Santo Domingo looked increasingly to the migrant community for financial assistance. Though there are no official data supporting these claims, party leaders estimated that between 10 and 30 percent of the party's operating budget, and as much as 50 percent of the funding for specific campaigns, came from migrant contributions.[8] During the 1994 elections, Dr. Peña Gómez visited New York seven times in a thirteen-month period, raising hundreds of thousands of dollars (Sagás 1999). New England section leaders said they raised more than $150,000 during Peña Gómez's visits to the region.

Opposition Parties and the Dominican State

The PRD was not the only party encouraging Dominicans to participate politically in two places or creating the institutional arenas that enabled them to do so. The Partido de la Liberación Dominicana (PLD) also established a U.S.-based organization. In 1998 there were eleven base-level *comités intermedios* (intermediate committees) in the United States that were equal in status to comparable groups on the island. The Boston committee, founded nearly twenty years ago, had twenty-one full members and fifteen individuals working toward membership who met on a weekly basis.[9]

Unlike the PRD in New England, which is autonomous, the PLD falls under the jurisdiction of the New York party chapter. Migrant and nonmigrant party members remain in contact with one another in a number of ways. Every two weeks an *enlace,* or contact person, travels between New York and Boston to supervise the party's activities. Similarly, *enlaces* travel biweekly between New York and Santo Domingo. Three members from the party in the United States sit on the PLD's Central Committee in Santo Domingo. These representatives were elected under an unofficial quota allowing 3 out of 150 seats to be filled by migrants. These provisions grant migrants some voice in party governance but also limit their influence. PLD members living outside the country have also formed their own commission, the PLD Commission for Dominicans Living Abroad, to better represent migrants' interests. While its current president lives in New York, many members are return migrants who lived in the United States for many years and only recently returned to Santo Domingo.

By 1992 all the principal political parties claimed to be in favor of dual citizenship and expatriate voting. In fact, in a televised address, then-candidate Leonel Fernández actively encouraged Dominican migrants to naturalize. He said they must protect themselves from changes in U.S. laws limiting government services to noncitizens and assured them they would not lose their rights as Dominican citizens if they did so.

If you, young mother, or you, elderly gentleman, or you, young student, feel the need to adopt the nationality of the United States in order to confront the vicissitudes of that society stemming from the end of the welfare era, do not feel tormented by this. Do it with a peaceful conscience, for you will continue being Dominicans, and we will welcome you as such when you set foot on the soil of our republic. (Fernández, cited in Graham 1997)

Calls for dual citizenship and the expatriate vote had grown stronger throughout the 1970s and 1980s due to the efforts of an emerging entrepreneurial class with business interests in the United States and on the island (Guarnizo 1998). Entrepreneurs and migrant civic associations arranged a number of conferences in New York and the Dominican Republic to advocate for a constitutional amendment that would institute such changes in the interest of national unity and economic growth. These calls went largely unheeded until the mid-1990s, when several factors converged to bring about their approval.

First, it became clear to Dominican leaders of all political persuasions that the diaspora played a decisive role in the economy. Though migrants made up only 1 percent of the electorate in 1996, they clearly influenced how nonmigrants voted (De La Garza et al. 1998). As a result, when migrants' calls for improved consular services, investment incentives, and greater incorporation into the political system grew louder, the government and political opposition had strong incentives to listen.

While Balaguer publicly supported dual citizenship and expatriate voting, he actually blocked their implementation because he feared migrants' potential political opposition. The former president's position weakened considerably, however, when the international community agreed he had tampered with the 1994 election results. European and U.S. governments, along with international observers, forced Bala- guer to accept the Pact for Democracy to remain in office for a re- duced two-year term. This agreement allowed Dominicans to acquire a second citizenship without losing their original one (Sagás 1999).[10] The reformed constitution, approved in 1996, gives full citizenship rights to Dominicans who opt for a second citizenship, though they cannot be elected president or vice president. The new constitution also grants citizenship to those born outside the country to Domini- can parents, thus ensuring the formal inclusion of the second genera- tion and beyond.

All presidential candidates in 1996 also supported a bill that would allow Dominican migrants to vote from abroad rather than having to return to the island to do so. This measure was passed in Decem- ber 1997 (Electoral Law 275-97), when the Dominican National Con- gress approved a new electoral code allowing Dominicans permanently residing overseas, including those who are naturalized Americans of Dominican descent, to vote in the country's presidential elections and to run for office (Sagás 1999). Dominicans in New York campaigned extensively for these measures, creating a Pro-Vote Movement for Dominicans Living Abroad (Sontag and Rother 1997). Once achieved, these electoral reforms effectively cemented the political importance of Dominicans abroad as contributors, as well as voters, by making New York the second-largest concentration of Dominican voters out- side Santo Domingo.

Though the expatriate vote has been approved, the Central Elec- tion Board, or Junta Central de Elecciones, is still debating how to im- plement this legislation. Many ask how the Dominican government will be able to organize an election abroad when it has such a poor track record of organizing honest elections at home. Clearly there are administrative and financial challenges ahead. The U.S. Depart- ments of State and Justice do not have an official position on hosting large-scale expatriate voting on U.S. soil (Sagás 1999). The United States does not recognize dual citizenship for migrants who natural- ize, though in practice migrants are rarely required to officially re- nounce their former citizenship. If increasing numbers of Dominicans choose dual citizenship, what kinds of restrictions should be placed on where they cast their ballot?

Questions about voting are just one part of a broader set of concerns about the Dominican government's changing relationship with its expatriate members. The state made few systematic attempts to maintain contact with migrants prior to the 1990s. When mass migration began in the late 1960s, government efforts focused on channeling the money migrants sent back to the island through official, state-controlled channels. In his 1982 inaugural speech, for example, President Salvador Jorge Blanco outlined a plan to increase interest rates on special savings accounts designed to attract remittances (Messina 1988).

Since the PLD's election in 1996, however, the government has systematically reached out to migrants and, by so doing, extended the borders of the Dominican state. It no longer refers to Dominicans abroad as *migrantes* or Dominicanos Ausentes but as Dominicans Residing in the Exterior. Several U.S.-based Dominicans served in the Dominican Congress, including two PLD members from New York. The fact that the PLD designated three legislative seats on its ticket to Dominicans living abroad aided their election. Candidates for these seats ran from their hometowns because there was no formal mechanism to elect representatives from abroad. Those elected officially represent districts on the island but unofficially represent their constituencies offshore (Itzigsohn et al. 1999).

There has also been some discussion within the government about redistricting the island to include communities living abroad. President Fernández was said to support this idea, though no official proposals were made. Such reforms would increase migrants' political clout considerably, giving New York alone as many as ten congressional seats. There have also been calls to elect a "diasporic representative" to the U.S. Congress. This position would be similar to the Puerto Rican "resident commissioner" in Washington, who represents the Puerto Rican government in Congress (Sagás 1999). Finally, several legislators have proposed the establishment of a bipartisan Comisíon de Dominicanos Residentes en el Exterior, or a Commission for Dominicans Residing in the Exterior, within the Dominican Congress. The commission's goal would be to collect information about migrants' concerns and to propose legislation in response. One possibility under consideration was to establish a government secretariat dealing specifically with migrant affairs.

In addition to these efforts, the government initiated several programs aimed at strengthening migrants' economic and cultural ties. It allocated funds to set up *casas de cultura,* or cultural centers, in cities where there were large numbers of Dominican residents. The Dominican consular service encouraged community development. The consul in Boston helped create six *comités,* or provincial committees, from the regions sending the greatest numbers to New England. These groups aimed to reinforce Dominican national identity and to foster community development by encouraging migrants to support projects in their sending communities. Each group raised money and collected donations of equipment and supplies, which the consulate then shipped back to the Dominican Republic. Customs policy reforms allow return migrants to transport their belongings, including one car per household, without paying taxes. The government placed customs officers at each consulate to help migrants complete the paperwork they need while they are still in the United States. Finally, the government built 1,373 housing units in Santo Domingo specifically for return migrants. Prospective buyers take out mortgages with designated U.S. banks, which they have up to 15 years to repay; the government covers 60 percent of the original down payment (Dominican Consul 1998).

In sum, a complex web of transnational political relations spans Boston and Miraflores, formed by interpersonal ties between migrants and nonmigrants and by connections among local, regional, and national actors in the United States and the Dominican Republic. Transnational goals, and the creation of organizations with which to achieve them, do not always result in transnational outcomes. To date, Dominican political parties have acted transnationally but have seen results only uni-directionally. As I show below, despite calls for dual involvements and the mechanisms enabling them to sustain these, most Mirafloreños continue to participate more in island politics.

Political Change in Boston

Dominicans migrating to Boston during the past two decades encountered a complex political panorama. Politics was sharply divided along ethnic and neighborhood lines. Minorities have never been adequately represented in the city. In 1998, when they constituted nearly 50 percent of all residents, there were only two black city councillors (Walker 1998). A small group of middle-class Latino professionals and business owners generally spoke for the wider Latino community. Divisions within and among country-of-origin groups thwarted efforts to organize Latinos as a whole (Jezierski 1994). Puerto Ricans dominated most political groups because they were citizens and because they were the largest, best-established group in the state.

Although Latinos were the fastest-growing minority in Massachusetts during the past two decades, the Republican and Democratic Parties did little to reach out to them. The Latino population is still relatively small, and many community members are too young to vote. The Republican Party did not become a serious political force in the state until William Weld was elected governor in 1990. Most Latinos, with the exception of the Cuban community, support the Democrats.

As a result, Latinos achieved only modest political gains. In 1999 there were three Latino elected officials in the Massachusetts House of Representatives; there were no Latinos in the State Senate.[11] Two Latinos served on the Boston School Committee, though there were still no Latino representatives on the Boston City Council. In 1995, in Lawrence, Massachusetts, where nearly two-thirds of the 71,000 residents are Latinos, only two of the nine City Council members and seven School Committee members were Latino. This prompted a federal lawsuit calling for the city to elect its School Committee by districts, rather than citywide, and for council district lines to be redrawn to increase Latino access to political office (Walker 1998). These reforms have met with some success. In 1999, three out of the seven Dominicans who ran for office in Lawrence won (Rodriguez 1999).

Dominicans in the Boston area, however, have remained on the political margins. The PRD and PLD had no formal ties to any U.S. political organization. In 1993 mayoral candidates in Boston met briefly with PRD leaders, but only because the candidates happened to make a campaign stop in front of party headquarters. PRD members, acting as private individuals, worked on campaigns or formed relationships with particular politicians. These ties resulted in the proclamation of Dominican Independence Day by former State Senate president William Bulger: a public ceremony is held on the State House steps each year. Bulger also officially welcomed presidential candidate Peña Gómez and other high-level PRD leaders during their many visits to Boston.

To be a serious political player, new groups must become citizens, vote, make campaign contributions, and work on election campaigns. Dominicans in Massachusetts have largely failed to do so. In 1990, only 20 percent of all Dominican residents in the state were naturalized U.S. citizens (U.S. Census 1992). Figure 1 shows changes in naturalization rates among foreign-born Dominicans in the United States between 1975 and 1993. Figure 2 illustrates these same trends for Massachusetts, New York, and the United States as a whole. Though naturalization increased among Dominicans in general, particularly in the 1990s, the numbers were still quite low. There was a 64 percent increase in naturalizations between 1990 and 1993 in Massachusetts, compared to more than 100 percent increases in New York and the nation as a whole. However, in Massachusetts, as figure 2 illustrates, this represents an actual numerical increase from only 171 naturalizations in 1990 to 281 in 1993. Table 13 compares naturalization rates among the major ethnic and racial groups in the United States by year of entry into the country (see Appendix A).

Here again, naturalization increased among those Dominicans who arrived after the 1960s, though it is still somewhat low compared to blacks and Asians. Citizenship was slightly higher among Dominicans than among non-Dominican Hispanics, however.

Dominicans have achieved greater political gains in New York than in Massachusetts. Guillermo Linares, who initially served on the New York City School Board, went on to become the first Dominican to be elected to the New York City Council in 1990. Adriano Espaillat became the first Dominican-born member of the New York State Assembly in 1996. Though Dominican parties did not participate officially in these campaigns, individual party members worked actively on them. Candidates for mayor of New York regularly travel to the island to campaign, attesting to the Dominican community's increasing clout. Former Mayor David Dinkins, for example, received the endorsement of Rafael Corporán de los Santos, the mayor of Santo Domingo, when he campaigned in the capital in 1992 (Moreno 1992).[12]

The New York Dominican community also created a large number of social service organizations that represent their interests in the informal political arena.[13] The Dominican-American National Roundtable (DANR), which focuses on health care, education, and immigration law, has purposefully distanced itself from Dominican politics. Dominicans 2000, based at the City University of New York, where more than 10 percent of the student body is Dominican, aims to increase education and empower Dominicans in the United States (Gonzalez 1998).

Several factors explain these differences in political integration between New York and Massachusetts. First, although the Dominican community in New York is also relatively young, it is much larger than its counterpart to the north. Dominicans in New York City constitute a critical enough mass of potential voters that the powers that be have begun to take them into account. The New York community is also better established. Migrants have had more time to educate and mobilize themselves. The large numbers of social service agencies that they established later shifted their focus toward promoting political participation (Guarnizo 1992). In contrast, in Massachusetts, the community is still quite young and relatively small. Because it does not have the same level of organizational development, Dominicans are less well represented in formal politics. There are fewer organizational contact points where migrants are encouraged to become politically active.

Second, in New York, Dominicans found a number of well-organized minority allies to work with. Sometimes they joined formal coalitions to promote issues like immigration reform or electoral redistricting. At other times, they worked informally with particular groups or politicians who could further their cause. When African-American representative Charles Rangel backed Linares' candidacy, for example, it was said to contribute in important ways to his success (Weyland 1999). In contrast, powerful minority coalitions are absent from Boston's political landscape. There are few examples of blacks and Latinos rallying together to get a single candidate elected to office. Infighting among country-of-origin groups within the Latino community has generally rendered ineffectual what little might qualify as "Latino politics."

Furthermore, when Dominicans first came to New York, they encountered activists who willingly tutored them in U.S. politics. Some of the PRD's original members in New York City recalled the invaluable assistance they received from Adam Clayton Powell and Basil Patterson's staff, who guided their first entrees into New York politics. These teachers showed them how to negotiate the U.S. political system and helped them form relationships with other well-connected individuals who could also help them do so. Again, in Boston, few individuals were willing or able to fulfill this orientation function. The Puerto Ricans who came prior to most Dominicans had not gained sufficient political clout. Little help came from African-American leaders, since few bridges had been built between the black and Latino communities.

As a result, despite transnational party structures, strategies, financing, and leadership that were all put in place, in part, to promote political participation in the United States, Mirafloreños integrated little into U.S. politics. They offered several explanations for this. First, many Mirafloreños strongly resisted naturalization.[14] They planned to return to the Dominican Republic and they wanted to be able to do so with the privileges of Dominican citizenship. Others said they felt pressure not to naturalize because they did not want to be seen as *vende patrias*, or traitors to their homeland. If nonmigrants already suspected them of having abandoned their homeland, it would prove they had done so if they changed their citizenship. Worse still, they might be viewed as siding with the *gringos* (Americans) who had consistently compromised Dominican sovereignty throughout the country's history.

A number of Mirafloreños claimed it was just too difficult to participate. They were too busy trying to earn a living and raise their families to take on anything else. Leaders attributed some of their difficulty organizing migrants to their poor language skills. Since so many members could not speak English, they said, it was difficult to mobilize them around the problems they faced in the United States. Migrants spent too much time "in the Latino ghetto" to understand the larger issues confronting them.

I think that what is going on in the U.S. doesn't matter to them because they are not educated. The vast majority don't have culture. They have not tried to continue their studies. Look at our community leaders. Look at each of the parties and see how many speak English, which one knows where to go in an emergency. There are people who have lived there for 20 years and they have never been to the Prudential Center. (Former Dominican consul, Santo Domingo)

Other respondents argued Dominicans were excluded from politics. The logistics of becoming a citizen were unnecessarily confusing and complicated. Latino political organizations were not taken seriously by people with influence because they were too weak and poorly organized. Since the Dominican community was small, the Democratic and Republican parties simply did not need them to win elections. And when U.S. politicians did reach out to Dominicans, they did so without a real sense of the kind of courtship required. This came through particularly clearly in an example given by an ex-PRSC consul in New York who was deeply offended when the first thing that former mayor Edward Koch inquired about when they were introduced was the opposition candidate, Dr. Peña Gómez.

Most important, many Mirafloreños simply continued to care more about the Dominican Republic. They participated politically as a way to remain connected to the island and to counteract how excluded and displaced they felt in the United States. They remained active as a way to express their continued patriotism and loyalty. As one Mirafloreño who had been living in Boston for more than 15 years said, in what was a fairly typical statement, "The fact is that I am still more worried about what happens in the Dominican Republic because it is my cradle, it is where I was born. It would be wrong for me to forget."

Mirafloreños' limited formal political integration, however, does not mean migrants are untouched by their experiences in the United States. They observed what took place around them and liked what they saw. They claimed to become more aware of politics. They listened to the news and talked with one another about what they heard.

Though I wasn't a member of a party in the U.S. I knew what was going on around me and how the American system worked. There was less of a carnival around politics in the U.S. They didn't make so much noise like they do here. They didn't stand on every corner with a big band. The day of the elections, you wouldn't have even known there were elections because the people just went out to vote and they didn't make a big scandal like they do here. I liked that it was more orderly. Here they say it is a democracy but que va. When I worked there and we would go to the bank on payday, I would say to my friends, *señores,* if we were in Santo Domingo they wouldn't let us into the bank being all dirty from work, but in Boston there were people who had on a shirt and tie and briefcase who were waiting behind me. Everyone had to wait on line. (Miguel, 51, return migrant, Miraflores)

Several Mirafloreños also participated in nonelectoral activities. Nearly half of all return and current migrants reported they attended meetings of community organizations, business-owner associations, school committees, church councils, and cultural clubs at least periodically. Over half of these individuals said they had not belonged to similar groups before they left.

There were a number of reasons for this. Mirafloreños' experiences in Boston gave rise to a set of concerns that could be addressed effectively through these kinds of groups. Since there was an even wider array of organizations in Boston than in Miraflores, migrants were more likely to find a group they felt inclined to work with. In some cases, outreach workers actively sought their membership. A Dominican store-owner, for example, personally invited Mirafloreño businessowners to attend the first meeting of the local merchants' association in Jamaica Plain. And participation served political and social ends—several respondents said they joined groups because they knew they would see their friends and neighbors at meetings.

Migrants also reported they had more contacts with government agencies in the United States than in Miraflores. They interacted with school officials, health care providers, and subsidized-housing-program managers on a regular basis.

Before I left, I had never had contact with a government official. We tried to avoid them like the plague because dealing with the government only spelled trouble. But when I lived in Boston, people started to tell me about the kind of help the U.S. government gives. That you could get help finding an apartment or paying for the doctor. When my husband left me, my sister and I were living together. We heard about the Section 8 housing program, where they give you vouchers so that you can afford to live in a better place. One day, Cecilia and I went down to the office. We were very shy. We did not know what to do. But the lady helped us. And after about 6 months of going down there every month, you know what? We finally got an apartment. That was when I learned that a government could do something good. (Helena, 38-year-old return migrant, Miraflores)

Consequently, many Mirafloreños first learned to negotiate bureaucracies in the United States. Since they had little prior contact with the Dominican state before leaving the island, it was in Boston that they learned what governments can provide and how to demand things from them. As Marcelo put it,

It never occurred to me that the government would provide these kinds of services, let alone that I would ask for them. It totally changed my mind about what a government's responsibility to its citizens could be. I started thinking, maybe I should participate. Maybe if I ask, I will really get some help. (56, return migrant, Miraflores)

The PRD and the PLD were much more successful organizing Dominicans around home-country causes. In 1994, the New England section of the PRD claimed to have more than 1,000 members stretching from the North Shore of Boston to Providence, Rhode Island. Party leaders said they raised close to $150,000 during the campaign. In 1999 the party raised an additional $50,000 in support of presidential hopeful Hipólito Mejía's candidacy (Rodriguez 1999). The community, however, was not large enough or mature enough to support committees of naturalized citizens or second-generation Dominicans the PRD had proposed. Party leaders also had difficulty sustaining their momentum during nonelection years. Mirafloreños complained that the issues the party tried to mobilize them around were just not important enough.

Some migrant PRD leaders claimed it was natural that their activities would ebb and flow between campaigns. But others accused their colleagues on the island of asking for migrants' support without giving them anything in return. They felt fustrated by island leaders' lack of real commitment to improve conditions in the United States.

The U.S. coordinator has been positive for Peña Gómez economically, but in terms of creating a political structure I don't see much progress. There has been too much of an economic thrust. We should have political education, consciousness raising, meetings to teach people and inform them about politics. We need to educate the masses of the party about why we are fighting. So far, we are not preparing them to be politicians but to be fund-raisers. . . . They are manipulating us. They are using us to get what they need and then forgetting that we have needs and concerns too. (PRD zone president, Boston)

As a result, conflict arose between the traditional party elite in Santo Domingo and a new U.S.-based elite. Though leaders in Boston occupied the lowest rungs of the "food chain," they still wanted to be recognized as big fish in their own small part of the pond. They deeply resented leaders who arrived from the island and tried to tell them what to do. These encounters reflected the sharpening divergence between migrant and nonmigrant interests.

There is an elite Dominican immigrant community in the U.S. that is conscious of its interests and has tried to put the brakes on those here. This emerging elite is not just political, it is intellectual, cultural, social. . . . It is achieving a place in City Hall and cannot be bossed around anymore. They want to be recognized and given their place in the sun. If the PRD is going to retain their support, some of the old guard has to move over. (Sociologist, Santo Domingo)

The party's message, migrant leaders claimed, was sometimes off the mark. It continued to speak to the realities of Dominican life without taking the problems of life in the United States into account.

Party leaders still don't understand because they don't know this setting. They think the PRD is organizing in Santo Domingo. The Dominican that lives in the U.S. is participating in a society that is highly developed and sophisticated. They have to work many hours each day to make enough money to live a life that is halfway decent. They work in third- or fourth-class jobs and they don't have time for politics. It is not easy to organize people who live in Roxbury with those who live in Jamaica Plain. Two hours on the subway to talk about nonsense—it just isn't worth it. . . . There is a real disconnection between what the party generally proposes, its actual attitude with respect to migration, and its capacity to understand the problems that migrants face. Politics is done there, not here. I do not mean that we are not important but that we do not have any real influence. (New England section leader, Boston)

The party would do better, some argued, if it were more responsive to migrants' needs. Migrants wanted help completing tax forms, locating housing, finding employment, and regularizing their immigration papers—help the party was unprepared to give.

The Impact of Transnational Politics in the Dominican Republic

Respondents expressed conflicting views about the impact of migration on local-level Dominican politics. About 15 percent felt that migration had no impact. They said that migrants were too poor and uneducated to learn much from their lives in the United States that would effect political change in the Dominican Republic. They were not smart or energetic enough to analyze their surroundings and interpret what they saw for those who stayed behind.

Immigrants have not been a catalyst for modernization because most of the people who have come back are poor, worked in a factory, earned little, and have not had the necessary education to understand the economic, social, and political problems. All those who live in the U.S. come back and the first thing they say is that they can't stand the disorder. But how to change or transform this, they have no idea what they would do. They appreciate the organization in the U.S., they realize there is chaos here, but the process of elaborating change escapes them. (PLD political committee member, Santo Domingo)

About 35 percent felt that migration was a negative or conservatizing force. These respondents said that migration diminishes activism by making politics obsolete. Mirafloreños did not need politics anymore because they solved their problems by migrating.

Before migration, Miraflores was a political community where the PRD was a powerful force, but today no party can say it has a major influence in Miraflores. There is great indifference to the electoral process. I think the proof is that Miraflores has one of the largest abstention rates in the municipality of Baní. It is not a question of not believing in the elections. It is not a question of political convictions. It is a question of economic conviction—they are not interested because their objective is undoubtedly to go to the U.S. Those in the U.S. have an influence because they transmit to the ones who stay behind an economic bonanza: the most TV antennas, the most satellite dishes, refrigerators are in Miraflores. [Migrants] transmit this same economic criteria to their people here and it makes them indifferent. It is inconceivable that in Miraflores we have only three base-level committees. That means 120 people. Before Miraflores had 900 registered members. (President of the Peravia Provincial Committee, Baní)

Respondents claimed that mobilizing young people was particularly difficult since so few of them saw themselves making their future in Miraflores.

Migrants undermined reforms by clinging to the ideas and practices that were in place before they left, though the political system had changed. This was felt to be especially true for those who did well in the United States. They assumed their new economic status automatically entitled them to greater political clout. They often expected to become leaders, but their old-style mentality worked against the grain of change.

They haven't changed. I think they come back with more economic power but with the same clientalist political culture. If you go to a small town, you will find many of them with a gun in their belt. . . . I don't want to be unfair. . . . I don't want to generalize, but it is obvious that though they are better off economically, they are not a factor in bringing about a better democratic order. . . . If anything they ask for more privileges. (Sociologist, Santo Domingo)

Futhermore, some social remittances introduced many negative role models. Several respondents argued that migrants absorbed the worst aspects of American society and then modeled these for their friends and family.

With respect to the development of a social or cultural consciousness, I see that each day we go from bad to worse. Things are very different than they were fifteen years ago, and I tell you this with a heavy heart. The youth of Miraflores don't think about a future. They are thinking about having fun, getting money to be able to drink beer and go out and dance, and some of them want to go out and get drugs. It is incredible the number of young men smoking dope. It is the fault of those who live in the U.S., who go back and encourage their friends to get into this. You know that in Miraflores there is not one house that doesn't have someone living in the U.S. These kids have never had to work to get their food. They stand around on the corner with their friends. Idleness is the mother of all vice, and since they aren't going to school or work, they fall prey to these vices. (Fausto, 29, migrant, Boston)

A remaining group saw migrants as catalysts for positive change. They claimed that even though migrants did not become citizens of the United States or participate directly in U.S. politics, they witnessed a fairer, better-functioning political system, which they described to those who stay behind. In response to migrants' narratives, nonmigrants also began to question the prevailing wisdom and envision a different kind of status quo.

I have never been to Boston, but my brothers say that the elections there are honest. Bill Clinton can't just tamper with votes because he wants to stay in power like Balaguer does here. In Santo Domingo, politics is a risk. Everything is personal. If I am from one party and you are from another, we can't share with one another. We can't discuss things. There you can say what you think. During the last elections, my brother told me how Bush and Clinton in a certain TV program said things to each other, and at the end they shook hands and one felt that the things that they said remained behind because it was a political thing. Here the same thing happens, but after the TV program is over they go outside and fight. Here, if there is a rally, the police are there and they hassle the parties on the Left. There the police have to supervise the entire rally and they can't favor one party over the other. (Freddy, 44, nonmigrant, Miraflores)

Proponents of this more positive view felt that migrants' experiences, and the ideas and practices they introduced, generated demands for a political alternative.

There are greater demands for more democracy within the parties, that the justice system should be separate from the executive branch, which is so corrupt. . . . Emigration plays a role, since the people who come back come with these ideas. Even though they haven't participated in the political heart of the U.S., they have lived there. They have a notion of the relationship between public and private and that these distinctions are clearer than those in the Dominican Republic. And these things, any person picks up on them because they see it when their kids go to school or when they pay taxes. If people live this in their daily lives, it produces a change in mentality. It is not that they have formed a movement in favor of the rights of citizens, but they have friends and neighbors, and they say to their cousins, "If you have a problem, go to a lawyer. Don't try to work it out through a friend." (PRD vice president, Santo Domingo)

These social remittances, along with other changes prompted by migration, raised questions about how politics should get done.

In the U.S. there is another style of politics. People don't fight with each other on the street. The candidates don't attack each other in an offensive manner. The Dominican Republic should be more like the U.S., where there is a complete democracy. In Santo Domingo there is limited democracy. The other parties can't participate as equals because the government uses state resources in the campaign, the cars that belong to the state. In the U.S., this doesn't happen. The government doesn't have its own TV or radio station. There are limits on campaign finances, but in Santo Domingo you can spend as much as you want. . . . Everyone in politics in the Dominican Republic is looking for something. It is not like the U.S. Everyone works, they support a particular party, but on the day of the election, they work, they vote, and they go home. Here, no one works on the day of the election, but they are interested in who wins. "Oh, we are going to win City Hall, and I will get a job for 1,000 pesos a month." That is what they are looking for. (José, 45, return migrant, Miraflores)

Said one village-level leader,

Here are a series of concrete examples of the things we have adapted from the U.S. We have begun to imitate U.S. publicity. We use slogans, posters, bumperstickers. We didn't do this before. We used to use photographs of the president but never posters. Also, people are more likely to form groups now. Neighborhood associations, associations of certain kinds of producers and business owners. They learned this in the U.S., where they felt the need to come together, to work together, to not be so dispersed. Many think that migration to the U.S. has made us more polarized, but it isn't like that. It has taught us how to work together better. . . . Also, people now want to know what the government's programs are. Before they didn't do this. It was purely emotional. We are starting to see change little by little. We have had ten elections since Trujillo died, and in that time Dominican politics has become more modern. This has a lot to do with the influence of Latin American democracy, but above all it is the influence of the U.S.

For at least some Mirafloreños, then, migration changed their expectations of politics and motivated them to seek political reform. When Juan returned to Miraflores after twenty-one years in Boston, for example, he said he had come home ready to challenge the system. "I want to play by the rules," he claimed, "and I believe that the rules can serve me well."

These hopes for a new kind of politics resonated with the PRD's espoused commitment to reform. In fact, PRD leaders promoted the process of *modernización* it has embarked upon as a way to achieve greater equity. The party would become more effective by pursuing its goals more systematically. It would perfect its vote-winning strategies by devising them based on computerized membership lists.

Still, though the PRD expressed concern for migrants, most respondents agreed its efforts were more symbolic than substantive. Despite individual calls for change, and the PRD's commitment to reform, the party in Baní continued to pursue business as usual.

Lucho's experiences illustrate this clearly. He is a sixty-year-old migrant who lived in the United States between 1983 and 1988. He worked as an agricultural day-laborer before migrating; in Boston he found work with an office-cleaning company. He returned to Miraflores with only minimal savings but borrowed enough money to purchase a small stand, where he sells dry goods. He also got a part-time job working for the Baní city government as a truck and road inspector. This was partially a reward for Lucho's long-term party membership. He joined the PRD in 1962 and was elected president of one of the three base committees in Miraflores soon after he returned in 1991.

The state figured only peripherally in Lucho's everyday life. He had never contacted a government official for help solving problems. He felt they were "corrupt," "ineffectual," and "only looking out for their family and friends." To prove his point he cited the example of the price control inspectors who came to his stand every day to collect their ten peso "tip." "Hardly a day passes when they don't come," he said, "and when they come, what am I going to do? I give them ten pesos, but they don't know how much I am charging. They don't check anything." Lucho knew this was wrong, but he never considered approaching the authorities to complain about it. This was just part of everyday life on the island and you had to learn to live with it. As a road inspector, he often opted not to fine violators, though he found many offenders and he had the authority to do so, because he feared that he would alienate his neighbors.

> I know everyone here and when I see a road that is dirty I go and talk to them about it personally. I don't like to have to bring anyone down to the police. My bosses won't back me up. And today I have this job, but tomorrow I may not. If I've made enemies in the community, I'll have problems. If you are dealing with the people you live with, you have to pressure them as little as possible.

When I asked Lucho to compare U.S. politics to Dominican politics, he said it was like comparing the sun to the moon. He said he had never been exposed to a system that worked so well or seemed to treat everyone so fairly as the system in the United States.

> Politics in the U.S. is something marvelous. There are more opportunities. Here you have to have a friend in the government to be able to get a job or get things done. There they respect your rights more. Here I go to the store and whatever rich one with a tie cuts in front of me, there everyone has to stay in line. Even Bill Clinton has to wait in line.

But when I asked him if his experiences in the United States changed his political activities when he returned, he said they had not. His ideas about politics changed, but the institutions he returned to had remained the same. He found the party and the political system in general to be as corrupt as ever.

> I came back thinking, what would it be like if the Dominican Republic was like the U.S.? What if things really did work according to the rules? What if every person was treated equally? When I started working in the party again, I said, you know, it isn't like this everywhere. There are some places on this earth where the person who works hard gets the rewards, not just the person who is related to those in power. And they just looked at me like, what are you talking about? The same old people were doing the same old thing. So even if I want to change, the party doesn't.

Lucho wanted better politics, but when he tried to do something about it he encountered strong institutional constraints. He came back wanting something new but was unable to put these new ideas into practice.

Two additional examples echo his experience.

The first involves the PRD's commitment to incorporating women. When the Socialist International Party called on all its members to increase women's participation, the party dutifully modified its statutes.

There were more women on the PRD's municipal slate than ever before, though the party fell far short of the SIP's 25 percent goal. Just prior to the 1994 election, however, Dr. Peña Gómez formed an alliance with the Unión Democrática (UD) Party to improve his chances of defeating Balaguer. The two parties had to come up with a unified slate that included candidates from both groups, and the female candidates were eliminated in the process.

In Baní, a commission was formed from members of our party and the UD to divide up the slots for candidates. Where are the women? They are not there. They kicked Estela off the ticket. [We] ceded her slot to the UD. They didn't consult with us. We didn't have anything to do with it. When the leaders who came from Santo Domingo to do this arrived, the slate had already been decided upon. (President of the Peravia Provincial Committee, Baní)

In a second example, the need to maintain party unity seemed to counteract all attempts to decentralize decision making. Divisions within the party following the 1986 election weakened the PRD so severely that national leaders directed their colleagues at the local level to preserve unity at all costs. As a result, several so-called elections were really ceremonial enactments of decisions that had already been made. At meetings to elect the municipal committee directors of the Women's Federation and the Youth Group, the "real" party leaders in Baní had already agreed upon a single slate before the meeting took place. The general membership had no say in selecting the candidates, though they dutifully went through the motions of approving them. When asked to comment on what seemed to be a retreat from their efforts to democratize, municipal PRD leaders responded, "We cannot run the risk of even the slightest division in the party, so in some ways, we have to control our results."

In sum, the PRD is an organization that acted transnationally but did not achieve its transnational goals. Though some aspects of its structures, goals, financing, leadership, and strategies were carried out across borders, the outcome of these efforts was decidedly one-way. Despite the party's efforts to foster political integration among migrants in Boston, only a small group of Mirafloreños, and Dominicans in general, participated actively in U.S. electoral affairs. The party enjoyed greater success mobilizing its U.S. constituents around Dominican causes. Migrants contributed generously to the party budget and continued to influence how nonmigrant family members vote.

Mirafloreños in Boston did participate in nonelectoral activities. They joined church councils, parent-teacher boards, and community development groups. These encounters, their contacts with government providers, and their observations of the political world around them reshaped their expectations of politics and the state. The new ideas they communicated and the different kinds of management and leadership techniques they modeled generated calls for a different type of politics on the island. Both nonmigrants and migrants were no longer content to unconditionally accept the status quo. They tried to challenge authoritarian-style decision making and favoritism at local-level PRD meetings. They resisted giving bribes or bestowing favors on municipal officials in order to complete official paperwork. They expressed a desire for honest, accountable leaders. Their efforts, however, met with limited success. They could begin to unravel the edges of the local-level political fabric but the bulk of the garment still remained strong.

Chapter Six

"God Is Everywhere"

Religious Life across Borders

When Ana María passed away in Boston, her family sent her body back to be buried in the Miraflores cemetery. Her relatives in the village began the traditional nine days of mourning as soon as they heard the news of her death. Since Mirafloreños believe the spirit of the deceased remains in his or her home during this period, the women in the family sit *guardando el rincón* (guarding the corner), or accompanying the spirit in a closed-off room where it is resting. Ana María's spirit would not leave her family after the nine days had past, however. Death is viewed as a transition to another place, where the deceased, who is present in a different form, can be visited, consulted, or petitioned. Ana María's family would be able to visit her at the cemetery, where the benches, photographs, and flowers they placed in the family crypt would provide the backdrop for their encounters.

But Ana María's daughter, Susana, would not be able to reach her mother. Since she lived illegally in Boston, she was afraid to travel to the funeral because she thought she might be unable to get back into the United States. Susana felt an insurmountable distance between herself and her mother, spanning spiritual realms as well as continents. "If I am here," she said, "and they are grieving in my house in Miraflores, it is like my mother is there, not here—her dead spirit is there, not here, and I cannot accompany her on her journey."

Susana's pain attests to the ways in which a second sphere of activity—religion—has become transnational. In contrast to the PRD, which acted across borders but fell short of accomplishing its transnational goals, the church acts and succeeds transnationally. Membership in the religious organizational system linking Boston and the Dominican Republic allows individuals to move almost seamlessly between these two settings, thereby facilitating their continued involvement in their sending community at the same time that they are assimilating into the United States. It also integrates migrants into a powerful, resource-rich international religious institutional network they can access regardless of their political citizenship.

Dominican Religious Life

Mirafloreños leaving the Dominican Republic for the United States in the late 1960s reinforced a loose transnational religious network already connecting Boston and the island. Foreign-born clergy began working in the Dominican Republic in the early 1930s due to a shortage of native-born priests. Trujillo actively encouraged western religious orders to come to the country, hoping they would introduce white cultural models that would fuel anti-Haitian sentiments and increase popular support. He also gambled that foreign-born clergy would be unlikely to challenge his regime since so many of these men came from countries under authoritarian rule. Trujillo guessed correctly until the late 1950s, when Monsignor Reilly, a Redemptorist priest from Boston serving as bishop of one of the island's southern provinces, actively spoke out against the government. Emboldened by Reilly's efforts, Dominican clergy also began demanding Trujillo's ouster, calls that ultimately contributed to his downfall (Sáez 1987).

The first ties linking religious life in Boston and the island, then, were established close to fifty years ago. Foreign-born Redemptorist, Jesuit, and Franciscan priests were the primary disseminators of institutionalized Catholicism throughout the country. Particularly strong connections linked Boston and the island because Redemptorist and Diocesan priests from Massachusetts were the principal orders working in the Dominican south.

The Dominican church has always had close relations with the government. Trujillo signed a *Concordato* with the Vatican in 1954 that granted the church special rights and privileges in exchange for its patronage and support. Under this agreement, the state funds most church construction projects, exempts it from taxes, pays for religious teacher training, and generally leaves the church to its own devices. In exchange, the church tends not to interfere with government policy. These close church-state ties, and former President Balaguer's particularly close relationship with Cardinal Nicolás de Jesús López Rodríguez,[1] circumscribed the church's role in social reform. In general, the Dominican church tolerated a variety of political tendencies, ranging from liberation theology–like base communities to very conservative Christian-renovation groups, as long as they did not directly challenge the government.[2]

This does not mean, however, that churches are not important sites of local-level political activity.[3] In fact, Mirafloreños often look to the church for help in solving problems because they distrust politicians and law enforcement officials so strongly. For instance, when some of the women in the community tried unsuccessfully several times to get police to shut down a prostitute bar, they eventually went to the bishop, who got it closed immediately. Community members also claimed it was the bishop who finally got the roads paved in Miraflores and El Llano, since his residence is located there.

These examples of church intervention weaken democracy because the bishop essentially substitutes for the politician as *patrón* and because the church solves problems that are the state's responsibility. There are cases, though, in which participation in religious groups generates social capital and imparts important skills (Verba, Schlozman, and Brady 1995). The Dominican church has a strong tradition of lay participation and leadership. When Mirafloreños lead services, organize celebrations, and study together they are learning skills they can apply to other arenas. When the community successfully carries out a church improvement project, it creates a model for future collective efforts.

This is particularly true for women. Despite the church's efforts to bring men into the fold, women are much more active. Though the majority of the men I interviewed answered unconditionally *"Soy católico"* (I am Catholic) when asked about their religious affiliation, they claimed that organized religion had little impact on their daily lives.

I am Catholic, I believe in God, but I am not much of a churchgoer. I go when someone is being baptized, a funeral, but I don't go to mass. In the U.S. it was the same. I would prefer to read a paragraph from the Bible in my house.

And I think I believe more in God than many that go to church. (José David, 48, return migrant, Miraflores)

As a result the church afforded women a protected space where they could become leaders without competition from men. They independently organized and directed the majority of the church's activities. They formed close relationships with one another by participating in small prayer and study groups that they ran on their own. In the process, they learned skills, acquired confidence, and interacted with people they might not have come into contact with.

Belonging to the charismatic Catholic group has changed my life. Before, I felt empty, timid. I almost never went out. I hardly talked to anyone. I felt a terrible loneliness. Almost all the time I was quiet, doing my chores alone. Then when I began the catechism, I began to feel different, like my spirit was being renewed again. I am more relaxed now. I stand up and read the Word during our groups; I have shared with a lot of other charismatic communities. I go to meetings with many people from many different places. (Carolina, 28, nonmigrant, Miraflores)

These interactions produced social capital that spilled over into women's personal and collective lives. When Carolina went through financial or emotional hard times, for example, she knew she could count on the other members of her charismatic group for help.

Participating in religious groups also strengthened other organizations in the community, as Belvis, a twenty-five-year-old nonmigrant, described:

What do you think about when you are praying as a group?

Señor, I hope to see everyone with the eyes of Christ. I want to act like he acted and to love the way he loved. The rejections one gets, don't return them, just try to keep going. I bring this when there are conflicts in the neighborhood and when there are conflicts in the party [the PRD]. I say, "Oh God, you are the one who knows," or if someone is accusing me of something, I just look at them and say, "I pardon you. You are not telling the truth, but I pardon you." They realize, sooner or later, that it wasn't true and we are able to keep working together.

When the Miraflores Development Committee needed help stocking the health clinic or distributing school supplies to kids who could not afford them, the church women constituted a skilled volunteer pool it could turn to.

The Church in Miraflores

During the last half of the 1900s, the Dominican Republic continued to be plagued by a shortage of religious personnel despite the many foreign-born priests serving on the island. Because the church directed most of its resources toward urban areas in the north, Baní was particularly underserved. It fell under the jurisdiction of the Archdiocese of Santo Domingo until 1987, when a new archdiocese was created. Until then, few clergy were based permanently in the area, and religious services were held only infrequently. The community worshiped in a thatched-roof sanctuary, or *ermita*, until the late 1950s, when Trujillo built a chapel as part of his sugar-colony project. Weekly masses did not begin until the late 1980s. As a result, many Mirafloreños had limited experience with the formal church, and they felt only weakly connected to it.

Instead, Mirafloreños developed their own private, personalized worship style, combining official and folk rituals, which they practiced in their homes and at informal gatherings. Though Dominican Catholicism generally synthesizes African, Haitian, and Catholic rituals, in Miraflores these outside elements were weaker because the Spanish and Canary Islanders who settled the area resisted contact so adamantly with their black neighbors. A syncretic mix of predominantly Catholic popular folk practices developed, manifesting only weak Haitian influences.

Miraflores is an enclave where the hegemonic subculture is very influenced by the Spaniards. The African influence is very hidden in Miraflores; it is almost subconscious, but it exists. But there is no such thing as a religiousness that is totally Catholic. There is Catholic primacy with a syncretic presence of the element of African culture. (Folklorist, Baní)

The Receiving-Church Context

When large numbers of European immigrants came to the United States in the early 1900s, the Catholic Church responded by creating national parishes that provided specialized services to each country-of-origin group. When Puerto Ricans arrived in Boston, however, church officials did not establish a national parish because they did not consider Puerto Ricans to be foreign-nationals. One church, located in the South End neighborhood where many Latinos initially settled, became the de facto hub of all Spanish-language activities. This strategy worked well until gentrification forced many migrants from the area. A small cadre of Anglo, Spanish-speaking priests then began providing itinerant religious services throughout the diocese. Each Sunday they celebrated mass, performed the sacraments, and gave baptismal instruction at churches with large Spanish-speaking populations, though they had little ongoing contact with these parishioners.

When I first went to Marlboro, the old pastor told me that while I was welcome to use the church, anything that was consumable I had to bring with me because "they are not really our folks." So that meant I had to bring my own candles because wax burns, bring my own bread and wine because that was consumable. For all intents and purposes we were having mass in basements because we were not welcome upstairs. (Diocesan priest, Boston)

Services to Spanish-speakers expanded in the early 1960s, when the first members of the Missionary Society of St. James of the Apostle began returning to Boston. Cardinal Cushing organized the St. James Society in 1958 to respond to Pope John XXIII's call for first-world countries to tithe their priests to Latin America. When these men returned to Boston from Bolivia, Ecuador, and Peru, they were dispatched to serve the burgeoning, geographically dispersed Latino community that had since moved to the area. By 1968 the community had grown sufficiently large that all activities for Spanish-speaking parishioners were subsumed under a newly created Hispanic Apostolate (HA).

In 1993 thirty-three parishes, staffed by thirty-four Spanish-speaking priests, belonged to the HA; just five priests were foreign-born. A Puerto Rican auxiliary bishop, Msgr. Roberto González, directed the office. Instead of promoting eventual assimilation, as earlier officials had done, Msgr. González claimed that the goal of the Hispanic Apostolate was to integrate new parishioners into their new church while allowing them to maintain their unique identity, pray in their own language, and celebrate their homeland festivals. The HA coordinated a range of services, including Spanish-speaking mass, Bible study, and prayer groups; Latino youth groups; and celebrations of country-of-

origin holidays. Most parishes also organized a separate Latino council, which sent a representative to the general parish-wide council.

Though Protestantism has spread to the Dominican Republic and
to Latin America in general, few Mirafloreños converted to Protestant
groups. In 1994 there were two Pentecostal churches in the village
with about 25 members each. One pastor traveled to Boston frequently
but had not established any formal ties to churches there. Though numerous Spanish-speaking Protestant congregations were also forming
in Boston, they tended to attract more Puerto Rican and Central American than Dominican members.

United States–Dominican
Transnational Religious Ties

Ties linking Boston and the Dominican Republic formed a horizontally
and vertically integrated religious transnational system. Though there
were few actual formal organizational structures, frequent, informal
exchanges of parishioners, labor, resources, programs, and training systematically connected religious life in Boston with that on the island.

Parishioners traveling back and forth established the most basic
relations. Churchgoers generally attended the same two or three
churches in Boston since Mirafloreños often lived in the same neighborhoods. When nonmigrants went to church with their relatives during their visits to Boston or when Mirafloreños attended mass during
their visits home, they created a thin but steady stream of individuals
circulating between sending- and receiving-country parishes.

Relations between churches also grew out of contacts between individual priests. Some Dominican priests sought out their U.S. colleagues because they were concerned about their flock. They knew
that many Banilejos had gone to Boston and they still felt some sense
of responsibility toward them.

I went to Boston thinking about getting in touch with the Banilejos. I was on
vacation, but I got permission from the bishop to visit some families. The Banilejos do not usually tend to be very religious, and so they do not participate
that much in the church. I was worried about this and thought that by building on the pride and loyalty the Banilejo feels about his patron saint's day, I
would try to build a bridge like we had done in New York. I thought I would
throw out the idea and see if it caught fire. We could organize a mass to cele-

brate the Virgen de la Regla Day so that people would participate and then become committed to other activities in the church. (Bishop, Dominican Republic, formerly served in Baní)

Other priests viewed the Catholic establishment in the United States as a potential source of aid or supplemental income. They realized they might receive donations or supplies if they formed a close relationship with a particular parish. They could also earn additional income, in dollars, if they spent their vacations working in the United States.

For many of us, the church in the U.S. is a refuge to go and look for money. It is a cheap vacation for us and cheap for U.S. parishes that need replacements. They pay airfare and stipends. It is a way we supplement our salaries. . . . Also, the Dominican church does not have enough resources to progress forward. We have to look outside for help. Most of the country should still be on horseback and using candles, but someone arrived with a Mercedes-Benz so now we need gas. We haven't had a gradual enough development to be able to sustain what we have. (Diocesan priest, Dominican Republic)

Some clergy turned to the United States as a refuge during times of personal difficulty—a place to make a fresh start, escape from problems with superiors, or rethink their commitment to the priesthood. "In one sense," one priest said, "the U.S. becomes a dumping ground for priests with personal problems or problems with the church hierarchy who leave the country to get away."

Relationships between Dominican and U.S. clergy have deepened and proliferated over the years. As a result, priests from Massachusetts have visited the island and built social networks of their own. Some of these ties remain highly personal, informal relations among friends. Others develop into systematic exchange arrangements. Several Dominican priests, for example, worked regularly in parishes in New York and Boston during "high-demand periods" such as Holy Week. Semi-permanent placements were also arranged. "Adopt a Parish"–type relationships evolved, becoming an important source of financial and material support for particular Dominican parishes. A priest who spent a number of summers and vacations working in Brooklyn, for example, received sacramental items and religious ornaments for his newly established parish in Santo Domingo. The bishop in Brooklyn in charge of the diocese where he served later visited Santo Domingo on a "needs assessment" mission, resulting in additional contributions.

Cooperative ties also resulted in a seminarian summer-abroad program. Approximately twenty students worked in northeastern U.S. parishes each summer throughout the 1980s. They gained practical experience and also learned what it was like to live where so many migrants had gone. Dominican leaders canceled the program in 1992 because of disagreements over the relative importance of gaining work experience in the United States or in Santo Domingo and because too many young men overstayed their visas. One continuing result of this program, though, is the exchange of Catholic television programming. Between 1992 and 1995, Padre Domínguez, who hosted a religious program on Dominican TV, sent tapes of his shows to Father Torres, a priest he met while studying in Boston, who aired them on Boston's Catholic cable station. The Boston Archdiocese also contributed funding to offset production costs.

A growing sense that Dominican and U.S. church manpower and training needs were increasingly linked prompted discussions about coordinating labor sharing. Church officials in both countries agreed they needed to reach an agreement about who was responsible for the immigrant flock.

Few people in the U.S. are entering the priesthood now. In the past there was always a surplus of priests and they could offer priests to us. In Latin America there has always been a shortage of priests. Now we are growing vocationally but our priests are still very young. We need them to mature. Even though they receive theoretical preparation at the seminary, they still need real-life experience. If we send them now, they get work experience in the U.S. but not in the Dominican Republic, which is not necessarily the best thing for us. (Bishop, Dominican Republic)

In response, the Dominican Bishop's Conference planned to create a separate Office of the Immigrant Apostolate. This new agency would oversee seminarian and priest exchanges, advocate for migrants and expatriate priests in the United States, and oversee services to tourists and Haitians.

Just as the PRD belongs to the Socialist International Party, so these religious relationships form within the context of the universal Catholic Church. Ties between Boston and the island make sense because migrants and nonmigrants are all part of a worldwide organization. Catholics are Catholics wherever they live and they must be welcomed and served regardless of their nationality. An extensive institutional infrastructure already facilitates international coordination and cooperation. Meetings of the Pan American Bishops' Conference,[4] for example, bring religious leaders from both countries into regular contact. These events could serve as forums to iron out the details of labor sharing or training agreements. Migration, then, fleshes out and deepens this long-standing transnational system even further.

Local chapters of the Catholic renewal movements growing throughout the United States and Latin America form the final strand of this transnational tie. These movements aimed to restore a sense of ecclesiastical community to popular Latino religion and to bring spiritual renovation to the church. They created communities of prayer, organized and directed by lay individuals, which met regularly in members' homes. Just as Mirafloreños circulated back and forth between individual parishes, they also entered and exited movement chapters in Miraflores and Jamaica Plain.

Religious Life in the United States

Puerto Ricans and Cubans who came to Boston in the early 1960s filled the pews left empty by traditional white-ethnic parishioners, who were leaving the city in droves. Dominicans, who arrived somewhat later, entered a church that already had a great deal of experience incorporating Spanish-speakers. The Latino members who arrived before them created a vibrant, but separate, religious world of their own. While they occasionally crossed paths with Anglos at mass, at specially planned bilingual celebrations, in parish governance, or at the after-mass coffee hour, they generally remained within a Latino domain.

Church leaders expected Mirafloreños to assimilate into this pan-Latino market niche. Latinos, in general, were their proximal hosts, or the group that the wider society defined as their co-ethnics (Mittleberg and Waters 1992). These migrants, however, came from all parts of Central America, South America, and the Caribbean. Each group brought different practices, affinities toward particular saints, and distinct understandings of the relationship between religion and society. Churchgoing Mirafloreños had to adapt to this least-common-denominator Catholicism and let go of their Dominican-specific one. They also had to adapt to the ways in which this Latino Catholic space had been customized to fit within Anglo structures.

The Catholic Church acts and achieves transnationally. Unlike politics, where they have been only minimally incorporated into the U.S. arena, Mirafloreños have been integrated more fully into the U.S. church and remained active in their sending-community. In the following paragraphs, I describe how Mirafloreños' beliefs and practices have been modified to fit within the U.S. context before turning to the impact of these changes on religious life in Miraflores.

Changes in Beliefs and Practices

At one end of the continuum of change are norms about God and faith. Beliefs about God are, in some sense, intrinsically transnational. There is no need to modify them when someone migrates because they are highly personal and they are not dependent on other members of a group. God is present, in whatever form, wherever the believer is.

Certain home-based, informal folk practices, traditionally at the core of Mirafloreño religious life, transfer easily to Boston. It is as simple to create an altar, practice devotions or light candles to a particular saint, make *promesas*,[5] or say the rosary in Boston as it is in Miraflores. Local *colmados* in Jamaica Plain sell all the necessary religious supplies. Everyone knows about Marli, a woman who leads prayers in people's homes for a small fee. As a consequence, Mirafloreños can stay on the margins of the church when they migrate, and many do. It is only when they want or need to express their beliefs in more organized, institutionalized settings that the transformation of religious life begins.

Mirafloreños gravitated toward the church for a number of reasons. Some said they sought comfort and support. It was one of the few places where they found a community of like-minded individuals. For others, going to church, like participating in political and community groups, fulfilled a social function. They knew they would see people from home at mass. Other Mirafloreños used the church as a stage from which to act on their enhanced social status, where they experimented with new styles of dress and socializing with Anglos.

Others had to go to church to fulfill their religious obligations. They had to go to mass if they wanted to officially baptize their infants. Children had to go to religious-school classes to receive their first communion. These prerequisites pushed Mirafloreños toward the formal church. Still others were drawn to the church for reasons of expedience. They said it was easier and more reliable to have a mass said in honor of a deceased parent than to organize home-based prayer sessions. You could never be sure if enough people would come so you could actually hold the ceremony.

When Mirafloreños did go to church, they had to adjust their beliefs and practices accordingly. The Catholic templates they shared with Anglos provided some common ground. They were already familiar with many of the prayers and rituals. The services offered by the Hispanic Apostolate lowered barriers to their entry. Some Anglo priests were bilingual and familiar with Dominican culture. But in many cases, different national worship styles, administrative requirements, and new lifestyle arrangements meant that Mirafloreños had to fundamentally change their religious practices.

For example, the substantive content of the sacraments in the United States and the Dominican Republic was the same, but the prerequisites for participating in these rituals differed. They were also expressed in different ways. To be baptized in Boston, one had to belong to a particular parish. "People don't know what parish they belong to in the U.S. because there are so many of them," one priest said. "It is not like Miraflores, where there is only one church." The archdiocese also required that to baptize a baby, its godparents must be married in the church, a practice that is fairly rare among Mirafloreños.

Basic stylistic differences also characterize the mass in each country. In Miraflores, religious services go on for varied lengths of time. Lay people actively plan services, form choruses, organize readings, and take responsibility for the upkeep of the church. The liturgy includes many rhythmic songs.

The Anglo mass at our church is more reserved, private, individualistic. Mass in the Dominican Republic is more communal and more sensual. There is more music, community participation, a sense of gathering people together. Children are brought to mass at an early age. There is an emotion or drama that gets acted out, like when we reenact the stations of the cross on Good Friday. (Father John, Diocesan priest, Boston)

Though Spanish-language masses in Boston incorporate some of these elements, institutional constraints limit how much accommodation can occur. Mass in Boston can last only an hour because a new group of parishioners is waiting outside the church for the next service to begin. For the same reason, the *Saludo de la paz*[6] becomes a quick handshake with the person sitting in the next chair instead of the noisy, social, ten-minute stroll around the church that it is in Miraflores.

Confession was also more complicated for migrants in Boston. Unlike the predetermined baptismal ceremony or mass, the priest-parishioner exchange is a matter of the heart. Meaningful encounters require a cultural as well as an organizational fit.

Banilejos are very hard workers and like to earn money. They don't have time to come to church. They might not be able to come during the hours set for confession. I understand how they are, and I listen to them. I can orient them in a different way than other priests who aren't Latinos because I know where they come from, what their strengths are, how they live their lives. I know how to help them better than other priests, and they understand me better because I speak to them in a language they can assimilate. The same thing would happen to me in English. The culture in which I have lived, in which I have learned, makes me different and people come to me to confess with more trust. Now, there may be Dominicans who speak English well who prefer confessing to an American priest because they'll finish more quickly. I've done confessions in English. In 70 percent of the cases they don't come looking for guidance. They want a confession where there are ten other people waiting and the priest just listens and absolves them quickly. (Padre Nelson, Dominican priest, Boston)

The changing character of Mirafloreño immigrants' lives further transformed their religious practices. As with politics, the climate, pace of life, and difference in the balance of work and leisure in Boston and Miraflores changed how faith was expressed. In Miraflores, most families finish work by midafternoon. They have the rest of the day free to participate in religious activities or to visit with priests. In Boston, since many Mirafloreños worked a second, part-time job in the evenings, in addition to their full-time day jobs, they had much less time to be active at church. It was normally too cold to organize events like religious processions during Holy Week. And since Mirafloreños lived farther away from one another than they did at home, it was not as easy for them to meet spontaneously to pray.

In this country (the U.S.), life moves very quickly. You have to work on Good Friday. The days I used to observe as holy, I cannot observe anymore because I have to work at 8 A.M. One lives alone. In Baní, if I came home late from teaching, I found three plates of food waiting for me. I did the same for my neighbors. If I said, "I am sick," my neighbor would say, "Ah," and the next minute she would appear with a cup of tea in her hand. Loneliness changes you a lot. And the fact that you have to work on Good Friday and on the 24th of December, you don't feel like doing it anymore. In Baní, on the 24th, I would begin making *pastelitos* in the early morning. Here, I can't because my life isn't the same. I have to live quickly. The food doesn't turn out the same. You come to an unknown culture, you have to adapt rapidly. To survive, you begin losing some of your cultural roots. (Julita, 32, migrant, Boston)

Once Mirafloreños started attending church on a regular basis, even popular rituals changed. The practice of *echar agua* (pouring on water) provides a good example. Many villagers believe that newborns are susceptible to *mal de ojo* (the evil eye). Adults who admire or are envious of a new baby can cast a spell, making the infant ill. Since priests visited the rural parts of the island so infrequently, Dominicans developed an alternative, popular baptismal ceremony that protected children until they could be formally baptized. The tradition of *echar agua* remained strong among migrants. It was easy for them to hire someone to perform the ceremony at their homes. But as Mirafloreños became more frequent church attenders, some families began holding two baptisms:

. . . the first when the baby is small and then when it is older in the church. In the first, a person comes to pray to the saint which protects children. We give thanks to God for the baby and ask God to make the baby healthy. We put holy water from the church on the baby's face and a little salt on its head. This baptism protects the baby from *mal de ojo*. The baptism in the church would also protect him, but one has one's customs. I am Catholic. I believe in God. The baptism that one does in the house and the baptism that one does in the church for me mean the same thing. (María, 35, migrant, Boston)

Changing Relations
with the Secular Aspects of the Church

Administrative differences between the Dominican and U.S. church are more pronounced than differences in religious practices. As a result, Mirafloreños have had to modify their behaviors more with respect to the management and secular functions of the church than with respect to religious rituals. To remain viable, the church in Boston needed new members to conform to its norms about financial contributions, lay participation, and priest-parishioner relations.

Several priests, for instance, claimed they had to teach new parishioners to feel a greater sense of financial responsibility to the church.

Migrants arrived, they said, accustomed to receiving and they had to be trained to give instead. According to Father Peter, a Diocesan priest in Boston: "Latinos come naturally to the church looking for social services. They are used to being on the receiving end of missionaries. Here they don't understand that the church has finite resources and that it depends on their contributions."

Ideas about the parishioner-priest relationship also differed. While Boston clergy complained that Latinos expected them to be available at all times, Dominican-born priests felt it was their responsibility to come when a parishioner called. These divergent expectations created conflict. One Dominican priest recalled being criticized by his superiors for creating unrealistic demands among church members by being always available to them. In an interesting twist, a second priest working in Boston attributed his difficulties in reaching parishioners to the fact that they

have been Anglicized by the priest that came before me. In the U.S. there are certain times for confessions, certain times to visit the priest. He is not on call twenty-four hours a day. I might have been willing to do that, but Latinos have already adjusted to a more scheduled, organized version of faith. The people do what the priest tells them to do. If he says, "Don't call me at this hour," they won't call. So now I don't get calls. They are directed to a nun, but she has an answering machine in English. (Padre Santiago, Dominican priest, Boston)

Restricting priest availability and limiting their scope of work shifts the focus of the clerical role from one of service to one of professional worker. Rather than looking to the priest as a companion or guide who is an integral part of their family and community, parishioners begin to think of him as their employee. In the Dominican Republic, one priest said, he was always needed, while in Boston he felt isolated and underutilized.

In Latin America the priest cannot confine himself to just saying mass. He has to go to meetings, look for help, clothing, or housing. In this country, it is not that there aren't needs, but I am just one more person. In my country, people offer me their houses for church activities, here I have to ask for them. There I was always in demand, always receiving invitations, here I am lonely. Many times I tell people, "I am here whenever you need me." I would like to go and help out, but I am not sure that I am wanted. I no longer feel comfortable saying, "I'll be over in a little while," even among those people I knew in Baní. In the Dominican Republic, people have fewer commitments. They are not so busy. They are more at peace. Here you have to fight hard to get a little of people's time. You can't ask them for a lot, and they don't ask a lot of you. (Dominican-born priest, Boston)

The role of laypeople in the church also changed in Boston. Though Mirafloreños arrived with the skills and experience needed to run many church programs, priests in Boston were not accustomed to such high levels of lay involvement. Some priests were reluctant to let parishioners assume such prominent roles, claiming that migrants were too busy and that it burdened them unfairly.

Here people often become accustomed to not taking the initiative and there is a perception on the part of church leaders that they can't. We tried to organize a small prayer group that met on Wednesdays. Each member had to prepare a reading before the meeting. And because of the two or three hours that this required, the members tired, they lost interest, and soon the group broke up. In the Dominican Republic we organized the same thing, and these communities are still running. Here the nun working with me said it was a lot to ask of people. (Diocesan priest, Boston)

Apart from their occasional participation in parish council meetings or special celebrations, Mirafloreños generally participated far less in the secular aspects of church life.

The church's role as a social-service provider also changed in Boston. While migrants were accustomed to looking to the church for assistance in Miraflores, they could seek help in any number of places in addition to the church in the United States. Mirafloreños who received welfare could turn to their social workers for advice instead of their priests. They were less dependent on the church for donations of food and clothing. "Those who do well," commented one priest, "seem to need God less."

The Impact on Religious Life in Miraflores

Widespread migration from Miraflores coincided with a heightened church presence in the village. Clergy began holding mass, organizing programs, and offering religious instruction on a much more regular basis in the late 1980s. As a result, the church's more integral role in village life complemented and sometimes intensified the changes in religious practices stimulated by migration.

One set of changes in religious life resulted from social remittances.

Migrants in Boston sent back the new religious ideas and practices they observed in the United States to those at home. They introduced different notions about God and faith, as Miriam, a forty-five-year-old nonmigrant, described:

I have never been to Boston, but my sister tells me all about it when she comes back to visit. She told me about the church with the stained-glass window and the gold plate where they put all the communion wafers. I can imagine how beautiful it is. She also told me that some of the things we did here were bad. You should go to church, you should have a mass dedicated to a person when they die. But we should forget about all this other stuff of casting spells and superstitions.

She went on to explain that she thinks the way the church is run in Boston is also different.

My sister said it is not like here where the priest walks down the street and everyone is inviting him to eat something, to have a cup of coffee. He is always visiting in our homes. There, you see the priest once a week up on the fancy altar dressed in fancy robes. He is like a teacher you are afraid of rather than a family member or friend. And you can't organize prayer groups or lead services unless he says its okay. Here we all take part in the planning. We form our own little groups to pray and study together. But there, it seems like you have to do what the priest says. I'm not sure I would like that so much. It sounds like it is well organized, but it also sounds like it is very cold.

Mirafloreños also remitted notions about religious identity. Most villagers had a clear idea about what it meant to be a good Catholic. They generally described this in terms of their affiliation with the Catholic *pueblo* (community); their identity was rooted in their affective ties to other members of the group. This view stands in stark contrast to the notion of religious identity in the United States, where an individual is Catholic because he or she belongs to a church, participates in its associations, and identifies with its structures (Fitzpatrick 1987). Individuals manifest their membership by taking part in these organized structures of faith. Migrants seemed to modify their notions of good "Catholicness" as their participation in the formal church increased and to talk about this to those who remained behind.

Carmen María says it is not enough to say the rosary in your home. She says that in Boston you have to go to church regularly, at least once a week. You can't just feel Catholic, you have to act Catholic. You have to do something about it. And you can see that here, in Miraflores, more people are going to church. They may not all be going to mass on Saturday night, but they are joining these charismatic groups and getting their kids baptized and educated. (María Rosa, 32, nonmigrant, Miraflores)

Community members have become more responsive to overtures from the church as a result.

My sister never went to church before she went to Boston. But when she was there, she told me that she met an old friend of our family who took her to a meeting of a charismatic group. Now she goes every week and she began going to mass on Sundays as well. So when Alicia came and asked me to join the charismatic group, I decided to try it. Now I also go to weekly meetings and I go to the prayer sessions on Thursday nights. I am also sending my daughter to catechism classes. (Elena, 22, nonmigrant, Miraflores)

By talking about and modeling these social remittances, migrants gently nudge their nonmigrant family members and friends away from popular religious practices toward more officially sanctioned, church-based rituals. "We are more educated now about the church," Julita, a twenty-six-year-old return migrant said, "So when our last child was born we knew what we wanted and took him to the priest to be blessed in the church. With my older children, we did *echando agua* and placed a red ribbon around the babies wrist to protect it from *mal de ojo*."

Dominican priests and seminary students who served in the United States were also social remittance carriers. One priest liked the "organized sociability" at the parish he visited. When he came back to the Dominican Republic, he instituted an after-mass coffee hour and began personally greeting parishioners at the end of each service. After observing lay ministers give communion, a second priest organized a training school where Dominican parishioners could learn these functions. He also wanted to introduce the "personalized collection envelopes" he noted as a way to teach his parishioners a stronger sense of financial responsibility to the church.

A second group of changes in the Dominican church resulted from the new demands that migration places on religious institutions. The U.S. embassy, for example, transformed the church into a gatekeeper by requiring that Dominicans present a birth *and* baptismal certificate to obtain a visa. The archdiocese in Baní had to create a new office to cope with the increased paperwork. The relationship between priest and parishioner assumed instrumental overtones because more and more parishioners turned to the church for immigration papers rather than for religious guidance. Parishioners pressured church leaders and administrators to give them counterfeit documents. According to one priest, individuals offered parish secretaries in Baní as much as $1,000 to forge priests' signatures on false baptismal certificates. The church became just one more hurdle along the road to the coveted goal of migration—an opponent rather than a partner.

Migration also resulted in the commercialization of the sacraments. Marriages consecrated solely to obtain visas became common. Dominicans who were legal residents in the United States were known to charge as much as $5,000 to "marry for business." The demand for baptismal classes increased when baptism became a requirement for migration. While most priests felt that "sacraments for visas" depreciated these rituals, some felt it offered them a unique outreach opportunity. "Once we get them to come to church," one priest said, "we can take advantage and bring them more firmly into the fold."

Priests also reported that migration created a whole new set of problems that required a church response. They said they received many calls from families whose relatives had been killed or imprisoned for their involvement in the drug trade. Parishioners who lost their homes because they could not make payments on the mortgages they took out to finance their children's trips to the United States also turned to the church for assistance. The sisters at the parochial school had to enlist priests' help to mediate between students and the grandparents who were raising them.

The other afternoon Sister Carmen came to the door. She had a boy and his grandfather with him. There were so many problems at home between the two of them that the boy was starting to have trouble at school. The boy had spent most of his life in Boston, but his parents sent him back to live here last year. He and his grandfather were at each other's throats. The boy thought his grandfather was much too strict and didn't understand him. The grandfather thought the boy was terribly disrespectful. The sister only knew that the kid was becoming a real behavior problem. (Father Julio, Diocesan priest, Baní)

Selecting baptismal godparents also assumed economic overtones. Mirafloreños now tend to choose migrants rather than their closest friends and family members on the island as the *madrina* (godmother) or *padrino* (godfather) for their children. They feel that migrants will offer their children greater financial support. As a result, a new type of godparent has developed. One set stands in for *los ausentes* (the absent ones) at the actual ceremony and takes care of the godchild's day-to-day needs. The other "real" godparents, who live in Boston, take care of "big ticket" items like special clothing for a first communion or a party to celebrate a fifteenth birthday.

A third group of changes in religious practice and organization stemmed from the social consequences of migration's economic rewards. Religious practice changed because most Mirafloreños had more disposable income and could do things they would not have been able to do in the past. They could afford, for example, to make pilgrimages to holy places for the first time. When the community organized a trip to Higüey, where there is a shrine to the national patron saint, most members could afford to go.

But since migration's rewards were not equally distributed, some members were left out. After the Miraflores Development Committee built its funeral home, some families decided to use the new facility rather than mourn in their homes. Some of their friends and neighbors felt uncomfortable with these new ceremonies, claiming they could not afford the right clothes or hairstyling to be able to attend.

Each of these three types of change catalysts pushed Mirafloreños toward the organized church. They went to mass more frequently. They attended baptism and catechism classes and joined Catholic renovation movement groups. Community members increasingly substituted church-based, official ceremonies for the home-based, popular folk rituals they had practiced in the past. Because religious involvement became a stepping-stone toward migration, some individuals participated to further nonreligious goals. Their relationship to the church became more formal and instrumental. The church created new structures and rules to respond to these demands. The religious lives of subsequent émigrés, though still Dominican, reflected this more systematic, bureaucratic tone. Their religious formation was shaped by both U.S. and Dominican influences, and the beliefs and practices they brought to their lives in Boston reflected this dual character.

In sum, migration between Boston and Miraflores produced a series of horizontal and vertical religious ties that stimulated sending- and receiving-country religious convergence while reinforcing a continued place for "Latino" Catholicism in the United States. Unlike its political counterpart, the church acted and achieved transnationally and, by so doing, facilitated migrants' continued participation in the sending- and receiving-country church. It also transformed religious life in Miraflores such that nonmigrants participated in a local-level organization that became transnational in and of itself.

The Catholic Church in Boston needed a new constituency after longtime parishioners left the inner city. It created an infrastructure that offered newly arriving Latinos a panethnic product. Administrative requirements, lifestyle constraints, and the search for social and spiritual comfort both pushed and drew many Mirafloreños into the formal church. Migrants assimilated into this panethnic market niche, which offered them a generic, rather than a country-of-origin-specific, product. Though they also brought a wealth of lay leadership experience with them, they were not able to use this as much in Boston, except in the context of small prayer groups.

Migrants introduced these changes in religious ideas and practices to those in Miraflores. These social remittance transfers, in conjunction with the church's stronger presence in the village and other changes prompted by migration, altered the nature of religious life. It became more formal, instrumental, and church-based. Villagers replaced popular folk rituals with officially sanctioned practices.

Relations at other levels of the Dominican-U.S. transnational religious system further encouraged these parish-level changes. Ties between priests and seminarians, donations of money and supplies, and the institutionalization of mechanisms to meet the needs of expatriate parishioners reinforced them. Subsequent émigrés arrived in the United States as better-educated consumers. They were inculcated transnationally about the ways of the U.S. church and integrated more easily into its activities. A happy convergence of supply and demand resulted. New migrants continued to infuse the U.S. church with new Dominican blood, though it was more Anglicized in tone. Migrants circulated in and out of the sending- and receiving-country church without conflict. Nonmigrants also adopted many ideas and practices from the United States. These qualities heighten the durability of transnational religious ties and ease the way for long-term dual religious membership.

Chapter Seven

Transnationalizing Community Development

Meetings of the twenty-member Miraflores Development Committee (MDC) take place each Sunday at a member's home in Jamaica Plain. These gatherings usually last about three hours. When it is warm, members, who begin arriving at about 5 P.M., gossip about sports and politics on their host's front porch. When it gets colder, they relocate their conversations to the living room. In warm weather or cold, though, no one ever seems to get down to business before 6:30 or 7.

Mirafloreños created the MDC to improve living conditions in Miraflores. Between 1992 and 1994 the committee raised more than $70,000. They built an aqueduct, providing Mirafloreños with a reliable water supply for the first time in its history. They funded renovations to the village school, health clinic, and community center. They also began construction of the funeral home and baseball stadium.

The Boston committee has a sister chapter in Miraflores. Though this group also raises funds, its primary function is project implementation. The two chapters communicate regularly by phone to update one another about their progress, exchange village news, and resolve disputes. When disagreements about project management arose in Miraflores, for example, MDC leaders in Boston asked the committee's nonmigrant leadership to organize a community-wide meeting to be held at the same time as their weekly meeting in Boston. The two groups then conducted a transnational town meeting via conference call during which they discussed their concerns and agreed on a project-implementation plan.

This chapter examines a third type of transnational organization, a community development group. Unlike its political and religious counterparts, the MDC acts transnationally to achieve locally. It intentionally uses resources, money, and skills acquired in the United States to promote community development in Miraflores. Horizontally integrated chapters in Boston and on the island articulate goals, make decisions, and implement projects across borders, but these are all aimed at improving life in Miraflores rather than Boston.

The MDC's transnational character enhanced organizational performance at the same time that it constrained it. By organizational performance, I mean the group's ability to effectively articulate and achieve its goals. The Miraflores Development Committee (MDC) contributed significantly to Miraflores community development. A larger, more diverse, highly skilled group of migrants and nonmigrants participated in its activities than in previous development efforts. The committee functioned more efficiently and accountably. And the community bolstered its bargaining position vis-à-vis the state.

The benefits of transnational activism, though, were not without cost. An increasingly well-defined division of labor between migrant donors and nonmigrant beneficiaries meant that nonmigrant interests sometimes received short shrift. Since migrants funded so much of the MDC's work, their vision for Mirafloreño community development often took precedence over the needs and goals of those still residing there. The unique challenges of sustaining participation across borders resulted in frequent ebbs and flows in activism. Finally, the community's heightened ability to solve its own problems absolved the state of its responsibility to provide adequate services and infrastructure in Miraflores and allowed the government to continue pursuing policies that hurt rural development.

These concerns notwithstanding, the MDC and other organizations like it represent an important, emerging arena for coordinated transnational community development efforts. These transnational migrant organizations (TMOs) are likely to become increasingly important as transnational communities grow and strengthen over time.

Migrant Organizations Past and Present

Much of the research on immigrant associations analyzes their impact in a single context. These studies generally describe the organization's accomplishments with respect to home-country affairs or focus on activities affecting the host country without paying much attention to the interaction between the two.

How migrant associations affect local sending-country communities is not always clear (Sassen-Koob 1992). They often try to influence U.S. foreign policy toward their countries of origin, particularly when members are official or de facto political refugees (Zabin and Escala-Rabadan 1998). They are said to contribute significant financial and material support to the communities they come from. However, Georges (1988a) found it was not migrants but middle-class, nonmigrant community members who were the strongest proponents of community development. Other studies indicate that migrant organizations impede change. Both rural-to-urban and international migrants often invested heavily to preserve cultural institutions that would attest to their continued membership in their sending communities.[1] Castro (1985) found that migrant associations exerted a conservative influence by introducing new practices like evangelical Christianity.

Research on the impact of migrant associations in host countries is also inconclusive. Such groups clearly play an important role in creating the social networks that facilitate migration and settlement (Boyd 1989; Massey et al. 1987). Some researchers also claim they ease migrant adaptation (Gonzáles 1970). Others argue they prevent needed resocialization by reinforcing homeland ties and re-creating traditional power arrangements (Hendricks 1974). Georges (1988b), however, suggests that migrant organizations are an indicator of, rather than means to, adjustment because so many of the Dominican groups she studied gradually shifted their goals from social and cultural preservation to increased political integration.

When, as in the case of Miraflores, migrants and nonmigrants remain strongly connected to one another, the terms of these debates shift. The question becomes not about sending- or receiving-community development in isolation but about how these two are mutually linked and about the best kind of organizational arenas to achieve transnational goals. What projects should be carried out and who should choose them? How can migrant and nonmigrant concerns both be adequately addressed? What resources and skills arise from transnational activism that are not present when sending- or receiving-community members act on their own? What kinds of unique challenges result?

Several recent works shed some light on these questions. While Salvadoran and Guatemalan hometown associations in Los Angeles primarily support development projects in their sending communities, some groups are becoming more concerned about the needs of their immigrant constituents. One federation established a credit union to serve low-income residents and workers in a neighborhood with large numbers of Central American residents. The same group made an agreement with a savings and credit association in El Salvador to allow migrants' family members access to credit as well (Hamilton and Stolz Chinchilla 1999). Zabin and Escala-Rabadan (1999), however, found that although the Mexican hometown associations they studied mobilized against anti-immigrant Proposition 187 in California, this did not translate into regular political organization around U.S. causes. Though these groups held political sway with their hometowns, states, and the federal government in Mexico, they did not contribute to political integration in the United States.

Prior Experience
with Community Development

Despite their limited experience with democratic governance, Mirafloreños have strong traditions of collective organization and sharing labor with one another. In the late 1960s the community created a mutual aid society that continues to help defray burial expenses. Each year Miraflores organizes a large, nine-day-long celebration in honor of its patron saint that is attended by Dominicans throughout the province. Farmers have a long-standing custom of helping one another during the peak of the harvest. Each day, a group of neighbors helps one family harvest its fields, successively rotating until each one is cleared.

After Trujillo's downfall, the Dominican government actively promoted the growth of Dominican civil society. State workers came to Miraflores to create farmers', youth, and mothers' associations. Mirafloreños established the Sociedad de Progreso y Cultura (Society for Progress and Culture) to promote cultural and educational activities in the community. They set up a library and convinced foreign diplomats to donate books. They founded a savings and loan cooperative at which community members who deposited their money earned interest on their savings and were entitled to loans they would not have been eligible for at a bank. The cooperative, though initially successful, later disbanded amid accusations of corruption. In fact, almost everyone claimed to know exactly who stole the money, though this happened almost 30 years ago.

People lost faith in the cooperative and it fell apart. They thought that if you put in 1,000 pesos, you could get 1,500. Even I believed it. The whole cooperative movement throughout the country came before its time. You have to educate people first before about what a cooperative is and how you use it. This is why they all failed and so few are still left. (Roberto, 62, nonmigrant, Miraflores)

Two new organizations emerged from the failed co-op. Farmers established their own association to improve access to technical assistance, equipment, and credit. The community at large created the Movimiento para el Mantenimiento y Obras de Miraflores (the Movement for Construction and Maintenance of Miraflores) to promote community development. That organization was the predecessor of today's MDC.

Mirafloreños living in Boston also began getting together informally during the mid-1970s. At first these gatherings were primarily social events until someone suggested that the group organize activities to better the community.

Our meetings were a place we could feel at home because at work and on the street we were still having a hard time getting adjusted. Then Pepe had the idea to try to do something for Miraflores. We had a big meeting on Mozart Street, where he was living. One of the people wrote a letter back saying we wanted to work with the Movimiento and help them. The idea to build the park originated in Boston. And after that we were always doing something. We would finish a project and the group would stop meeting. But then someone would come up with a different idea and we would get going once again. (Carlos, 42, return migrant, Miraflores)

All Mirafloreños are automatically members of the MDC, regardless of their place of residence. Each chapter has its own leadership and organizational structure. In 1994 seven *directores* (leaders) in Miraflores and eight leaders in Boston ran the organization. In addition to their weekly meetings, the group periodically organized larger meetings when a new project was starting or when committee members felt they needed additional help. The MDC in Miraflores organized community-wide *asambleas* (assemblies) about once a year to elect new leadership. Community-wide meetings also took place when a particularly difficult problem arose or a decision had to be made requiring a broader consensus. Members in Boston communicated their views by phone before these events, though they did not actually vote. Migrants chose their leaders separately, by informal agreement. When members of either chapter visited Boston or Miraflores, they were expected to attend the meetings held during their visits. As Rosita, a thirty-two-year-old nonmigrant, described it:

Last summer, I went to visit my sister in Boston for two months. While I was there, I used to go the *comité* meetings every Sunday night. People expected me to do this. And it helped. I could tell the people in Boston what was going on in Miraflores, and when I got home I was able to give the other members of the committee a better idea about what was going on.

When migrant leaders returned to the village to live, the community expected them to assume a leadership role in the MDC. "We are just waiting for Marcial to get settled," said Alfredo about a new returnee. "He's been back only five months, but when he's ready, we are counting on him to be very active with us."

The MDC does not receive technical assistance or financial support regularly from the Dominican government. It does not belong to a national or international nongovernmental organization (NGO) network. Independence has its advantages and disadvantages. Clearly these kinds of relationships can produce needed resources and enhance migrants' influence. In the Mexican case, however, while the government's Program for Mexican Communities Abroad extended resources and invited greater participation among immigrants, it also formalized and standardized many of these activities under the direction of the Mexican government.[2] Some argue that these transnational activities reproduce long-standing inequities because those already in power and an emerging migrant elite monopolize their benefits (Guarnizo 1998; Goldring 1999). Though migrant leaders' increased social status and economic weight earns them substantive citizenship rights they did not enjoy as residents of Mexico, it is at nonmigrants' expense.

The MDC is, however, operating in an environment that is favorable to NGOs. In the past two decades, international development agendas have devoted significant resources toward strengthening civil society and building institutions. The United States Agency for International Development supported such programs in the Dominican Republic as a way to circumvent government corruption and encourage the growth of alternative political forums. Organizations have also been created that directly address migrants' concerns. The Fundación para la Defensa de Dominicanos Residentes en el Exterior (Foundation for the Defense of Dominicans Living Abroad), a group formed primarily by return migrants, works to improve the image of Dominicanos Ausentes because they are so often associated with the drug trade and prostitution (Itzigsohn et al. 1999).

The MDC's Accomplishments

For twenty-five years various incarnations of the MDC have strategized, raised funds, and implemented projects across borders. These activities produced significant improvements in village life. Monies raised by the MDC purchased more than 80 percent of the land that the communal facilities were built on. The MDC also constructed the community center, health clinic, park, cemetery, and bridges over the irrigation canals that traverse Miraflores. In 1993, in addition to renovating the school and health clinic, the MDC also funded physicians' salaries and medical supplies.

Some combination of community and state resources generally supports these projects. The MDC funds at least some portion of all its projects, by either paying for the entire project or leveraging monies it raises to secure matching funds from the government. Fund-raising generally took two forms. The groups in Boston and on the island organized large fund-raising events, such as dances and fairs, which often took place simultaneously. The radio telethon in Boston, for example, during which Mirafloreños called in to pledge donations to the MDC, was broadcast at the same time in Miraflores. The Boston group held its big dinner dance during the village's *fiestas patronales* (patron saint celebration), which was also the most important fund-raising time for the MDC on the island. In Boston committee members also recruited villagers to contribute a $10 *cuota,* or donation, to the MDC each week. They visited their contributors every weekend to collect money, exchange news, and offer updates on the committee's progress. During this study, anywhere from 40 to 150 community members contributed money on a regular basis.

The MDC's contributions to community development in Miraflores, however, go far beyond physical improvements and fund-raising. The committee fosters positive change in the community in several other ways. First, the MDC solidified and expanded upon the informal solidarity that was such an integral part of Mirafloreño community life. Despite their regular exchanges of labor, food, child care, and clothing, attempts to formalize this social capital and use it systematically had generally failed. In addition to the previously mentioned co-op story, respondents recalled a number of other incidents in which they felt they had been taken advantage of. It was simply a fact of life, many said, that when funds are raised, someone pockets something for themselves.

I remember I was living in Boston and they came around asking for donations. They wanted to build a sewing workshop where they could teach women in the village how to sew and they could earn some extra income. I said I would donate the machines but not money. I was not going to give money and have it stolen another time. I never heard back from them. And now, look around you, do you see anyone making dresses anywhere? (Rolando, 46, return migrant, Miraflores)

As a result, the community was very suspicious of its leadership and had difficulty working together as a formal group. There were few community members considered honest enough to be leaders. After all, in a world where everyone must struggle to make ends meet, why wouldn't someone take advantage of an opportunity that presented itself? Don Miguel went so far as to say, "If you don't want to be called a thief, then you shouldn't belong to any organization." Added Juline, a sixty-seven-year-old nonmigrant:

It is very curious because we are a very generous people. We give to each other all the time. But any time someone tries to get us to work together as a group on some joint project, we all get suspicious of one another. We accuse each other of cheating and stealing or of trying to get something for ourselves. The people are right in this. There are too many instances where people cheated their fellow community members. That makes it very hard to trust someone who is not part of your family.

In the MDC's case, however, both the social remittances migrants introduced and the clear rewards resulting from the MDC's efforts helped convince a critical mass of Mirafloreños that community organization could work. In the same way that migrants encouraged calls for a different kind of politics, they also contributed to demands for an

MDC that was more accountable to its members. Some of the management and administrative techniques they introduced made this possible. Furthermore, increasing numbers became convinced once the MDC established a successful track record of completing projects that clearly made a difference in the community. The committee's activities stood in sharp contrast to the corruption and inefficiencies pervading Dominican life. While these examples could not counteract years of disillusionment with the state, they did provide models of success that could be emulated.

We still do not trust one another. And every time we start a new project, you know by the end that someone will be the bad guy. But we also have seen that if we work together, we can succeed. People see that we are finishing the funeral home. We're finishing the baseball stadium. These are clear examples that people see and say to themselves, we can do this. We can make things better around here without someone profiting for themselves. (Laura, 58, nonmigrant, Miraflores)

A second way that the MDC promoted community development was by fostering organizational growth. The community took on more projects, addressing a wider variety of concerns, because of the large sums migrants raised in Boston. As a result, greater numbers of migrants and nonmigrants participated in a more diverse set of activities, which in turn required a wide variety of skills.

In 1993, for example, committee leaders restructured the MDC in Miraflores to be able to manage its activities more effectively. They created health, education, and sports subcommittees supervised by an overarching coordinating committee. Someone uninterested in sports could work on health. A person worried about schools could go to the education subcommittee's meetings without having to sit through the entire meeting of the MDC. This made it easier and more attractive for Mirafloreños to focus their time and energies. Leaders estimated that participation in some kind of group rose from about 10 to 20 percent of all community members. More people also participated in Boston. Though the Boston chapter continued to meet as a whole, rather than dividing around specific activities, leaders felt that more migrants either attended meetings or kept informed about the group's activities because the MDC addressed a wider set of concerns.

Participation taught some respondents a new set of skills. Maribel, a twenty-six-year-old nonmigrant, said she learned some basic accounting and that this helped her manage her finances better at home. Mayra, a thirty-four-year-old nonmigrant, improved her social skills:

I gained a lot more confidence about speaking in front of a group. It used to be that I hardly ever went out, let alone got up in front of people and said what I had to say. But little by little, after going to meetings, I started feeling more comfortable. We were working together and it began to feel like a team. And one day, I finally raised my hand and said something. After that, they couldn't keep me quiet.

The creation of subcommittees particularly encouraged women to participate. As the MDC became more prominent and respected for its accomplishments, community members became more open to the idea that *mujeres serias* could be active in its work. Decentralizing the organization created "windows of opportunity" where women could assume more responsibility and have more say. Though in general men continued to dominate the organization and women took on traditionally female roles, their participation increased.

Women have always participated in the church. It is considered okay for even a woman who is married to go to mass and to attend meetings of the parish council. But very few women were active in the MDC. It wasn't considered proper. Now, though, that they have the health committee and the education committee—these are things that people feel it is okay for women to be involved in. They will not accuse a woman of going to a meeting to flirt with men. They will say she is there because she cares about her children. (Pedro, 58, return migrant, Miraflores)

The MDC also needed to improve its management and accounting practices. It was managing more projects involving larger sums of money and, at the same time, its members wanted a more thorough record of how things were done. In response, the committee formalized its administrative structure and delegated roles and responsibilities to its leaders in a much more systematic way than it had done before. Each subcommittee was ordered to maintain its own records and accounts and report back to the larger group.

This level of formalization and standardization contrasts sharply with earlier MDC projects, which were often run according to their organizers' whims. In the late 1970s, for example, Don Manuel Ricardo worked with the MDC to raise money to build a baseball stadium. He collected the money, purchased the land, and constructed the bleachers. Several years later, however, when he decided he wanted the land for himself, there was little villagers could do. The land legally belonged to him because he had purchased it in his name. Now, all purchases made on behalf of the community require three signatures. Such rules prevent future mishaps and also give community members more confidence about collective development efforts.

These new systems have made project implementation more effective and more transparent. Initially Boston committee members sent their contributions directly to the subcommittee in Miraflores in charge of the project they were working on at the time. They sent migrants' donations for the baseball stadium, for example, directly to the head of the sports committee. Members of the coordinating committee, however, felt these lines of communication did not allow them to supervise projects adequately. They also felt that if some subcommittee members had more friends in Boston, they would receive more support for their projects than other groups. As a result, all migrant contributions must now be channeled through the coordinating committee. In this way, leaders can distribute funds more evenly among projects and supervise how funds are spent.

A third way that the MDC promotes development is by generating some modest employment opportunities. The committee needs bookkeepers, watchguards, and manual laborers to help with construction projects. Though these are only temporary, part-time positions, they have been a help to some families.

When we began building the baseball stadium, we realized we had to hire several people to help us. We needed an architect. We needed men to help carry supplies and do some of the labor. We needed someone to keep watch over the site so no one stole the materials once we bought them. All of these needs made the MDC into an employer, which we had never been before. It was good because we could hire some of the men in the community. (Jesús, 48, nonmigrant, Miraflores)

Finally, the efforts of MDC members in Boston and Miraflores enhanced villagers' ability to make demands of the Dominican state. In some areas, such as health care, the community was able to provide for itself what the government did not provide for them. Before the PRD government (1978–86) built rural health clinics throughout the country, it was the MDC that financed health care provision in Miraflores. In other cases, the community leveraged the monies it raised to secure additional funds. Leaders convinced municipal authorities in Baní, for example, to match the $10,000 they collected to build the community's park.

Migrant support also ultimately enabled the MDC to pressure the government to provide for them. The committee raised approximately $50,000 to construct its aqueduct. Members planned to finance and implement the entire project on their own because they were tired of waiting for the government to do it for them. After the MDC raised enough money to begin work, committee members visited provincial water supply authorities to get the permits they needed. When months passed and no permits arrived, they began making weekly trips to Santo Domingo to complain at the National Palace. Though each time officials assured them that the permits were on their way, they never materialized. Finally, after several months, the MDC learned that President Balaguer was coming to Baní to inaugurate another public-works project and they arranged to meet with him.

We found out that Balaguer would be coming to Baní, so we asked the Reformistas in town to arrange a meeting for us. As the MDC president, I went as the representative of the entire group. I said, Dr. Balaguer, our village goes without water for days at a time. We want to build an aqueduct, and with the help of those who are living in Boston we have raised the money to do so. We have been asking the provincial water authorities for months to give us the permits we need, but there is always some excuse. We would like you to help us. And the old man looked at me and he said, "You can tell your community members to keep their money. I will build your aqueduct." (Ramón, 48, nonmigrant, Miraflores)

Migrant contributions enabled the MDC to advance the project far enough to capture Balaguer's attention and pressure him into helping them. Since one way he ensured the Dominican public's continued support was to bestow favors on them, Balaguer was unlikely to allow Mirafloreños to solve problems on their own. Such successful community organizing should ensure that politicians of all persuasions will find it more difficult to ignore Miraflores in the future.

The MDC also functioned as the logical counterpart to the state in subsequent public-works projects. Committee members were better at advocating for themselves and negotiating their way through the government bureacracy because they were more experienced at these challenges. In the case of the aqueduct, in particular, MDC leaders were more educated consumers. Since they had already paid an architect to draw up construction plans, and had advanced the project to the point they did, they could supervise the building process in a much more knowledgeable manner than they would have had the project been completed by the state alone.

The Limits to Change

The MDC acted transnationally to promote community development in Miraflores. It raised funds, acquired organizational skills and management strategies, and implemented projects across borders, but the fruits of these efforts registered in Miraflores alone and they were not all positive. The additional resources, skills, and opportunities for participation engendered by the group's transnational character came at a price.

First, when communities get better at solving their own problems, it lets the state off the hook. Because migration enabled Mirafloreños to meet their own needs more effectively, the Dominican government could continue to pursue policies that hurt rural development and caused migration to begin with. While high-migration communities like Miraflores are in a better position to withstand state negligence and to make stronger claims on the state, neighboring communities, from which few migrants leave, are double victims. They still have few resources with which to bargain and the Dominican government has even fewer incentives to help them (Goldring 1992; Smith 1995). Uneven development is exacerbated by the unequal distribution of migration's rewards.

Second, transnational community development created a sharp cross-border division of labor within the MDC that empowered migrant community members at nonmigrants' expense. Who decided what was in the community's best interest and how it should be acted upon changed such that migrants enjoyed greater influence while nonmigrants' interests were often given short shrift. Ostrander and Schervish's (1994) view of philanthropy as a social relation offers a useful way to examine the changing dynamics between migrants and nonmigrants by highlighting shifts in philanthropic arrangements over time.

When the MDC was first reconstituted, all of its members were both donors and recipients. Nonmigrants contributed to and benefited from the MDC's efforts. Many migrants also thought of them-

selves as beneficiaries because they planned to return to live in Miraflores as soon as they could. During these early stages, both migrants
and nonmigrants engaged in consumption philanthropy (Schervish
and Herman 1988). They were all donors who contributed to causes
from which they directly benefited.

These relations changed over time. As migrants' economic status
improved, they assumed the lion's share of responsibility for fund-
raising. Though nonmigrants also raised money, everyone agreed they
could not possibly contribute as much as migrants. Instead, they took
responsibility for project implementation or, in the case of the aqueduct, for advocating to make sure the project got done. Sharp lines developed between donors and recipients. Though migrants still saw
themselves as reaping the rewards of the MDC's efforts, they began
to want different kinds of benefits from those nonmigrants wanted.
The way in which power was distributed between these two groups,
and the extent to which each took the other's interests into account,
was constantly renegotiated. Different visions of the "future Miraflores" and how to create it were proposed. Nonmigrants wanted jobs,
youth programs, and a better baseball facility. Migrants wanted a Miraflores where they would be comfortable vacationing or retiring to.
They wanted cultural programs that preserved the community traditions they remembered so fondly from their youth.

Among migrants this new focus signaled a shift from consumption
to a combination of empowerment and therapeutic philanthropy. In
this second type of giving, donors take charge of their own "wealth"
and their desire to empower others (Schervish 1996). Migrant MDC
members used giving as a way to understand their new lives and to
orient the course of change in Miraflores in a particular direction.
In many cases migrants contributed out of a strong sense of responsibility to their birthplace. They felt that they were indebted to their
friends and family and to the place they came from. As one leader put
it, "We are sons of Miraflores and it is our responsibility to share our
good fortune by giving back to the place where we were born."

In other cases migrants gave to make their personal difficulties easier to bear and to counteract their fatigue and loneliness. Just as individuals felt somehow compensated for their hardship when they gave
gifts to their friends and neighbors during their visits home, so MDC
members derived a similar sense of satisfaction from being able to
give to their community. Still others gave to show off their success. Ri-

cardo, who left Miraflores in the early 1970s, contributed $1,500 toward the baseball stadium and requested that a dugout be named for his family. Those who donated benches to the park had their names inscribed in them to affirm their continued membership in the community and to demonstrate their new social standing. Finally, a last group contributed to preserve the Miraflores they left behind. They supported poetry contests and patron saint's day celebrations because this is what they remembered most fondly about their childhoods and what they most wanted to return to.

The project selection process reflected the growing divergence between migrant and nonmigrant community goals and how difficult it was to make decisions across borders. The funeral home provides a case in point. Though pleased with the final product, both migrants and nonmigrants felt that far too much money had been spent. They seemed perplexed when I asked them how the actual decision to build the funeral home had come about. Each group felt that the other had supported the project more avidly.

Some wanted a funeral home because El Llano, a neighboring *campo,* already had one and villagers did not want to be outdone by their long-standing rival. Others felt it was migrant community members who wanted the project because their priority was to create a comfortable place to vacation and return to in their old age. Others argued the project was misguided.

> If they had left it up to me to decide, I would not have built it. We are going to break a tradition that we have always had, and we are going to bring a modernization here that we don't have and that we don't need. . . . If you ask other Mirafloreños, I bet there would be 70 percent who would prefer to be laid out and mourned in their own homes. They wouldn't want to go to a funeral home. . . . I also realize that when people die in the U.S. and are sent home to be buried, if they are laid out in the homes, all of Miraflores goes. But if it is in a funeral home, women have to go to the beauty parlor, men have to wear ties, and you have to have the right clothes and this destroys something about it. Many people prefer not to go. They wait until the family goes back to their home to pay their respects. I know that this is going to happen. It was not a priority. (Gustavo, 43, return migrant, Miraflores)

Additional disagreements between migrants and nonmigrants arose over the baseball stadium and the health clinic. Members in Boston objected when the sports subcommittee hired nine replacement players from outside the community to play on the Miraflores baseball team. Even if Miraflores wins, they said, it would not be a real victory for the community because these players were not from Miraflores. They felt that only young men from the community should play because the character-building aspect of playing was more important than whether the team won or lost. Nonmigrants, however, cared little about these larger social goals. They wanted to win and saw nothing wrong with hiring people from outside the community if it enabled them to do so.

In the case of the health clinic, the community was at odds with doctors who had been stationed there by the government as a mandatory part of their medical training. Boston members made matters worse when they gave the MDC's contributions directly to these physicians. They diminished the community's already weak sense of ownership toward the clinic and bolstered the physicians' position at the community's expense. This working at cross purposes occurred, in part, because migrants wanted to be seen as benefactors and because they did not have their fingers on the pulse of daily village life.

As the line between donor and beneficiary became more pronounced, nonmigrants grew increasingly dependent on migrants. Though community members in Boston recognized that it was hard for nonmigrants to raise money in Miraflores, they still felt that those who remained behind should at least try to do their fair share. In fact, Boston members withheld funds twice during the course of this study to register their displeasure with the management of the baseball-stadium project. They said they would not send more money down, even if they had it sitting in the bank, until those in Miraflores made more of an effort to raise funds on their own.

The Possibilities for Transnational Community Development

Doing development transnationally heightened conflicts between migrants and nonmigrants, but it also strengthened organizational performance and produced significant gains for Miraflores. The MDC's efforts improved infrastructure, increased participation, created jobs, improved skills, and bolstered organizational effectiveness.

But immigrant Mirafloreños face problems, too. They often found it difficult to raise their children in the new environment in which they found themselves. They lacked adequate English-language skills. They did not always know what kinds of services were available to them or how to get access to them. How can organizations like the MDC, which successfully help nonmigrants, help migrants as well?

Several issues need to be resolved before a truly transnational community development strategy becomes possible. The first is that the solidarity that is so plentiful when it comes to Miraflores does not always apply to life in Boston. According to Raúl, an MDC leader, a different set of social rules is gradually taking hold in the United States. While in Miraflores, he feels it is his right and responsibility to scold a teenager who misbehaves, in Boston he feels that young people are "too far out of control" and that "they don't respect adults the way they do at home." There is a feeling of every man for himself—that when it comes to Miraflores, "we are all members of the same family, but when it comes to life in the U.S., we are beginning to compete with one another."

Second, committee members tended to view community development as a zero-sum game. They claimed they had limited time, energy, and resources and that devoting themselves to making life better in Boston would detract from their efforts to help those at home. "If we work on the problems that we face here," Doña Juana said, "it will take away from what we are trying to do for Miraflores." By turning their attention to Boston, they would also be facing up to the fact that they were unlikely to return. "If we begin working to help the community here," Don Héctor said, "it means admitting that we are here to stay."

These issues are not necessarily insurmountable. Social-service providers could reinforce community ties before they weaken further. Practitioners could convince Mirafloreños that addressing the problems they face in Boston does not mean they will permanently remain. Foundation program officers can support pilot transnational development efforts involving projects in Boston and on the island.

These efforts could take a number of forms, from the very simple to the more complex. The social remittances migrants send to their families regularly contribute in small, individualized ways to positive social change. Because we understand the mechanisms of social remittance transmission, and because the source and destination of these transfers is clear, many kinds of ideas and practices could be purposefully transmitted to particular audiences with positive results. Health behaviors, business and technical skills, and organizing techniques, for example, could be channeled toward specific target groups with beneficial effects.

These kinds of information transfers should not be one-way. Migrants are circulating in and out of U.S. and Dominican schools, health care institutions, and churches. Some workers enter and exit specific factories and service-sector industries. Information about Dominican life could be targeted at health care providers working with this community. Exchanges between U.S. and Dominican educators could improve school performance. Transfers of information about Dominican work culture could also help integrate migrants more successfully into the U.S. workforce.

Conclusion

Not very much about Cecilia Jiménez's life changed when she returned to Miraflores after fifteen years in Boston. She had the refrigerator and television she had always wanted. She had enough money to live comfortably because her children sent her something every month from the United States. In general, though, things were pretty much as they had always been. The tin roof on her house still leaked. The family still used an outhouse instead of an indoor bathroom. And she complained that there were still too many noisy children running around her yard in the afternoon when she was trying to rest.

This was not the case for Pablo Liriano. He returned to a new home with air-conditioning and marble-tile floors. He had all the latest appliances in his kitchen. His children played with imported toys and always wore clean, neatly pressed clothing. Community members elected him leader of the MDC's sports committee. But although he had dreamed for years about his return to Miraflores, it was not as easy as he had thought to readjust to village life. He had trouble figuring out how to form new relationships with his neighbors and old friends. They either kept him deferentially at bay or treated him as if his pockets were lined with gold. And though he spent months searching for some business idea to invest in, he was still living off his savings more than a year after his return.

Both Cecilia's and Pablo's experiences speak to the paradoxical relationship between transnational migration and development. Most Mirafloreños have more income and enjoy a more comfortable lifestyle since migration began. They have a better school, health clinic, and water supply. They feel a stronger sense of civic responsibility and a desire to challenge the political status quo. But they have achieved these gains only through the graces of those in Boston. They cannot sustain this higher standard of living on their own. They have lost faith in Dominican values and in their country's ability to solve its own problems. They have become so dependent on the money, ideas, and values imported from Boston that migration has become an integral part of their everyday lives.

Immigrant life also yields ambiguous rewards. Most Mirafloreños work at jobs that pay more than they have ever dreamed of. The new furniture and electronics that fill their homes please them. They are proud of their English-speaking children when they do well in school. On the weekends, they go to the mall, where they can choose from a range of products so vast it is almost unimaginable. But work consumes them. They leave at five o'clock in the morning, return at two, eat, bathe, and then work again until ten at night. Their jobs give them little besides a paycheck. Many live near the bottom of the socioeconomic ladder. Since they often work alone, they generally learn little English and few new skills, meaning they have few opportunities to get ahead. They watch the Anglo world from its margins, not knowing how to negotiate their way in. They feel more capable when they compare themselves to those who remain in Miraflores and diminished when it comes to their dealings in the larger world. Those who regret their choices find it difficult to turn back because so many family members and friends depend on their support.

Transnational migration opens up opportunities for some and constitutes a deal with the devil for others. One factor shaping this relationship is class. Those who start out with more generally finish with more. Mirafloreños who arrived with more education, money, and contacts were more likely to get ahead. Those with more human and social capital could raise families, start businesses, and express political demands across borders more easily. Pablo had completed primary school when he arrived in Boston. He already spoke some English. He had an uncle already living in the city who helped him get a job at a factory where he eventually became a supervisor. He worked hard and learned how to handle himself among Anglos. When he moved back to Miraflores, he did so with more than $50,000 in his bank account.

Cecilia, on the other hand, left Miraflores with much less on her side. She could barely read and write and spoke little English. She did not know anyone who could help get her a "good" job where she had a chance to get ahead. While migration catapulted Pablo into the elite ranks of Miraflores, Cecilia's minimal social and cultural capital meant that for her, migration was like treading water. With some slight improvements, her life upon return was very similar to the one she led before she left.

The experiences of the five Paniagua family siblings further highlight the equivocal relationship between transnational migration and development. They also underscore how status and power differences within households are renegotiated such that norms of bounded solidarity and enforceable trust still hold sway across borders. Teresa Paniagua ascended into the American middle class. She married a small business owner who is a widely respected leader of the Latino community in Boston. Together they run a successful children's clothing store and own several residential and commercial properties in Jamaica Plain. Her children are doing well in school. Teresa sends back money regularly to her mother in Miraflores and generally visits at least once a year. Success has been more elusive for her brother Ricardo. After working two part-time jobs for nearly ten years, he also tried his hand at small business ownership but went bankrupt within a year. He is now trying to put together another strategy for escaping out of permanent part-time employment. Things are looking up. He recently moved to Providence, Rhode Island, where he and his wife both found work easily. He also purchased a home with help from a program for first-time home buyers.

For Anthony, migration has been a disaster. During his first stint in Boston, he and his wife, Ana, lived separately for three years until she got a visa and was able to join him. Together they saved enough money to return to Miraflores, where they opened a small *colmado* and bar. When this failed, after only six months, Anthony returned to Boston, but this time, by the time Ana and their children could follow him, he was living with another woman; he and Ana subsequently divorced. Anthony later got arrested on a drug-related charge and spent three years in prison before being deported back to the Dominican Republic. He now works as an itinerant barber, traveling to Santo Domingo several times a week to cut hair, which is exactly what he did before migrating more than twenty years ago. He also sells hotdogs in front of one of Miraflores's main squares—a newly acquired taste among visitors and nonmigrants alike.

Teresa and Ricardo support their mother, Doña Silvia and, by default, their older sister Concepción, who lives next door. Doña Silvia is satisfied, though there are times when she waits anxiously for her money because she owes so much on credit at the corner grocery store. She and Concepción never complain. They are grateful for their family's support and know that receiving without ever directly asking for anything is their part of the bargain. Last year Teresa and Ricardo finally had enough money to renovate the family's home. They expanded the kitchen and added an extra bedroom, where they stay when they visit. And their youngest sister, Iris, who had been *loca por irse* (crazy to go) ever since she was a teen, finally made it to the United States on her second try at crossing the border. Her fate remains to be seen.

The Impact of Dual Memberships

Though many scholars have abandoned the notion of fixed identities for one that acknowledges their malleability, much research still assumes that individuals have a "master," overarching identity that is fundamentally rooted in a single place. In contrast, transnational community members develop several fluid, sometimes conflicting identities. Rouse (1991) called the Mexican Americans he studied "bifocal" because their multiple roles enabled them to view the world through different types of lenses simultaneously. Mahler (1998) described the migrant who left El Salvador as an impoverished peasant but eventually earned enough money to buy a house and land back in his village. While he worked in the United States, he hired a man to care for his property, paying him barely a subsistence wage. By asking if he is exploiter, exploited, or both, she brings to light the contradictory roles migrants play and how each repositions the individual with respect to the locus of power in the sending- and receiving-country context.

In the case of Miraflores, and other transnational communities like it, identity construction is even more complex. Mirafloreños simultaneously managed several sometimes-contradictory roles and identities that divided their attachments between their home and host countries. The same individual is not just peasant or owner, leader or follower, exploiter or exploited, but a political, religious, and social actor who might earn her livelihood in the United States, dedicate most of her time toward achieving political goals on the island, but feel equally comfortable as a member of a transnational Dominican–U.S. church. She is able to maintain these multiple, partial memberships without conflict. One can see such individuals as hedging their bets. A more accurate description is that they belong to and are making a future in two places. They are assimilating and remaining transnational at the same time. Increasing numbers of migrants and nonmigrants now understand their roles of parent, moral compass, breadwinner, and political claims maker as ones they will carry out across borders over time.

The individual and household-level connections that form across borders reinforce and are reinforced by the transnationalization of organizational life. How individuals distribute their loyalty and energy between sending- and receiving-countries depends upon how political, religious, and social life is organized across space. The organizations I described here each manifested their transnational character along different dimensions. All three groups were structured transnationally, though in distinct ways. In the case of the church, autonomous chapters of the same global institution were connected to one another through informal, interpersonal ties between religious and lay individuals. The PRD created a franchise in the United States that was supervised directly by its organization on the island. The Miraflores Development Committee, also an entirely Dominican group, consisted of linked chapters in Boston and the Dominican Republic that were, at least initially, equal partners.

These organizations were also transnational to the extent that they carried out their activities across borders. They each raised funds, recruited members, and carried out strategies and goals in two settings. The Miraflores experience demonstrates, though, that articulating a transnational agenda and acting transnationally to accomplish it does not automatically produce transnational results. While the Catholic Church acted and achieved transnationally, cross-border politics and community development had a much greater impact in the Dominican Republic. The proliferation of political, religious, and community organizational transnational membership challenges the meaning and content of citizenship and participation. More and more residents of contemporary nation-states are non-nationals or hold multiple citizenships. Many aliens enjoy political and social rights previously reserved only for citizens. However, a high proportion of ethnic minority members, regardless of their citizenship status, are excluded, discriminated against, and treated as second-class citizens. Furthermore, naturalization does not necessarily signal a shift in allegiance from one national culture and identity to another. Instead, a number of sometimes-conflicting motivations underlie citizenship choices. These trends take place in a world in which rights can be claimed, demands articulated, and interests organized at multiple levels. It is not just the nation-state that endows individual rights but also international and supranational organizations that guarantee certain basic protections.

A number of researchers convincingly argue that earlier migrants and nonmigrants also sustained strong ties to one another. As far back as 1927, Thomas and Znaniecki observed that nonmigrants held fast to their hopes that migrants would return and take up their original place in their communities of origin. Earlier migrants managed business and real estate transactions transnationally and supervised the emotional affairs of their nonmigrant kin through their letters, telegrams, and visits just as migrants do today. Their loyalty and worth were also measured against the yardstick of how much money they remitted. And migrants' home-country political focus, and the efforts of sending states to perpetuate it, persisted over time, in some cases up through World War II (Morawska 2001a; Foner 2000; Glick-Schiller 2000).

But clearly these relationships have also changed. The strength of migrants' attachments ebbed and flowed depending upon sending- and receiving-country opportunities and constraints. The motivations underlying them also shifted, ranging from mere interest in keeping up with home-country news to actively mobilizing against home-country rule. Morawska (2001c) argues that the New Deal and immigrant-friendly labor organizations encouraged the foreign-born to become more active in U.S. politics. Their transnational attachments did not wane, however, but were "reconfigured through the ethnicization process into new compositions" as their experiences in America gained preeminence in shaping their reference frames (Morawska 2001c, 15–16). They could do so, she argues, because they enjoyed a great deal of flexibility with which to create the meaning and content of their ethnic and immigrant identities, as well as their home-country attachments. The present-day U.S. context endows migrants with even more room with which to invent who they are and gives them access to an even broader range of elements, including transnational ones, to use in identity construction.

Several additional factors reinforce contemporary transnational attachments. Ease of transport and cheap travel increase the intensity and immediacy of these relationships. Unlike the 1920s, when restrictive laws dramatically reduced the numbers entering the United States, migration that began in the 1950s is likely to continue at a steady rate. Because sending states need migrants' remittances, they are allowing expatriates to assert their continued membership from their host-country base. More and more states are putting into place formal mechanisms, such as dual citizenship, the expatriate vote, and various investment incentive schemes, that enable migrants to maintain official, long-term dual loyalties. Finally, conditions in the United States make it more difficult for some low-skilled individuals to assimilate to the same degree as migrants in the past. Institutions like political wards and unions that fostered political integration among earlier groups are on the decline. Economic restructuring during the past two decades narrows opportunities for social and economic mobility. Contemporary migrants, who are more likely to be nonwhites, often encounter discrimination. Transnational practices allow some individuals to compensate for these limits to their economic advancement. They choose to remain transnational to overcome the blocked opportunities they face in the United States.

Increasing numbers of migrants, then, have the ability and the incentive to sustain some combination of long-term formal or informal political, religious, and civic attachments to their countries of origin even as they assimilate into the United States.[1] The rest of this section highlights what Mirafloreños' experiences reveal about the consequences of different membership choices. It also examines the relationship between transnational political, religious, and civil-society memberships. Tens of millions of people are said to live in one state as citizens but be subject to another state where they are also citizens. The 1997 European Convention on Nationality reflected a heightened recognition among governments that dual nationality is not a short-term aberration that should be eliminated, but a growing reality that must be accommodated (Aleinikoff and Klusmeyer 1998). Thus far, dual citizenship has not posed a major threat to the security and stability of the nation-state regime, nor do I expect it will do so in the future. Isolated examples, such as that of the U.S.-Israeli dual citizen Samuel Scheinbein, whom the Israeli government refused to extradite to the United States, where he was accused of murder, highlight some of the practical problems that need to be addressed (Katzenell 1999).

States need to iron out which government is ultimately responsible for these individuals and where dual citizens will vote, pay taxes, be punished for the crimes they commit, or serve in the military. They need to decide where dual citizens will fulfill the duties and responsibilities of citizenship. They need to sort out how best to protect transnational actors' interests without neglecting the needs of those who stay behind.[2] Though some states may do so by disallowing dual membership, it makes more sense to acknowledge that increasing numbers of individuals already live their lives across borders and to create mechanisms to allow them to contribute fully and equally to both polities. The issue is not whether migrants should or should not belong, in some way, to two polities but that, given that increasing numbers live transnational lives, how their rights and representation can be best guaranteed.[3]

If migrants do not have the option to hold dual citizenship, or they decide not to exercise it, they can configure their membership in a number of ways. They can become U.S. citizens but still continue to participate in home-country affairs, or they may opt for long-term resident alien status, participate in civic and religious groups, and exercise their political citizenship rights in their countries of origin.

To date, most Mirafloreños have chosen long-term partial membership in the United States as legal resident aliens in combination with continued full, though often unexercised, membership in the Dominican Republic. As noncitizens, many participated in nonelectoral forums. Membership in church, school, or civic groups allowed them to address their everyday concerns fairly effectively. These kinds of groups successfully pressure government officials to keep the local health clinic open, provide after-school care, or install more streetlights in their neighborhood. Belonging to the Catholic Church also integrated Mirafloreños into a strong, well-endowed institutional network that afforded them some basic protections and representation.

Even the largest, most well-organized groups, however, will not sway politicians if their members do not vote or make campaign contributions. Participation and representation through local-level civic groups still leaves migrants out of the loop with respect to electoral politics. While citizenship cannot predict social and economic status or guarantee that those who hold it will exercise their rights or receive equal representation and protection, long-term partial membership leaves individuals without an electoral voice.[4] It also excludes them from the political agenda-setting process. They have little say over what issues are put on the table and who is invited to discuss them.

Until 1996, permanent resident aliens enjoyed almost the same set of rights and privileges as citizens. Green-card holders could not vote, serve on juries, run for certain elected offices, or hold government positions considered politically sensitive (Schuck 1998). Apart from this, though, they received the same basic protections and benefits as citizens. Legislative reforms subsequently scaled back welfare benefits and food stamps for many legal immigrants. Though some states reinstituted benefits, and Congress restored some benefits at the national level, the tenuousness of social rights without full political membership in the United States is clear.[5]

In some areas, long-term permanent residents have won the right to participate in local politics. Noncitizens can vote in New York City School Board elections and in elections for Chicago school advisory boards.[6] Takoma Park, Maryland, granted noncitizens the right to vote in municipal elections in 1992. For the second time since 1993, noncitizen voting is being considered by the Cambridge, Massachusetts, City Council (McNaught 1999). The New York State Assembly's Task Force on New Americans recommended a similar proposal in 1992 (Sontag 1992). Some level of local political rights has also been granted to noncitizens in a half-dozen European countries since the 1970s (Miller 1989). While these arrangements mediate against complete disenfranchisement, limited, localized citizenship still means migrants have minimal say over state and national issues. They enhance migrants' ability to sustain multiple memberships but allow them to do so only from a position of second-class membership. Furthermore, noncitizen voting rights are still reversible. In fact, the eighteen states that granted some form of noncitizen suffrage between 1789 and 1924 repealed these rights in the face of heightened anti-immigrant sentiments (Jones-Correa 1998a).

Given their limited rights as noncitizens in the United States, migrants may turn to their sending states for protection and representation if the need arises. But to what extent can this compensate for partial host-country membership? There are an increasing number of cases in which sending states have intervened on migrants' behalf. In 1998, for example, the Paraguayan government, acting through the World Court, tried unsuccessfully to stay the execution of a Paraguayan national sentenced to death in Virginia (Jacobs 1998). Clearly, some countries are in a much stronger position to advocate for their citizens than others. The Mexican government, for example, is more likely to be successful at protecting its emigrants than smaller, less influential states because Mexico sends such large numbers and plays such a significant role in U.S. economic and political affairs. Countries that send fewer migrants and that are less important economically and politically have much less bargaining power.

And what of migrants' continued political participation in their home countries? The rise in multiple, differentiated memberships is important not only for receiving-country politics but also for the politics of the homeland. Not only do increasing numbers of sending-country politicians campaign and raise money regularly among their migrant constituents in the United States, but migrants' participation in the civil societies of the countries that receive them, and their exposure to the political life around them, also has the potential to transform their political culture and behavior. The social remittances they send back can contribute to local-level reform just as the political skills and resources they bring with them can heighten participation and introduce new ways of doing politics in receiving states.

How migrants' long-term participation without residence will affect Dominican formal politics is difficult to predict. By allowing dual citizenship, and by mandating that all those born to Dominican parents outside the country are eligible for Dominican citizenship, the Dominican government institutionalized the long-term incorporation of its expanding diaspora. It also granted formal recognition to an emerging transnational elite who could challenge traditional power holders (Guarnizo 1998). Before expatriate voting was approved, Dominicans often returned to the island to cast their ballots (Sontag 1997; Rohter 1996a). Thus, presidential candidate José Francisco Peña Gómez acknowledged that "the part they [migrants] play is absolutely decisive, especially in terms of campaign finances." Migrants' influence will increase considerably if and when the Dominican government agrees on an implementation plan for the expatriate ballot.

Though it is too soon to assess the effect of expatriate voting in the Dominican Republic, voter turnout among expatriate Brazilians and Colombians has been low.[7] These numbers may increase as registration and vote casting become easier. The Brazilian consulate in Boston, for example, planned to open three polling stations during the 1998 election to allow migrants to vote closer to their homes and workplaces.[8] If participation remains low, despite efforts to encourage it, this may indicate that migrants are satisfied with their ability to influence politics through their financial contributions or through reciprocal exchanges, such as lobbying host-country legislators in exchange for home-country legislation favorable to migrant interests. It may also indicate that transnational actors are being left out or are opting out of the political process on both sides of the border and that they will remain marginal to politics for the long-term in both settings.

It is important to remember, however, that transnational political outcomes are context-specific. The Dominican community in New York has been much more successful than the community in Boston at acting and achieving transnationally. Dominicans play an increasingly important role in New York City politics while they continue to influence political outcomes on the island. Several factors, unique to the New York experience, encouraged this, including the Dominican community's growing numbers, long history, and ability to form alliances with other racial and ethnic minorities who have served as their guides.

Migrants from larger, more distant countries that have less history of political and economic dependence on the United States are unlikely to play such a significant role in national-level, home-country politics as those from the Dominican Republic. There are a number of reasons for this that a comparison with Mexico brings to light.

First, the high residential concentration among Dominicans in the United States is unmatched by most other groups. Though there are large communities of Mexicans in Texas, California, and Illinois, it is much more difficult to organize them around a united agenda than it is to mobilize Dominicans, nearly two-thirds of whom live in the Northeast.

Second, when 10 percent of the Dominican Republic's 7.5 million residents migrate from several parts of this small country, it affects the nation as a whole. When 10 percent of 90 million Mexicans enter the United States from specific regions, its impact on Mexico is concentrated in just those regions. When many people leave particular cities or states in large countries, regionalized political effects, similar to those occurring nationally in the Dominican Republic, are more likely to result.

A number of cases come to mind. Significant numbers have migrated from the Brazilian city of Governador Valadares and the Mexican state of Zacatecas, to name two; both send significant numbers who tend to residentially cluster near one another in the United States. These migrants send high levels of remittances that the sending-country regional economy is increasingly dependent on. The strength of Mexican and Brazilian migrants' influence over home-country regional electoral politics depends upon the distribution of power between federal and state governments. It also hinges on the likelihood that migrants will be granted the right to vote in state or provincial elections.[9] Whether they are allowed to vote or not, however, migrants may still shape nonmigrant voter preferences, encourage reforms, and influence campaigns in their home country region in much the same way that migrants from smaller countries do nationally.

The Miraflores experience also sheds light on how transnational religious affiliations interact with political memberships and shape the relationship between transnational religion and politics. Transnational religious membership involved few costs. Mirafloreños belong to the Catholic Church wherever they reside. Their home- and host-country religious practices often had much in common. Unlike the PRD, which had to forge relationships with a host-country organizational partner to achieve transnational results, migration merely extended and deepened the scope of this already transnational religious institution. Organizational and ritualistic similarities allowed Mirafloreños to circulate fairly effortlessly between religious arenas in Boston and on the island.

Mirafloreños left a church that often substituted for or pressured the state to solve their problems for them. They also brought with them a strong tradition of lay leadership. Migrants' interactions with the church in Massachusetts taught them new skills but also allowed them to introduce their own traditions into the receiving-country arena. They modeled these experiences for fellow church members and by so doing opened up space for greater participation and voice in the receiving church. Because of the ease of entry and exit afforded by these transnational connections, iterative skill transfers and democratization between sending- and receiving-countries are likely to continue. Verba et al. (1995) have demonstrated the role that churchgoing plays in encouraging civic engagement, but the Miraflores case makes clear that skill development and institution building are processes that occur increasingly across boundaries.

Religious participation also encourages mobilization and voice indirectly because it can result in panethnic participation and cooperation that other groups are unable to achieve. Efforts to create panethnic economic and political coalitions in Boston have met with limited success. The Latino Democratic Committee in Massachusetts, for example, has undergone several waves of active mobilization to near collapse. In contrast, at church, different country-of-origin groups consistently come together around worship and parish governance. Under the right circumstances, these alliances could be mobilized more explicitly to achieve political goals.

Finally, transnational religious membership incorporates migrants into potentially powerful, politically influential institutional networks where individuals can also express their interests and make claims. They are transnational religious members, regardless of their political citizenship. Though migrants' direct ties to states may weaken because of their divided political membership, they are reconnected to the state by virtue of the church-state relationship.

Variations in this church-state relation shape the extent to which transnational religious memberships compensate for or complement partial political membership. Religion has been a catalyst for opening up totalitarian and authoritarian regimes, raising new democratic demands in established democracies, and in building stronger institutions (Casanova 1994; C. Smith 1996). It has also clearly thwarted political change. In countries like the Dominican Republic, where there is a close marriage between the government and the church, religious institutions are unlikely to be effective platforms from which to challenge the state. In countries like Brazil, where the church has a strong history of advocating for the poor, religious participation integrates migrants into an influential, well-endowed organization that can represent them and help them access resources.

How the relationship between religion and politics changes when it is negotiated across borders has to do with the match between sending- and receiving-country churches. At the local level, the direction and impact of these activities depend upon each clergyman's particular vision, how much autonomy he grants his followers, and how much autonomy he is granted by his superiors. In the Miraflores case, some priests have played an active role in community-development efforts. It was parish priests, for example, who convinced the first commercial bank to locate in Jamaica Plain and who fought to convert what had been a French Canadian and Italian national parish in Lawrence, Massachusetts, into a church dedicated to the growing Latino community.

But there are also many cases where the church has done little to raise concerns about social justice despite the growing impoverishment of its members. In their current incarnations, the Boston and Dominican churches are fairly conservative. In contrast, similar transnational ties linking Brazilian Catholics and their sending church bring new members from a much more liberal religious environment into the fold. Depending upon how much freedom the archdiocese grants its new Brazilian parishioners, these differences could act as catalysts for liberalization in Massachusetts. In Brazil, these cross-border ties could make the church more conservative as leaders back away from their social reform agenda and focus on individual spiritual growth.

Community organizational participation is a third way that Mirafloreños exercise dual membership. To date, participation in the MDC has done little to encourage incorporation into U.S. society or to compensate for migrants' political marginalization. In fact, it strongly reinforces their ties to their sending communities and privileges migrant members over those who stay behind. In addition, these activities have not taken into account that transnational villages need transnational development strategies. Community development is not a zero-sum game, in which migrants must rob Peter to pay Paul, but one in which outcomes on both sides are inextricably linked.

Proponents of postnational or transnational citizenship would argue that rights guarantees by the sending or receiving states are increasingly irrelevant because individuals are ensured a set of universally accepted rights regardless of their membership in particular states. There are, indeed, a growing number of examples where extra-state entities bestow rights. In exchange for greater access to Indian and other markets by U.S. financial services corporations, the United States agreed to grant 65,000 visas for professionals entering as temporary workers as well as the continued admission of intracompany transferees. Although mirroring provisions already in domestic law, these guarantees were made in the context of negotiations over the General Agreement on Trade in Services (GATS) and, having treaty status, can be made more restrictive only with the consent of other signatories.[10] The Working Group on Migration and Consular Affairs of the U.S.-Mexican Binational Commission on Migration, which began meeting as an independent entity in 1992, has also become a useful mechanism for bilateral dialogue and for coordinated efforts between Mexican and U.S. officials (Mexican Ministry of Foreign Affairs and U.S. Commission on Immigration Reform 1998).

While I believe we are moving toward a world in which some rights are universally accepted and guaranteed by extra-state entities, there is still a long way to go. States still matter. The institutional mechanisms that guarantee universal rights are weak at best. States regularly disregard international treaties they have signed when it is in their perceived best interest. The United States, for example, ignored the World Court's recommendation to stay the Paraguayan's execution, saying that the court did not have the jurisdiction to order it to do so.[11] Though the U.N. Declaration of Human Rights was signed more than fifty years ago, a 1999 U.S. State Department report on the state of human rights in the world documents a significant increase in abuses (State Department 1999). In the interim, more and more migrants sign on to dual, partial memberships that postnational citizenship does not, at present, adequately compensate for.

Variations in Transnational Community Forms

Miraflores exemplifies one type of transnational community, which I call a transnational village, that emerges when large numbers of people from a small, bounded sending community enact their lives across borders. But migrants and nonmigrants create other kinds of transnational social groups through their enduring ties.

Relations between Boston and the sending city of Governador Valadares in Brazil produce a second kind of community. Governador Valadares is a city of approximately 270,000 located in Minas Gerais, one of Brazil's largest states. North Americans came to Valadares during World War II to get minerals for their war efforts. Migration to Boston is said to have begun when mining-company executives brought back young Valadarense women to work for them as domestic servants when they returned to the United States.

An estimated 20,000 Valadarenses have settled in eastern Massachusetts (Sales 1999; Braga Martes 1999). Though significant numbers reside in other, smaller cities in the area, such as Allston and Somerville, one center of the Valadarense community is Framingham, where an estimated 5,000 Brazilians are living. Most work in restaurants, hotels, or cleaning homes, though a good number have started their own small stores and home- or car-cleaning businesses. The Valadares economy depends strongly on *Valadólares* (Valadollars), or migrant remittances, so much so that when the Brazilian government devalued its currency in 1999, Valadares was said to be the only place in the country where the devaluation had a positive effect.

The urban to urban transnational social group linking Boston and Valadares differs from the Mirafloreño transnational village. The strong connection between Valadares and Boston is widely recognized throughout Brazil. That "there is not one house in Valadares that doesn't have family in the United States" is a constant refrain. When one walks through both poorer and upper-class neighborhoods in the city, it is easy to identify the many houses that have been built or renovated with U.S. money. There are strong formal and informal ties between Protestant and Catholic churches in Valadares and those in Massachusetts. Yet not all potential members have joined elites' efforts to create a transnational community. Leaders have laid down a foundation for such a group but, so far, it does not figure large in the everyday lives of ordinary people.

The mayor of Valadares, for example, visited Framingham and several other East Coast cities with large concentrations of Valadarenses in 1997. Just as he visits his constituents in the neighborhoods of Valadares, he said, so should he visit those living in the United States. The publisher of the daily newspaper, *O Diario Rio Doce,* added a two-page section with news and advertising from community members in Massachusetts. The Banco do Brasil, in conjunction with the Mayor's Office, created a Valadares-focused investment fund that pays higher interest rates to those who deposit their remittances. The Federacao das Industrias do Estado de Minas Gerais (FIEMG, or the Federation of Industries in Minas Gerais) mounted a technical-assistance program to help return migrants set up businesses in Brazil. FIEMG also organized a trade fair at the Massachusetts Institute of Technology to attract recent graduates to return to work in Brazil. There is, however, no specific Valadares–Framingham association equivalent to the hometown associations created by so many immigrant groups. The Brazilian Workers' Party is the only Brazilian political organization that has been at all active in the area.

Unlike Mirafloreños, then, who continue to place a higher priority on staying involved in Dominican affairs, those Valadarenses who participate in politics and community organizations are directing more of their energy toward U.S. concerns. They seem to be traveling a more traditional route toward social and political incorporation, though religious arenas facilitate dual memberships for those who choose them.

Thus far, this urban transnational community is constituted primarily by a single class. Though many Valdarenses perceive themselves as being one of many who keep their feet in two worlds, they have largely rejected elites' invitations to express this collectively.

Migration between Gujarat, India, and Massachusetts forms a third type of normative transnational community, one that initially arises from shared geographic ties but gradually matures into a social group based on migrants' common identities and values. In 1990 there were more than 815,500 Indian immigrants living in the United States. An estimated 30,000 Indian immigrants currently reside in Massachusetts, more than half of whom arrived in the 1980s. Many of those living around the city of Lowell are Patidars or Patels, who belong to a subcaste from the Baroda and Anand Districts. Like Indians throughout the United States, they are likely to be college educated (49%), well represented in professional (49%) and technical (47%) occupations, and home owners (63%) (U.S. Census 1992). But there is also a growing number, originally from rural towns and villages, who find blue-collar jobs when they arrive in the States.[12]

At first glance, Patidars might be expected to be weakly united with one another and to be only weakly connected to Gujarat. Though there is a critical mass of Gujaratis in Massachusetts, there are also large communities in New Jersey, California, and Texas. The Indian government and Indian political groups have played a minimal role in reinforcing these ties. But geographic dispersion and limited transnational institutional development are counteracted by the multiple overlapping identities community members share with one another. Larger, more inclusive identities, such as being from Gujarat or belonging to the same caste, are reinforced by membership in smaller endogamous marriage groups of residents from particular towns or religious organizations. The requirements of membership in many of these groups, the values that guide them, and the substantive content of their activities, isolate members from the host society and constantly remind them of their attachments to their home state. In the case of Gujaratis, then, the nature of their transnational normative community may mean strong, continuous ties to Gujarat combined with abbreviated participation in U.S. political and civic institutions.

Indigenous Mexicans in northern Mexico and southern California form a similar normative transnational group. The goal of the Frente Indígena Oaxaqueño Binacional, a coalition of Mixtec-Zapotec groups, is to promote and defend the human rights of indigenous migrants and improve living and working conditions for indigenous migrants on both sides of the border. These groups are said to do better at organizing transnationally than their Mixtec counterparts because their shared ethnicity enables them to mobilize unique cultural and social resources, traditional forms of self-government, and a strong political identity. Their common ethnic ties supersede attachments to particular localities. Since the transnational goals of these indigenous groups are not rooted in tightly circumscribed geographies, people, regardless of their location, are the object of these efforts (Rivera-Salgado 1999).

What other types of cross-border communities does transnational migration give rise to, and how do we explain variations within and among them? What is the relationship between these transnational social groups and broader, diasporic ones? How do migration-generated, place-based, or normative communities compare to the epistemic, professional, or issue-oriented transnational social groups and movements that are becoming increasingly common? What does this tell us about how ordinary people live their lives in this increasingly globalized world? There is much research to be done.

Appendix A

Figures and Tables

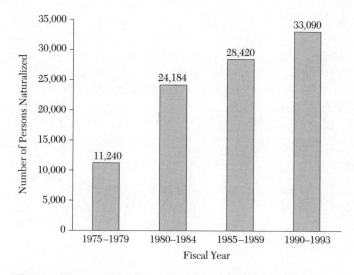

Figure 1. Foreign-Born Dominicans Naturalized by Fiscal Year, 1975–93.

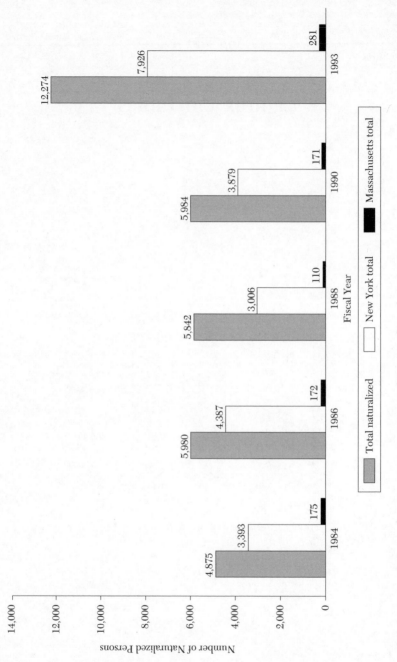

Figure 2. Naturalization of Foreign-Born Dominicans by State of Residence, 1984–93.

TABLE 1. Percentage of Sending-Country
Population Living in the U.S. in 1990

Sending Country	Percent of Sending-Country Population in the U.S. in 1990
Cuba	11.3
Dominican Republic	8.5
El Salvador	16.8
Guatemala	5.0
Jamaica	23.0
Mexico	9.4
Brazil	3.0
Trinidad and Tobago	16.0
Barbados	9.2

SOURCE: U.S. Census Bureau; 1990 U.S. Census.

TABLE 2. Percentage of Sending-Country
Population Living in the U.S. in 1920

Sending Country	Percent of Sending-Country Population in the U.S. in 1920
Germany	3.1
Ireland	23.6
Italy	4.0
Poland	3.8

SOURCE: Nugent 1992 and the World Almanac 1920.

TABLE 3. Selected Demographic Characteristics of Certain Racial-Ethnic Groups in the U.S., 1996–99

Racial-Ethnic Group	Persons (N)	Age				Sex		Marital Status of Adult Population				
		0–17 (%)	18–65 (%)	65+ (%)	Mean Age (%)	Male (%)	Female (%)	Married (%)	Widowed (%)	Divorced (%)	Separated (%)	Never Married (%)
White	193,073,611	23.8	62.1	14.1	37.2	49.0	51.0	46.3	5.6	7.6	1.4	39.1
African American	34,162,615	33.2	59.1	7.7	30.6	46.7	53.3	24.0	4.9	7.8	4.0	59.3
Native American	2,216,574	34.8	59.8	5.4	29.8	49.2	50.8	31.1	4.1	9.0	2.5	53.3
Asian	10,601,174	29.3	63.7	7.0	31.5	48.8	51.2	43.2	3.0	3.1	1.1	49.6
Dominican	921,883	38.1	56.0	5.9	27.7	45.5	54.5	25.4	2.7	6.5	4.7	60.7
Non-Dominican Hispanic	30,766,977	35.8	59.0	5.2	27.7	50.7	49.3	35.5	2.5	4.8	2.8	54.4

SOURCE: U.S. Census Bureau; Current Population Survey; March 1996–99; Public Use Data.
NOTE: Includes all persons 15 years and older. Population estimate from 1999 March CPS Public Use Data.

TABLE 4. Citizenship and Year of Entry into the U.S.
of Selected Racial-Ethnic Groups, 1996–99

Racial-Ethnic Group	Citizenship			Year of Entry				
	Native Born (%)	Foreign-Born Naturalized (%)	Foreign-Born Not a U.S. Citizen (%)	Before 1960 (%)	1960–1969 (%)	1970–1979 (%)	1980–1989 (%)	1990–1999 (%)
White	96.6	1.7	1.7	24.8	15.7	15.7	18.7	25.1
African American	94.8	1.9	3.3	2.6	9.0	20.5	36.5	31.4
Native American	97.3	1.3	1.4	10.5	14.2	28.1	25.3	21.9
Asian	39.5	25.8	34.7	2.2	5.2	19.4	37.7	35.5
Dominican	40.6	19.2	40.2	1.9	12.1	17.6	33.6	34.9
Non-Dominican Hispanic	62.8	8.4	28.8	6.4	10.3	18.5	33.7	31.1

SOURCE: U.S. Census Bureau; Current Population Survey; March 1996–99; Public Use Data.
NOTE: Includes all persons 15 years and older.

TABLE 5. Concentration by Region of Selected
Racial-Ethnic Groups in the U.S., 1996–99

Racial-Ethnic Group	*Region*						
	New England (%)	Mid-Atlantic (%)	North Central (%)	South Atlantic (%)	South Central (%)	Mountain (%)	Pacific (%)
White	6.0	14.3	27.5	17.0	15.7	6.4	13.1
African American	2.3	15.1	18.4	31.8	23.8	1.5	7.1
Native American	1.4	4.3	22.2	9.3	19.6	22.0	21.2
Asian	2.7	15.1	10.0	9.6	7.3	3.4	51.9
Dominican	5.0	81.0	1.6	10.0	1.3	0.2	0.9
Non-Dominican Hispanic	0.3	12.1	7.6	10.8	23.4	10.9	34.9

SOURCE: U.S. Census Bureau; Current Population Survey; March 1996–99; Public Use Data.

NOTE: Includes all persons 15 years and older.

TABLE 6. Home Ownership among Selected
Racial-Ethnic Groups in the U.S., 1996–99

Racial-Ethnic Group	Movement between Regions					Home Ownership	
	Never Moved (%)	Same State (%)	Different State within Same Region (%)	Different Region (%)	Abroad (%)	Owned or Acquiring Property (%)	Rented (%)
White	85.4	11.7	1.3	1.3	0.3	72.9	27.1
African American	80.7	16.6	1.5	1.0	0.2	46.5	53.5
Native American	78.4	17.3	3.0	1.2	0.1	55.5	44.5
Asian	80.0	14.5	1.7	1.2	2.6	52.9	47.1
Dominican	85.7	12.4	0.8	0.4	0.7	15.9	84.1
Non-Dominican Hispanic	78.6	18.1	0.9	1.0	1.4	45.7	54.3

SOURCE: U.S. Census Bureau; Current Population Survey; March 1996–99; Public Use Data.
NOTE: Includes all persons 15 years and older.

TABLE 7.   Education of Selected Racial-Ethnic Groups
in the U.S., 1996–99

Racial-Ethnic Group	*Educational Attainment of Adults*					
	0–8th grade (%)	9–11th grade (%)	High School Graduate (%)	Some College (%)	College Graduate (%)	Post Graduate (%)
White	5.2	12.7	32.3	26.3	16.0	7.5
African American	8.4	21.4	33.3	25.2	8.4	3.3
Native American	8.2	21.2	33.5	25.6	7.9	3.6
Asian	8.4	12.5	20.5	22.9	24.1	11.6
Dominican	25.4	26.7	21.5	20.0	5.0	1.4
Non-Dominican Hispanic	25.4	23.0	25.2	18.2	6.0	2.2

SOURCE: U.S. Census Bureau; Current Population Survey; March 1996–99; Public Use Data.
NOTE: Includes all persons 15 years and older.

TABLE 8. Employment of Selected Racial-Ethnic Groups in the U.S., 1996–99

Racial-Ethnic Groups[a]	Employment Status					Hours at Work		Earnings
	Employed (%)	Unemployed (%)	Retired[b] (%)	Disabled[b] (%)	Other[b] (%)	Full Time (%)	Part Time (%)	Self-Employed[c] (%)
White	63.4	2.6	17.6	3.5	12.9	45.6	15.6	11.4
African American	56.5	6.1	10.3	8.5	18.6	42.4	12.3	5.3
Native American	56.0	7.2	8.5	9.0	19.3	39.6	14.1	8.6
Asian	62.1	2.9	9.3	2.0	23.7	47.1	12.9	11.5
Dominican	48.9	5.7	7.8	6.3	31.3	36.8	10.3	5.7
Non-Dominican Hispanic	60.3	5.2	6.8	4.5	23.2	45.3	13.0	7.4
Total	62.1	3.3	15.3	4.2	15.1	40.3	13.5	10.3

SOURCE: U.S. Census Bureau; Current Population Survey; March 1996–99; Public Use Data.
[a] All persons 15 or older.
[b] Not in labor force.
[c] Non-farm self-employed household earnings from incorporated and unincorporated enterprises.

TABLE 9. Current Occupation of Selected Racial-Ethnic Groups in the U.S., 1996–99

Racial-Ethnic Group	Occupation					
	Managerial and Professional (%)	Technical, Sales, and Administrative Support (%)	Service (%)	Farm, Forestry, Fishing (%)	Precision, Production, Craft, Repair (%)	Operators, Fabricators, and Laborers (%)
White	31.8	30.2	12.1	2.4	11.0	12.5
African American	18.8	29.5	22.4	1.0	7.9	20.4
Native American	19.9	26.8	18.9	3.2	12.4	18.8
Asian	34.1	30.2	13.9	1.3	7.8	12.7
Dominican	11.6	25.7	27.8	—	4.7	30.2
Non-Dominican Hispanic	13.7	23.9	20.7	6.2	12.9	22.6
Total	28.5	29.4	14.2	2.6	10.8	14.5

SOURCE: U.S. Census Bureau; Current Population Survey; March 1996–99; Public Use Data.
NOTE: Includes all persons age 15 and older.

TABLE 10. Work Experience by Industry of Selected Racial-Ethnic Groups in the U.S., 1996–99

					Industry					
Racial-Ethnic Group[a]	Agriculture, Forestry (%)	Construction (%)	Manufacturing (%)	TCPU[b] (%)	Wholesale Trade (%)	Retail Trade (%)	FIRE[c] (%)	Services (%)	Government (%)	Never Worked (%)
White	2.2	4.8	10.5	4.6	2.7	12.3	4.6	24.9	3.4	30.0
African American	0.8	2.8	9.2	5.9	1.6	10.6	3.3	25.4	4.6	35.8
Native American	2.2	5.7	8.4	4.5	2.5	11.2	2.7	23.0	6.1	33.7
Asian	1.1	1.2	12.4	4.0	2.4	14.1	4.0	25.0	3.0	32.8
Dominican	—	2.1	10.8	4.3	1.8	14.8	2.9	17.4	1.1	44.8
Non-Dominican Hispanics	4.2	5.3	11.2	3.9	2.7	13.5	2.8	20.9	2.1	33.4

SOURCE: U.S. Census Bureau; Current Population Survey; March 1996–99; Public Use Data.
[a] All persons 15 or older.
[b] Transportation, communication, and public industries.
[c] Finance, insurance, and real estate.

TABLE 11. Household and Income for Selected
Racial-Ethnic Groups in the U.S., 1996–99

Racial-Ethnic Group[a]	Income[b]				Public Assistance
	Below Low Income (%)	100–149% Above Low Income (%)	150%+ Above Low Income (%)	Median Income[c] ($)	Households Receiving (%)
White	8.6	7.4	84.0	41,031	2.0
African American	27.3	13.8	58.9	25,000	10.3
Native American	25.8	12.4	61.8	27,841	9.0
Asian	13.9	7.2	78.9	45,833	3.7
Dominican	39.9	14.8	45.3	18,210	23.2
Non-Dominican Hispanic	27.4	17.1	55.5	26,982	8.4

SOURCE: U.S. Census Bureau; Current Population Survey; March 1996–99; Public Use Data.

NOTE: Includes all households excluding group quarters.

[a] All persons 15 or older.

[b] Income of persons below the federal poverty line calculated at $16,530 for a family of four in March 1998.

[c] Total household income in constant 1998 dollars.

TABLE 12. Racial Identification of Persons
of Selected Hispanic Origin in the U.S., 1996–99

	Race			
Racial-Ethnic Group	White (%)	Black (%)	American Indian (%)	Asian or Pacific Islander (%)
Dominican	83.3	15.3	0.3	1.1
Cuban	97.5	2.3	0	0.2
Mexican	97.9	0.6	1.1	0.4
Other Hispanic	90.8	7.0	0.8	1.4

SOURCE: U.S. Census Bureau; Current Population Survey; March 1996–99; Public Use Data.
NOTE: Includes all persons 15 and older.

TABLE 13. Citizenship of Selected Racial-Ethnic Groups in the U.S., 1996–99, by Race and Year of Entry into the Country

	Race and Citizenship[a]											
	White		African American		Native American		Asian		Dominican		Non-Dominican Hispanic	
Year of Entry	FBC[b] (%)	NC[c] (%)	FBC (%)	NC (%)	FBC (%)	NC (%)	FBC (%)	NC (%)	FBC (%)	NC (%)	FBC (%)	NC (%)
Before 1960	42.9	5.8	4.0	0.4	18.3	4.9	4.1	0.5	3.1	1.1	11.3	1.7
1960–1969	20.3	8.4	18.5	2.9	24.3	3.6	9.4	1.7	27.9	4.8	26.4	4.6
1970–1979	17.8	11.8	35.0	12.0	39.5	5.9	35.7	6.7	27.9	13.0	29.4	15.6
1980–1989	14.2	23.7	35.0	38.1	17.9	41.1	42.3	34.9	31.0	34.4	24.4	38.8
1990–1999	4.8	50.3	7.5	46.6	—	44.5	8.5	56.2	10.1	46.7	8.5	39.3

SOURCE: U.S. Census Bureau; Current Population Survey; March 1996–99; Public Use Data.
[a] All persons 15 and older.
[b] Foreign-born naturalized citizen.
[c] Foreign-born, not a U.S. citizen.

Appendix B

Methodology

This study grew out of earlier research I conducted on Latino entrepreneurship in Boston (Levitt 1994; Levitt 1995). Before I began that work, I thought that Puerto Ricans owned most of the Latino small businesses in the city. After only a few days of fieldwork, I soon realized that the majority of these businesses were owned by Dominicans and that many came from Baní and its environs. I also learned that many of those living around the Hyde Square area of Jamaica Plain came from Miraflores. I wanted to know how these strong transnational connections came to be and what their effects were.

Findings from this book are based on fieldwork carried out during an intensive three-year period (1992–95) and during subsequent, periodic visits to the Dominican Republic and Jamaica Plain. To find migrants specifically from Miraflores, I used a snowball sample, asking each respondent to recommend other people who might also be willing to participate in the study. While this approach allowed me to evaluate differences in transnational practices among Mirafloreños, it did not allow me to compare transnational connections among other *campos* (villages) around Baní.

I used six broad strategies to collect my data. First, I conducted 142 interviews with individuals working at the local, provincial, and national level of the religious, political, and community development organizations in the study. I interviewed churchgoers, religious movement group members, and individuals who led or participated in home-based religious practices in Boston and Miraflores. I spoke with parish priests who worked with the community in both countries. I interviewed members of the Dominican church hierarchy who had served or were serving in Baní or who helped formulate church policy toward migrants. In Boston I also interviewed religious and lay church officials responsible for making policy and implementing services to the Hispanic community.

I spoke with more than sixty members and leaders from the three principal political parties. These individuals worked in Miraflores, Baní, Santo Domingo, and Boston. Though the PLD and the PRSC were also active in

Boston when I carried out my fieldwork, I chose to focus on the PRD because it had the oldest, most well-developed organization in Boston and because it was the party that had most self-consciously articulated a policy toward migrants at the time. I interviewed many high-ranking officials who willingly shared their insights, opinions, memories, and written materials with me. Though I also conducted numerous interviews with PLD and PRSC representatives, I did not gain the same level of understanding about these other two groups.

I taped and transcribed approximately 75 percent of the interviews I conducted. More than 80 percent of the interviews were conducted in Spanish. I did not record my conversations when respondents refused my request to do so or in cases where I intuitively sensed that the respondent would be more comfortable if I took notes instead.

Second, I conducted a set of in-depth, semistructured interviews with twenty return migrant families in Miraflores and twenty migrant families living in Boston. These families ranged in size from three to eight members, for a total of 134 respondents. Our discussions focused on migration histories, migrants' work and social lives, their impressions of U.S. political and social life, their changing relationships with the organizations in the study, and, for returnees, their process of reintegration into the community. I asked each respondent the same set of open-ended questions but encouraged them to talk about other concerns if they were so inclined.

I initially planned to interview men and women and younger and older family members separately to hone in on differences in migration experiences among gender and age groups. This strategy proved untenable. In many cases, had I insisted on speaking with respondents alone, it would have made them more uncomfortable with what was already an unfamiliar interviewing process. My interviews were much more fruitful when I treated them as informal conversations with those who happened to be at home. I learned the most from these long afternoon talks or when, during the course of teaching me about farming or cooking, my companions spoke about their lives. About half the time, these conversations took place during two or more visits. They generally included the same three or four individuals, with other family members and neighbors periodically joining in.

My third research strategy entailed attending more than sixty-five meetings, rallies, and special events in Boston and the Dominican Republic. I participated in village, zone, municipal, and provincial political-party meetings. I took part in rallies and waited for the PRD caravans that went from Santo Domingo to Azúa. I also attended mass regularly and participated in the holiday celebrations taking place at the time of my visits. I met with men imprisoned in Baní and at the Massachusetts Correctional Facility in Billerica and observed trials at the Baní Municipal Court House. I worked with the Miraflores Development Committee (MDC) to organize and staff fund-raising dances, sell raffle tickets, secure permits to hold public events, and supervise building construction.

My fourth research strategy involved reviewing pertinent documents and bibliographic materials about each of the organizations in this study. These included financial records from the MDC; collections of pastoral letters published weekly in Dominican newspapers; PRD membership handbooks; analyses of the Dominican judicial and legal systems; and relevant newspaper and journal articles from Baní, Santo Domingo, and Boston. I also collected relevant survey and census data.

Finally, I carried out a survey in Miraflores of 184 households, or 806 individuals, in March and April of 1994. I designed the survey instrument, reviewed it with MDC members in Boston, and pilot-tested it among migrant community members.

The survey asked nonmigrant Mirafloreños two sets of questions concerning household members in Miraflores and migrant family members in Boston. The first set focused on nonmigrants' sociodemographic characteristics, economic status, and living conditions. The second set collected data on migrants' sociodemographic characteristics and, in addition, examined migration histories, employment in Boston, level of contact with Miraflores, and remittances.

In Miraflores I recruited and trained a group of community members to assist me in carrying out the survey. We divided up the 545 households in the village into six sectors or neighborhoods. A complete census of all the households in each sector was completed, from which a random sample of households to be surveyed was drawn. We interviewed one-third of all the households in Miraflores.

Two-interviewer teams were assigned to each sector. It took each pair approximately five days to cover the thirty-odd households in their area. Each evening I reviewed the completed questionnaires for consistency and completeness. When there were inconsistencies in the data, we returned to the household and re-interviewed the family. The data were cleaned, processed, and analyzed in Boston.

In households where there were return migrants, interviewers explained the purpose of the survey and asked these individuals if they would be willing to participate in a follow-up interview. If they agreed, I returned to speak with them at length. At the end of these sessions, I inquired if there were return migrants living in neighboring houses who might also want to participate in the study. I also asked each household if I could contact their migrant family members in Boston. These individuals, plus MDC members and the individuals they referred me to, constituted the current migrant group that I interviewed in Boston.

These data were supplemented with data from the U.S. Census and from the Current Population Survey (CPS). A multiyear sample was constructed from the four consecutive March Current Population Surveys carried out between 1996 and 1999. Once the Census Bureau includes a household in the CPS, it remains in the study sample for four months, is excluded for eight months, and is included again for four more months. Thus, households typically have two records in the March CPS. We included all persons listed on the latest record for each household in our multiyear sample to utilize the most current information and to minimize duplication. All persons were included from 1999, and approximately half of those persons interviewed were included from the 1996, 1997, and 1998 household surveys (see table A). Methodological changes in the CPS over the three-year period were relatively minor.

The CPS does not record information on respondents who self-identify as Dominican. Three survey variables were used to derive Dominican origin: Hispanic identity, place of birth, and parental birthplace. All persons born in the Dominican Republic and whose response to the question on Hispanic identity was coded as either "Central or South America" or "Other Spanish" were included as first-generation Dominicans. All persons with two Dominican parents and who identified themselves as any of the Latino categories (including Mexican, Cuban, Puerto Rican, Central and South American, or Other Spanish) were counted as second-generation Dominicans. All persons with one Dominican parent, but who identified as "Central or South America" or "Other Spanish," were also included in the second-generation category. All other persons who identified in any of the Latino categories were categorized as non-Dominican Hispanics (see table B).

TABLE A.   Respondents Included
in the Multiyear Sample 1996–99.

	Respondents Selected	Total Unweighted Respondents
March 1996 CPS	64,921	130,476
March 1997 CPS	65,460	131,844
March 1998 CPS	65,444	131,627
March 1999 CPS	132,324	132,324
Multiyear Sample	328,149	526,271

TABLE B.   Race and Ethnicity of Respondents
Selected for Multiyear Sample 1996–99.

Race and Ethnic Identification	Selected Multiyear Respondents Unweighted
White	229,540
African American	31,780
Native American	3,756
Asian and Pacific Islander	11,233
Hispanic Origin	51,840
Dominican	1,672
First generation	1,027
Second generation	645
Non-Dominican Hispanic	50,168
Total	328,149

Notes

Introduction

1. The Dominican Revolutionary Party, one of the principal opposition political parties during the course of this study. In May 2000, the PRD candidate, Hipólito Mejía, was elected president.

2. The Social Christian Reform Party, the party in power for much of the last three decades.

3. Triple-deckers are typical of the housing in certain neighborhoods in Boston. They are three-story houses, generally with one apartment on each floor.

4. Gans (1979) predicted increasing assimilation with each generation, while Hansen (1940) formulated the notion of "third generation return." In his view, the third generation would identify increasingly with its grandparents' ancestry, which in turn would result in an ethnic revival.

5. For a more in-depth discussion of various types of assimilation, see Gordon (1961), Portes and Zhou (1993), and Alba and Nee (1997).

6. For work on the changing nature of ethnic identity, see Gans (1979), Waters (1990 and 1999), and Nagel (1994).

7. Morawska (2001a) describes two general approaches to the study of transnationalism. The first, based primarily on scholarship from North America, focuses on the international migrants who engage in economic, sociocultural, and political activities that cross borders and "deterritorialize or extrapolate (rather than undermine) the nation-states interlinked by them" (2001a:2). The second broad perspective, coming primarily from European scholars, views transnationalism as a shift beyond or past the nation-state to political claims and memberships based on universal rights, suprastatal membership/entitlements (e.g., in the European Union), or panreligious solidarities (e.g., Muslims in Europe). A third approach comes from cultural studies. These writers emphasize the ways in which identity formation is linked to multiple sites, both real and imagined, such that new hybridized and creol-

ized identity forms emerge (Appadurai 1996; Gilroy 1993; Hall 1991). Identities shift and are negotiated in response to forces from above and below and therefore are never fixed or bounded (Bhabha 1990). These scholars also stress the underlying power dynamics that shape identity construction. They highlight the multiple axes of racial, ethnic, and national domination that are brought to bear in these processes and the circumstances under which resistance and challenge become possible (Gupta and Ferguson 1997; Ong 1993).

This study falls within the first approach to transnationalism, though all three are clearly related. As more individuals are guaranteed certain basic rights, regardless of their residence and citizenship, and as more suprastatal institutions are created to guarantee them, the foundation upon which migrants build their transnational social and political lives grows stronger. The Miraflores story is also clearly one about identity construction and the underlying power dynamics shaping this process.

8. Rouse (1992, 1989) called these spaces transnational circuits, while Guarnizo (1994) called them binational societies. Landolt et al. (1999) argue that the circulation of resources between home and host country does not necessarily give rise to a transnational social sphere of action.

9. Mahler (1998) distinguishes among those who travel regularly to earn their livelihoods; those who visit on a routine, though less frequent, basis; and those whose lives take place within a transnational social field though they have never migrated. Itzigsohn et al. (1999) call "transnationality in a narrow sense" those people involved in economic, political, social, and cultural practices requiring regular movement, a high level of institutionalization, and constant personal involvement. They use *transnationality* in the broad sense to refer to a series of material and symbolic practices in which people move only sporadically, with less institutionalization and personal involvement, but still use both countries as reference points.

10. Transnational villages are most like what others have described as translocalities (Smith 1998) or bilocal communities (Rouse 1991; Guarnizo 1994; Glick Schiller, Basch, and Szanton Blanc 1992).

11. These estimates vary. Some sources place the number of Dominicans living in the United States as high as 14 percent of the country's population (Georges 1990).

12. See, for example, Smith (1995), Goldring (1992), Landolt (1999), Popkin (1999), Mountz and Wright (1996), Duany (1994), and Hendricks (1974).

13. Phillips and Massey (1998), for example, have argued that in some regions in Mexico the social networks underpinning migration are so well entrenched that migration will continue regardless of U.S. laws designed to prevent it.

14. Though the expatriate vote was approved in 1997, the Junta Central Electoral, or the board that oversees Dominican elections, is still debating how it should be implemented.

15. See, for example, Kibria (1998), Levitt (1998b), Smith (1998b), and Glick Schiller and Fouron (1998).

16. For more in-depth discussions of the similarities and differences between older and more recent transnational practices, see Foner (2000), Glick Schiller (1999), and Morawska (2001a).

17. It is true that migrants today enjoy certain opportunities not available to either foreign or native-born minorities 100 years ago. Earlier in the twentieth century, even native-born minority men, including those with Ivy League degrees, were barred from certain jobs in universities, industry, and the public sector. Present-day migrants also benefit from government initiatives like affirmative action (Gold 2000).

18. While this is the case for unskilled workers, it may not be true for the new cadre of professional, highly trained workers who are coming to the United States. Indeed, these individuals enjoy more opportunities for assimilation because many of the elite schools, social clubs, and work settings that might have been closed to them in the past are now much more accessible (Gold 2000).

19. In fact, Spiro (1999) argues, we are in the midst of a profound crisis about what it means to be American.

20. Throughout this book, I use the term *migrant* to highlight Mirafloreños' strong connections to two places. As Glick Schiller (1999) argues, it is not possible to classify them as emigrants or immigrants because they do not exchange one position for another. •

Chapter One

1. People from the city of Baní are called Banilejos. Miraflores is situated near this city of approximately 100,000, located 65 kilometers from the Dominican capital.

2. In 1855, fighting between liberals and conservatives in Nicaragua weakened the state to such a degree that Walker installed himself as president until 1857.

3. *Cebollines* are small onions, much like thick scallions.

4. This book builds on what is now three generations of scholarship on U.S.-bound migration from the Dominican Republic. Some of these earlier researchers also studied individuals "between two islands." Grasmuck and Pessar's (1991) study compared emigration from a rural village, town, and urban area. They also conducted research among a nonprobability sample of Dominicans living and working in New York, though not directly connected to the places of origin they studied in the Dominican Republic. Georges (1990) described migration's social and economic transformation of a mountainous rural village. Though she also emphasized the influence of those in New York, she did not conduct fieldwork there. Hendricks (1974) studied in-

dividuals from the same village in New York and on the island as I do here. This book, then, owes its greatest debt to him, though it also pays tribute to these other scholars. In fact, it echoes many of Hendricks's findings. He also found that "in many senses the village is an economic and social appendage of New York and vice versa" (1974, 84).

This book, and the most current wave of research by scholars such as Itzigsohn et al. (1999), Graham (1997), and Guarnizo (1992), describes migration within a mature and highly institutionalized transnational social field that was in formation when Hendricks began his work nearly thirty years ago. For many, transnational practices have become an accepted way of life rather than a temporary strategy. This book explores the consequences of long-term, if not permanent, transnational lifestyles that are carried out in a context that depends upon them and facilitates their implementation. It also differs from these other works because it describes transnational migration between the Dominican Republic and Boston, a destination with social and economic characteristics quite different from those of New York.

5. See Gonzáles (1970), Peña and Parache (1971), Hendricks (1974), Garrison and Weiss (1979), Kayal (1978), Castro (1985), Bray (1987), and Georges (1990).

6. See Pérez (1981), Ugalde and Langham (1980), Gurak and Kritz (1982), Guarnizo (1992), and Grasmuck and Pessar (1991). For a broad overview, see Báez and Ramírez (1986), and Del Castillo and Mitchell (1987).

7. This includes those working as motorcycle drivers.

8. One hectare is equivalent to 2.47 acres.

9. Eleven percent of current migrants left before 1980, 21 percent left between 1980 and 1984, and 47 percent migrated between 1985 and 1990. An additional 21 percent departed beween 1990 and mid-1994.

10. In that same year, 20 percent of central-city Boston residents were foreign-born—the tenth highest proportion among the top seventy-seven central cities in the country. Haiti, China, and Ireland now send the largest numbers of migrants to the city (Bluestone and Stevenson 1998).

11. The 1992 Greater Boston Social Survey, carried out by the John W. McCormack Institute of Public Affairs at the University of Massachusetts in Boston, is based on 1,820 household interviews carried out in 154 towns and cities in the greater Boston metropolitan area. It found that 45 percent of the white respondents felt that current immigration rates diminished their political influence; 52 percent also felt they had fewer economic opportunities. All the Hispanic respondents claimed to have experienced discrimination, including 50 percent who said they faced limited opportunities in the labor force.

12. Boston is located in Suffolk County.

13. Many of these characteristics are corroborated by results from a household survey completed in Miraflores in 1994. The average household

had five members. There were slightly more females (55 percent) than males. The community was generally quite young. More than one-third were under twenty years of age; 55 percent were between the ages of 20 and 59. More than one-half (52 percent) of those 16 years or older were either married or living in union. Nearly 80 percent of the respondents had not completed primary school, though 28 percent were currently attending. The profile of return migrants differed somewhat from nonmigrants. Returnees were more likely to be married or living in union, older, and slightly better educated than their nonmigrant counterparts. They were also somewhat more likely to be male (56 percent) than female (44 percent).

Chapter Two

1. See Portes and Manning (1986), Light and Bonacich (1988), and Waldinger et al. (1990) for work on ethnicity and economic incorporation. See Kasinitz (1992) and Jones-Correa (1998a) for the role of ethnicity in politics.

2. Westney (1987), for example, described the western-style police and postal systems that Japanese leaders self-consciously selected and "imposed" on their public in the late nineteenth century. She argues that variations in their acceptance were due to relative differences in the authority of the officials that disseminated them, the strength of competing indigenous cognitive models, and the availability of supportive organizations in the immediate environment.

3. Portes and Sensenbrenner define social capital as "those expectations for action within a collectivity that affect the economic goals and goal-seeking behavior of its members, even if these expectations are not oriented toward the economic sphere" (1993, 1323). Value introjection, reciprocity transactions, bounded solidarity, and enforceable trust are four sources of social capital through which "individual maximizing behavior is constrained" in a fairly predictable way so that these expectations can be utilized as a resource. Coleman (1990), Bourdieu et al. (1991), and Putnam (1993), among others, offer their own slightly different versions of this concept. What is important here, as Portes and Landolt (1996) correctly point out, is that social capital can be used with positive *and* negative consequences.

4. See Hughes (1975), Hall (1989), and Domínguez (1997).

Chapter Three

1. The impact of migration on the sending community has long been an interest of migration scholars. Neoclassical migration theorists claim that migration benefits sending communities. Remittances provide investment capital, support the balance of payments, and stimulate a demand for locally produced goods and services (Friedlander 1965; Griffin 1976; Hume 1973). A

new version of this approach, called the New Economics of Migration, still views migration as positive because it enables households to diversify risk by engaging in a variety of income-generating strategies (Stark 1991). Historical structuralists, in contrast, are more pessimistic about the relationship between migration and development (Rhoades 1978; Weist 1979; Portes and Walton 1981; Portes and Borocz 1989; Sassen-Koob 1978; Cornelius 1976). Since migrant workers earn low wages, they are too busy meeting their own consumption needs to be able to send remittances. When migrants do send remittances, they are often spent conspicuously rather than productively.

2. See, for example, Grasmuck and Pessar (1991), Georges (1990), Mahler (1996), (Hondagneu-Sotelo 1994), and Kibria (1993).

3. For example, Hondagneu-Sotelo and Avila (1997) described transnational mothering. Guarnizo (1997) told of migrants who form multilocal, binational families in which parents and children were distributed in households across national borders. Wolf (1997) discusses the costs of emotional transnationalism among Filipino immigrant families. Like Mirafloreños, Ong (1993); Wiltshire (1992); Basch, Glick Schiller, and Szanton Blanc (1994); and Rouse (1991) found that those in the United States were able to participate in family events and decisions from a distance.

4. Dominicans often use "Santo Domingo" to refer to their entire country.

5. Kibria (1993), Zhou and Blankston (1998), Espiritu and Wolf (1999), and López and Stanton-Salazar (1999) have also described how children take on this role of cultural broker. Waters (1999) found that the West Indian parents she studied also changed their disciplinary styles for fear of U.S. government reprisals.

6. Children are required to attend school through the eighth grade in Miraflores.

7. See Grasmuck and Pessar (1991) and Hondagneu-Sotelo (1994) for a discussion of the effects of status declines in the United States. For an account of how migrants use their enhanced status in their sending community to compensate for status declines in the United States, see Goldring (1998).

8. Prior work on Dominican migration indicated that the intention to return often turned into a proclivity toward circular mobility (Grasmuck and Pessar 1991; Georges 1990; Ugalde and Langham 1980; González 1970; Hendricks 1974). Returnees were often unsuccessful economically or felt culturally ill-at-ease, so they migrated once again. Some developed economic strategies that depended on their permanent circulation between the United States and the island.

9. Grasmuck and Pessar (1991) also found that the returnees they studied could not sustain their middle-class lifestyles.

Chapter Four

1. Prior to the 1970s, much migration research left women out. Many of the first studies seeking to rectify this imbalance asked either/or questions. That is, they tried to determine if migration either enhanced women's autonomy or made them more dependent upon men (Pessar 1999). Subsequent studies concluded that migration did not change the status of women equally in the workplace, community, and home. Women might enjoy gains in one sphere while experiencing contradictions and strains in another (Morokvasic 1984). There is now broad agreement that immigrant women achieve some limited, albeit uneven, benefits from migration and settlement. They generally achieve greater independence, despite inequalities in the labor market and workplace, at the same time that men tend to lose ground. To protect these advances, women are more likely to want to remain in the United States than men (Grasmuck and Pessar 1991; Chávez 1992; Hondagneu-Sotelo 1994; Hagan 1994; Guarnizo 1994; Goldring 1998). Despite this, there is little evidence that migration profoundly changes gender ideologies or that power within households is radically redistributed.

2. South Boston is a neighborhood in the city with predominantly white, Irish-American residents.

3. Ewick and Silbey (1998) describe legal consciousness as the reciprocal process by which meanings given by individuals to their world become patterned, stabilized, and objectified. It is participation in the construction of legality.

4. In 1993, the president of the Dominican Bar Association, commenting on what a terrible year it had been for the judiciary, cited police violations of court decisions to release prisoners, corruption scandals involving judges of higher and lower courts, and underfunding of the judicial system as just some of the problems plaguing the judicial system; of the 109.8 million pesos assigned to the judiciary in 1993, only 60 percent was actually allocated (Espinal 1996).

5. The term *caso* is used when someone purposefully orchestrates an accident at work and is able to collect disability insurance.

6. *Sweep* refers to the indiscriminate rounding-up of people who happen to be at the scene of a crime. These are allegedly quite common.

Chapter Five

1. I am grateful to Amelia Brown for her research on the PLD.

2. See Hartlyn (1993); Espinal (1994, 1995, 1998); and Brea Franco (1985).

3. *Neopatrimonialism* refers to "a type of political regime with important within-type variations, which can crosscut authoritarianism and democracy (while constraining the latter)" (Hartlyn 1998, 6). One of its key characteris-

tics is the centralization of power in the hands of a leader who tries to limit his followers' autonomy by binding them to him through ties of loyalty and obligation. As a result, public and private interests and goals are blurred and democratic institutions are weak. According to Hartlyn (1998, 6), "As an explanatory factor, it helps to reveal why transitions to democracy from certain regimes are more difficult than from others, and it highlights how some kinds of political patterns can continue, and even be reinforced over time, in the absence of particular kinds of sustained social change or of concerted effort by political leaders from above."

4. Interestingly, Bates (1999) claims that eighteenth- and nineteenth-century campaigns in the United States shared similar characteristics. Campaigns and elections were also festive occasions complete with alcohol and entertainment.

5. Juan Bosch later broke with the PRD and formed a new party, the PLD.

6. Other parties of the Dominican radical Left, including the Partido Comunista Dominicano (the Dominican Communist Party), the Movimiento Popular Dominicano (Dominican Popular Movement), and the Partido de los Trabajadores Dominicanos (Dominican Workers' Party), also organized in New York (Sagás 1999).

7. In fact, Dr. Peña Gómez, the party's president, was SIP vice president for Latin America at the time of this study.

8. Graham (1997) estimated that monies raised in the United States make up 10 to 15 percent of overall party fund-raising for the PRD and the PLD.

9. The PLD requires all full members to undergo a program of study before officially joining the party.

10. The agreement also included reforms like the introduction of runoff elections and the separation of presidential elections from congressional and municipal contests (Sagás 1999).

11. Two state representatives are from Puerto Rico and the third is Cuban.

12. Ruth Messinger also traveled to the Dominican Republic during her campaign against incumbent Mayor Rudolph Guiliani in 1997. Though Guiliani has not visited Santo Domingo to campaign, he did travel to the island to supervise relief efforts supported by New York City after a severe hurricane in 1998.

13. Dominican organizations in New York include La Unión Dominicana, La Organización de Mujeres Dominicanas, the Dominican Association of Professionals and Businessmen, La Asociación de Dominicanos Progresivos, and the Immigrant Coalition of Washington Heights (Weyland 1999).

14. Until dual citizenship became an option in 1996, naturalization meant giving up their Dominican citizenship, something that many Mirafloreños were unwilling to do. Gilbertson and Singer (1999) demonstrate that the motives behind naturalization are not always what they might seem. Naturalization is a dynamic social process conditioned by national, community, and

family characteristics as well as individual ones. Some of the individuals in their study of a Dominican family in New York, for example, naturalized to gain greater control over how much extended family members depended upon them. In his study of Latinos in Queens, New York, Jones-Correa (1998a) explained low participation rates as a function of the high cost of activism. Established political actors did not want to expend their limited resources welcoming newcomers who were only partial participants. Latinos resisted naturalization because it entailed definitively cutting their ties to the place they hoped to return to.

Finally, a survey conducted by the *Washington Post,* Harvard University, and the Henry J. Kaiser Foundation found that the U.S. government's cumbersome naturalization process was responsible for low citizenship rates (Pan 2000).

Chapter Six

1. The archbishop of Santo Domingo at the time of this study.

2. There are isolated exceptions in which religious NGOs organized and improved urban neighborhoods. In general, however, Dominicans have not embraced liberation theology with the same fervor as some of their Latin American neighbors. The clergy interviewed for this study claimed that there were few Comunidades Eclesiales de Base (Christian base communities) in the Dominican Republic and that they had little impact on broad social issues. In other parts of the region, such as Brazil and Central America, these communities of fellowship and prayer have played a major role in promoting social reform.

3. Here, I define politics broadly to include not only electoral politics but other kinds of collective action that promote or defend immigrant or sending-country interests, including participation in political demonstrations, unionization efforts, involvement in community-based organizations or coalitions, and involvement in community affairs.

4. The conference includes clergy from the United States, Canada, and Latin America.

5. Promising to abstain from something or engage in a particular behavior if something one requests in prayer comes true.

6. The greeting of peace—a part of the mass when parishioners greet one another.

Chapter Seven

1. See, for example, Nagengast and Kearney (1990), Berry (1985), Arizpe (1982), and Goldring (1998).

2. Mexican migrants' increasingly strong opposition to the Cardenas

government, and the Mexican government's need for migrants to support NAFTA, prompted the Mexican state to reach out to its expatriates. A series of programs was put into place to encourage stronger ties. The most ambitious was the Program for Mexican Communities Abroad, which extended commercial, health, cultural, and social welfare programs and services beyond Mexico's borders for the first time. Formal agreements have been signed between many of the hometown clubs that migrants have formed and the Mexican federal and/or local governments to undertake community projects. Though these provide important services, they also limit migrants' autonomy because they are carried out under the auspices of the Mexican government (Guarnizo 1998; Smith 1998; Goldring 1999).

Conclusion

1. Many names have been proposed for this dual position with respect to two systems of governance, including multinational citizenship (Aron 1974) and multicultural citizenship (Kymlicka 1995). Laguerre (1998, 13) proposes the notion of diasporic citizenship, which "includes both the national and transnational outlook, attachment, and commitment." It presupposes some level of integration in the country of residence and some kind of attachment with the homeland. The intensity of these relationships may vary over time from one individual to another and from one generation to the next.

2. Some Indian scholars, for example, argue that elite nonresident Indians (NRIs), the term used by the Indian government to refer to its citizens abroad, should not be allowed to make decisions for those who continue to live in India (Papastergiadis 1998). In the Dominican case, nonmigrants have feared that Dominicanyork would gain too much influence over national affairs if they were allowed to vote.

3. Allowing dual citizenship eliminates the barriers to naturalization created by forcing migrants to choose between two polities (Gilbertson and Singer 1999). But as Jones-Correa (1998a) correctly points out, officially sanctioning dual citizenship does not reduce all the costs associated with entering the political sphere. Once Latin American immigrants naturalize, they tend to register to vote at high rates, though this has not always translated into actual participation. The NALEO National Latino Immigrant Survey found a significant disparity between the numbers who were registered to vote and those who actually voted (Pachón and DeSipio 1994). For additional, in-depth discussions of the changing nature of citizenship, see Pinkus (1998) and Schuck (1998).

4. Certainly we cannot hold migrants to higher standards of participation than we hold ourselves. Voter apathy in the United States is strikingly high. In 1996 barely 50 percent of all registered voters voted for president (Bates 1999). Nationwide, 60 percent of people summoned to jury duty fail to serve.

There is also considerable debate about the decline of civic engagement. Putnam (2000), for example, argues that American social capital and volunteerism are dangerously declining, while Skocpol (1999) argues that we continue to participate at the same rate but in different ways. Schudson (1998) observes that belonging to an organization reveals little about one's actual level of participation in it.

5. In January 1999 the Clinton administration proposed a $1.3 billion, five-year program to close the remaining gaps in medical and food-stamp benefits for legal immigrants created by welfare system reforms in 1996 (Janofsky 1999).

6. As part of school reform legislation passed in Illinois, each school must form a local school council. Noncitizens are eligible to participate in these groups, which play a role in hiring administrators and managing school budgets.

7. Jones-Correa (1998a) reports that fewer than four thousand of the more than one-hundred thousand Colombians in the New York City metropolitan area turned out to vote in the three presidential elections prior to 1998. According to Lucio Pires De Amorim, the director general for Legal and Assistance-Related Consular Affairs for Brazilians Living Abroad, only 50,000 Brazilian migrants registered to vote in the 1998 election, and of these only 25,000 actually cast their ballots.

8. The Brazilian government ultimately decided against this, saying it was too expensive.

9. I am grateful to Robert Smith for our discussions about these points.

10. Personal communication, Susan Martin.

11. The ruling in The Hague stemmed from a complaint from Paraguay that the accused had not been granted consular access in the United States as stipulated under the 1963 Vienna Convention. The World Court, the U.N.'s highest judicial body, does not have enforcement powers and relies on voluntary compliance (*London Daily Telegraph* 1998).

12. There is a long history of migration from Gujarat. In the early 1900s, Patidars, a subcaste from the region, went to East Africa to become traders. They maintained high levels of contact with India. Some respondents spent long periods in Uganda or Tanzania, followed by extended periods in India, before migrating once again to Africa. Others remained in Gujarat while their fathers worked in Africa and returned each year. The Gujarati immigrant community in Africa prospered while remaining socially distinct. When independence movements spread throughout Africa in the 1960s, African nationals associated Indians with the status quo. Many returned to India after they were forcibly expelled or their property was expropriated; others migrated to the United Kingdom and the United States.

References

Alarcón, Rafael. 1989. *La Nortenización: The Impact of Migration to the United States in a Mexican Town.* La Jolla: Center for U.S.-Mexican Studies, University of California, San Diego. Photocopied.

Alba, Richard, and Victor Nee. 1997. Assimilation Theory for a New Era. *International Migration Review* 31: 826–75.

Aleinikoff, Alexander, and Douglas Klusmeyer. 1998. Plural Nationality: Facing the Future in a Migratory World. Paper presented at the Conference on Demography and Security, 11–12 December, MIT Center for International Studies, Cambridge, Massachusetts.

Alexander, Victoria. 1998. Environmental Constraints and Organizational Strategies: Complexity, Conflict, and Coping in the Nonprofit Sector. In *Private Action and the Public Good,* edited by Walter Powell and Elisabeth Clemens. New Haven: Yale University Press.

Amiraux, Valérie. 1998. Turkish Muslims in Germany: Transnationalising Social Space. Paper presented at European Forum, May, European University Institute, Florence, Italy.

Appadurai, Arjun. 1990. Disjuncture and Difference in the Global Cultural Economy. In *Global Culture: Nationalism, Globalization and Modernity,* edited by Mike Featherstone. London and Newbury Parks: Sage Publications.

———. 1996. *Modernity at Large: Dimensions of Globalization.* Minneapolis: University of Minnesota Press.

Arizpe, Lourdes. 1982. Relay Migration and the Survival of the Peasant Household. In *Towards a Political Economy of Urbanization in Third World Countries,* edited by Helen Safa. Delhi: Oxford University Press.

Aron, Raymond. 1974. Is Multinational Citizenship Possible? *Social Research* 41 (4): 638–56.

Bacon, Jean. 1998. Transnationalism East and West: Transnational Tendencies Among Second-Generation Asian Indians in the U.S. and Their Contemporaries in India. Paper presented at the Transnationalism and the

Second Generation Conference, Weatherhead Center for International Affairs, Harvard University, Cambridge, Massachusetts.

Báez Evertsz, Frank, and Frank d'Oleo Ramírez. 1986. *La emigración de Dominicanos a Estados Unidos: Determinantes socio-económicos y consecuencias.* Santo Domingo: Fundación Friedrich Ebert.

Basch, Linda. 1992. The Politics of Caribbeanization: Vincentians and Grenadians in New York. In *Caribbean Life in New York City: Sociocultural Dimensions,* edited by Constance Sutton and Elsa Chaney. New York: Center for Migration Studies.

Basch, Linda, Nina Glick Schiller, and Cristina Szanton Blanc, eds. 1994. *Nations Unbound: Transnational Projects, Postcolonial Predicaments, and Deterritorialized Nation-States.* Amsterdam: Gordon and Breach Science Publishers.

Bates, Stephen. 1999. Reinvigorating Citizenship. *Society* 36 (3): 80–86.

Baubock, Rainer. 1994. *Transnational Citizenship: Membership and Rights in International Migration.* Brookfield, Vermont: Edward Elgar.

Berry, Sara. 1985. *Fathers Work for Their Sons.* Berkeley and Los Angeles: University of California Press.

Betances, Emilio. 1995. *State and Society in the Dominican Republic.* Boulder, Colorado, and Oxford: Westview Press.

Betances, Emilio, and Hobart Spalding. 1996. *The Dominican Republic Today: Realities and Perspectives.* New York: Graduate School and University Center of the City University of New York.

Bhabha, H.K. 1990. Introduction: Narrating the Nation. In *Nation and Narration,* edited by H.K. Bhabha. New York: Routledge.

Black, Jan Knippers. 1986. *The Dominican Republic: Politics and Development in an Unsovereign State.* Boston: Allen and Unwin.

Bluestone, Barry, and Mary Huff Stevenson. 1998. *Greater Boston in Transition: Race and Ethnicity in a Renaissance Region.* New York: The Russell Sage Foundation.

Boin, J., and J. Serullé. 1980. *La explotación capitalista en la República Dominicana.* Santo Domingo: Ediciones Gramil.

Bosch, Juan. 1983. *Composición social dominicana: historia e interpretación.* Santo Domingo: Alga y Omega.

Bourdieu, Pierre, Channa Newman, and Loic J.D. Wacquant. 1991. The Peculiar History of Scientific Reason. *Sociological Forum* 6: 3–26.

Boyd, Monica. 1989. Family and Personal Networks in International Migration: Recent Developments and New Agendas. *International Migration Review* 23: 638–70.

Braga Martes, Ana Cristina. 1999. *Brasileiros Nos Estados Unidos.* São Paulo, Brazil: Editora Paz e Terra, SA.

Bray, David. 1987. The Dominican Exodus: Origins, Problems, and Solutions. In *Caribbean Exodus,* edited by Barry Levine. New York: Praeger.

Brea Franco, Julio. 1985. *Cultural política dominicana*. Santo Domingo: Instituto Tecnológico de Santo Domingo.

Calder, B. 1984. *The Impact of Intervention: The Dominican Republic during the U.S. Occupation of 1916–1924*. Austin: University of Texas Press.

Campbell, John. 1995. Mechanisms of Evolutionary Change in Economic Governance: Interaction, Interpretation and Bricolage. Paper presented at the Conference on Evolutionary Economics and Path Dependence, May, Uppsala University, Sweden.

Casanova, José. 1994. *Public Religions in the Modern World*. Chicago: University of Chicago Press.

Cassá, Roberto. 1979. *Modos de producción, clases sociales y luchas políticas, siglo XX*. Santo Domingo: Alfa y Omega.

———. 1982. *Capitalismo y Dictadura*. Santo Domingo: Universidad Autonoma de Santo Domingo.

Cassá, Roberto, D. Ortiz, R. González, and G. Rodríguez. 1986. *Actualidad y perspectivas de la cuestión nacional en la República Dominicana*. Santo Domingo: Editora Buho.

Castells, Manuel. 1989. *The Informational City: Information Technology, Economic Restructuring, and the Urban-Regional Process*. London: Blackwell.

Castro, Max. 1985. Dominican Journey: Patterns, Context, and Consequences of Migration from the Dominican Republic to the United States. Ph.D. diss., University of North Carolina at Chapel Hill.

Chávez, Leo. 1992. *Shadowed Lives: Undocumented Immigrants in American Society*. Orlando, Florida: Harcourt Brace Jovanovich.

Cinel, Dino. 1991. *The National Integration of Italian Return Migration, 1870–1929*. Cambridge: Cambridge University Press.

Clausner, Marlin. 1973. *Rural Santo Domingo: Settled, Unsettled, and Resettled*. Philadelphia: Temple University Press.

Cohen, Robin. 1997. *Global Diasporas: An Introduction*. Seattle: University of Washington Press.

———. 1996. Diasporas and the Nation-State: From Victims to Challengers. *International Affairs* (72): 507–20.

Coleman, James. 1990. *Foundations of Social Theory*. Cambridge and London: The Belknap Press of Harvard University Press.

Coleman, James, Herbert Menzel, and Elihu Katz. 1973. Social Process in Physicians' Adoption of a New Drug. In *Social Change: Sources, Patterns, and Consequences*, edited by Amitai Etzioni and Eva Etzioni-Halevy. New York: Basic Books.

Cornelius, Wayne. 1976. Outmigration from Rural Mexican Communities. In *The Dynamics of Migration*. Occasional Monograph Series 2 (5). Interdisciplinary Communities Program, Washington, D.C.: Smithsonian Institute Press.

Debiaggi, Sylvia Dantas. 1992. From Minas to Mass.: A Qualitative Study of Five Brazilian Families in Boston. Master's thesis, Boston University.

De La Garza, Rodolfo, et al. 1998. *Family Ties and Ethnic Lobbies: Latino Relations with Latin America.* Claremont, California: Tomas Rivera Policy Institute.

Del Castillo, Jorge, and C. Mitchell, eds. 1987. *La Imigración Dominicana en Los Estados Unidos.* Santo Domingo: Editorial CENAPEC.

Del Castillo, Jorge, and Walter Cordero. 1980. *La Economía Dominicana durante el primer cuarto del siglo XX.* Santo Domingo: Fundación García Arévelo, Inc.

Derby, Lauren. 1994. Between State and Nation: The Dominican Republic and the U.S. World Order. Paper presented at the Latin American Studies Association, March, Atlanta, Georgia.

DiMaggio, Paul. 1988. Interest and Agency in Institutional Theory. In *Institutional Patterns and Organizations,* edited by L. Zucker. Cambridge: Ballinger Publishing Company.

DiMaggio, Paul J., and Walter W. Powell. 1983. The Iron Cage Revisited: Institutional Isomorphism and Collective Rationality in Organizational Fields. *American Sociological Review* (48): 147–60.

Domínguez, Jorge. 1997. Technopols: Ideas and Leaders in Freeing Politics and Markets in Latin America in the 1990s. In *Technopols: Freeing Politics and Markets in Latin America in the 1990s,* edited by Jorge Domínguez. University Park: Pennsylvania State University Press.

Dominican Consul. *Presencia Dominicana en Nueva Inglaterra.* Publication No. 3 of the General Consul of the Dominican Republic. Boston, Massachusetts. August 1998.

Dominican Party Ends Vote Alliance. 1996. *Boston Globe,* 13 July, final edition.

Dominican Republic. *The World Factbook 1999.* Available from http://www.cia.gov/cia/publications/factbook/dr.html.

Dorsey, Rick. 1994. Twenty-Five Are Picked to Help Hispanics Exhibit Clout in Political Affairs. *Boston Globe,* 30 August, final edition.

Duany, Jorge. 1994. Quisqueya on the Hudson: The Transnational Identity of Dominicans in Washington Heights. Dominican Research Monographs: City University of New York Dominican Studies Institute.

England, Sarah. 1999. Negotiating Race and Place in the Garifuna Diaspora: Identity Formation and Transnational Grassroots Politics in New York City and Honduras. *Identities* 6 (1): 5–53.

Escala-Rabadan, Luis. 1999. Political Empowerment, Immigrant Communities and Their Organization: Mexican Hometown Associations in Los Angeles, California. Paper presented to the University of California Comparative Immigration and Integration Program Research Workshop, 19 February, San Diego, California.

Espinal, Rosario. 1986. An Interpretation of the Democratic Transition in the Dominican Republic. In *The Central American Impasse,* edited by Giuseppe Di Palma and Laurence Whitehead. New York: St. Martin's Press.

———. 1987. Labor, Politics, and Industrialization in the Dominican Republic. *Economic and Industrial Democracy* (8): 183–212.

———. 1994. *Autoritarismo y democracia en la politica Dominica.* Santo Domingo: Editorial Argumentos.

———. 1995. Economic Restructuring, Social Protest, and Democratization in the Dominican Republic. *Latin American Perspectives* 86 (22): 63–105.

———. 1996. "The Dominican Republic: An Ambiguous Democracy." In *Constructing Democratic Governance,* edited by Jorge I. Domínguez and Abraham Lowenthal. Baltimore: Johns Hopkins University Press.

———. 1998. Los modelos de partido en la República Dominicana. *Revista de Reforma.* Julio-Septiembre: 53–77.

Espiritu, Yen, and Diane Wolf. 1999. The Paradox of Assimilation: Children of Filipino Immigrants in San Diego. Paper presented to the University of California Comparative Immigration and Integration Program Research Workshop, 19 February, San Diego, California.

Evans, M.D.R. 1988. Choosing to Be a Citizen: The Time-Path of Citizenship in Australia. *International Migration Review* 22 (2): 243–64.

Ewick, Patricia, and Susan S. Silbey. 1998. *The Commonplace of Law.* Chicago: University of Chicago Press.

Faist, Thomas. 1997. Cumulative Causation in Transnational Social Spaces: The German-Turkish Example. Paper presented at the International Sociological Association, 5–7 June, New York.

Falcón, Luis M. 1993. Economic Growth and Increased Inequality: Hispanics in the Boston Labor Market. In *Latino Poverty and Economic Development in Massachusetts,* edited by Edwin Meléndez and Miren Uriarte. Boston: University of Massachusetts.

Favell, Adrian. 1998. European Citizenship and Post-national Incorporation in Europe: Beyond Post-colonial Integration? Paper presented at the European Forum, May, European University Institute, Florence, Italy.

Fermi, Laura. 1968. *Illustrious Immigrants: The Intellectual Migration from Europe 1930–41.* Chicago: University of Chicago Press.

Fitzpatrick, Joseph. 1987. *Puerto Rican Americans: The Meaning of Migration to the Mainland.* Englewood Cliffs, New Jersey: Prentice Hall.

Foner, Nancy. 1987. West Indians in New York City and London: A Comparative Analysis. In *Caribbean Life in New York City,* edited by Constance Sutton and Elsa Chaney. New York: Center for Migration Studies.

———. 1997. The Immigrant Family: Cultural Legacies and Cultural Changes. *International Migration Review* 31 (4): 961–74.

———. 2000. *From Ellis Island to JFK: New York's Two Great Waves of Immigration.* New Haven: Yale University Press.

Franjul, Marcos Peña. 1991. *Los Franjul: una familia del banilejismo.* Santo Domingo: Instituto Dominicano de Ambiente y Sociedad, S.A.

Fraser, Nancy. 1991. Rethinking the Public Sphere: A Contribution to the Critique of Actually Existing Democracy. In *Habermas and the Public Sphere,* edited by Craig Calhoun. Cambridge, Massachusetts: MIT Press.

Friedland, Roger, and Robert R. Alford. 1991. Bringing Society Back In: Symbols, Practices, and Institutional Constraints. In *The New Institutionalism in Organizational Analysis,* edited by Walter Powell and Paul DiMaggio. Chicago: University of Chicago Press.

Friedlander, Stanley. 1965. *Labor, Migration, and Economic Growth: A Case Study of Puerto Rico.* Cambridge, Mass.: MIT Press.

Gans, Herbert. 1979. Symbolic Ethnicity: The Future of Ethnic Groups and Cultures in America. *Ethnic and Racial Studies* 2: 1 (January): 1–20.

Garrison, Vivian, and Carol I. Weiss. 1979. Dominican Family Networks and U.S. Immigration Policy: A Case Study. *International Migration Review* (12): 264–83.

Georges, Eugenia. 1988a. Dominican Self-Help Associations in Washington Heights: Integration of a New Immigrant Population in a Multiethnic Neighborhood. Working Paper No.1, New Directions for Latino Public Policy Research, New York.

———. 1988b. Political Participation of a New Hispanic Population: Dominicans in New York City. Paper presented to the Conference on Dominican Migration to the United States, Dominican Republic.

———. 1990. *The Making of a Transnational Community.* New York: Columbia University Press.

Gerstle, Gary. 1997. Liberty, Coercion, and the Making of Americans. *Journal of American History* 84 (2): 524–58.

Gilbertson, Greta, and Audrey Singer. 1999. Naturalization under Changing Conditions of Membership: Dominican Immigrants in New York City. Working Paper. Washington, D.C., and Canada.

Gilroy, Paul. 1993. *The Black Atlantic.* Cambridge, Mass.: Harvard University Press.

Glazer, Nathan. 1954. Ethnic Groups in America. In *Freedom and Control in Modern Society,* edited by Monroe Berger, Theodore Abel, and Charles Page. New York: Van Nostrand.

Glazer, Nathan, and Daniel P. Moynihan. 1963. *Beyond the Melting Pot.* Cambridge, Massachusetts: MIT Press.

Gleijeses, Piero. 1978. *The Dominican Crisis: The 1965 Constitutionalist Revolt and American Intervention.* Baltimore: Johns Hopkins University Press.

Glick Schiller, Nina. 1995. From Immigrant to Transmigrant: Theorizing Transnational Migration. *Anthropological Quarterly* 68 (1): 48–63.

———. 1999. "Transmigrants and Nation-States: Something Old and Something New in the U.S. Immigrant Experience. In *The Handbook of International Migration,* edited by Charles Hirschman, Philip Kasinitz, and Josh DeWind. New York: The Russell Sage Foundation.

Glick Schiller, Nina, Linda Basch, and Cristina Szanton Blanc, eds. 1992. *Towards a Transnational Perspective on Migration.* New York: New York Academy of Sciences.

Glick Schiller, Nina, and Georges Fouron. 1998. The Generation of Identity: Haitian Youth and the Transnational State. Paper presented to the Transnationalism and the Second Generation Conference, March, Harvard University, Cambridge, Massachusetts.

Gold, Steven. 2000. Transnational Communities: Examining Migration in a Globally Integrated World. In *Rethinking Globalization(s): From the Corporation Transnationalism to Local Intervention,* edited by Preet S. Aulakh and Michael G. Schecter. London: Macmillan, Ltd.

Goldring, Luin. 1992. Diversity and Community in Transnational Migration: A Comparative Study of Two Mexico U.S. Migrant Communities. Ph.D. diss., Cornell University.

———. 1998. The Power of Status in Transnational Social Spaces. In *Transnationalism from Below: Comparative Urban and Community Research (Volume 6),* edited by Luis Guarnizo and Michael P. Smith. Rutgers, New Jersey: Transaction Press.

———. 1999. El Estado Mexicano y las organizaciones transmigrantes: reconfigurando la nación y las relaciones entre estado y sociedad civil. In *Fronteras Fragmentadas,* edited by Gail Mummert. Zamora, Mexico: Colegio de Michoacán.

Gonzáles, Nancie. 1970. Peasants' Progress: Dominicans in New York. *Caribbean Studies* 10: 154–71.

González, Carolina. 1999. Young Dominicans Chart a New Agenda. *New York Daily News.* 27 February.

Gordon, Milton. 1961. Assimilation in America: Theory and Reality. *Daedalus* 90 (2): 263–85.

Graham, Pamela. 1997. Reimagining the Nation and Defining the District: Dominican Migration, and Transnational Politics. In *Caribbean Circuits: New Directions in the Study of Caribbean Migration,* edited by Patricia Pessar. New York: Center for Migration Studies.

Granovetter, Mark. 1973. The Strength of Weak Ties. *American Journal of Sociology* 78 (6): 1360–80.

Grasmuck, Sherri, and Patricia Pessar. 1991. *Between Two Islands: Dominican International Migration.* Berkeley: University of California Press.

———. 1996. Dominicans in the United States: First- and Second-Generation Settlement. In *Origins and Destinies: Immigration, Race, and Ethnicity in America,* edited by Silvia Pedraza and Rubén Rumbaut. Belmont, California: Wordsworth Publishing Company.

Griffin, K. 1976. On the Emigration of the Peasantry. *World Development* 4: 353–61.

Griswold, Wendy. 1992. The Writing on the Mud Wall: Nigerian Novels and the Imaginary Village. *American Sociological Review* 57: 709–24.

Guarnizo, Luis. 1992. One Country in Two: Dominican-Owned Firms in New York and in the Dominican Republic. Ph.D. diss., Johns Hopkins University.

————. 1994. Los Dominicanyork: The Making of a Binational Society. *Annals, AAPSS* 533: 70–86.

————. 1997. The Emergence of a Transnational Social Formation and the Mirage of Return among Dominican Transmigrants. *Identities* 4: 281–322.

————. 1998. The Rise of Transnational Social Formations: Mexican and Dominican State Responses to Transnational Migration. *Political Power and Social Theory* 12: 45–94.

Gupta, Akhil, and James Ferguson. 1997. *Anthropological Locations: Boundaries and Grounds of a Field Science*. Berkeley: University of California Press.

Gurak, Douglas, and Mary Kritz. 1982. Dominican and Colombian Women in New York City: Household Structure and Employment Patterns. *Migration Today* 10 (3–4): 14–21.

Hagan, Jacqueline. 1994. *Deciding to Be Legal*. Philadelphia: Temple University Press.

Hall, Peter A. 1989. *The Political Power of Economic Ideas: Keynesianism Across Nations*. Princeton: Princeton University Press.

Hall, Stuart. 1991. The Local and the Global: Globalization and Ethnicity. In *Culture, Globalization, and the World System,* edited by Anthony King. Binghamton: State University of New York.

Hamilton, Nora, and Norma Stoltz Chinchilla. 1999. New Organizing Strategies and Transnational Networks of Guatemalan and Salvadorans in Los Angeles. Paper presented to the University of California Comparative Immigration and Integration Program Research Workshop, 19 February, San Diego, California.

Hannerz, Ulf. 1992. *Cultural Complexity*. New York: Columbia University Press.

Hansen, Marcus Lee. 1940. *The Immigrant in American History*. Cambridge, Massachusetts: Harvard University Press.

Harrison, Bennett. 1988. The Economic Development Miracle of Massachusetts. In *The Massachusetts Miracle: High Technology and Economic Revitalization,* edited by David Lampe. Cambridge, Massachusetts: MIT Press.

Hart, Jordana. 2000. Sense of Duty to Homeland Compels Mass. Dominicans to Return to Vote. *Boston Globe,* 13 May: B3.

Hartlyn, Jonathan. 1993. The Dominican Republic: Contemporary Problems and Challenges. In *Democracy in the Caribbean: Political, Economic and Social Perspectives,* edited by Jorge Domínguez, Robert Pastor, and R. DeLisle Worrell. Baltimore and London: Johns Hopkins University Press.

———. 1998. *The Struggle for Democratic Politics in the Dominican Republic.* Chapel Hill: University of North Carolina Press.

Haug, Sonja. 1998. Transnational Migrant Communities: The Case of Italian Migrants in Germany. Paper presented at European Forum, May, European University Institute, Florence, Italy.

Held, David, Anthony McGrew, David Goldblatt, and Jonathan Perraton. 1999. *Global Transformations.* Stanford, California: Stanford University Press.

Hendricks, Glenn. 1974. *The Dominican Diaspora: From the Dominican Republic to New York City—Villagers in Transition.* New York: Teachers College Press.

Hernandez, Raymond. 1998. Guiliani, in Visit, Pledges Storm Help for Dominicans. *New York Times,* 4 October.

Hobsbawm, Eric. 1992. *Nations and Nationalism Since 1780.* Cambridge, Massachusetts: Cambridge University Press.

Hoetink, Harry. 1982. *The Dominican People 1850–1900.* Baltimore and London: Johns Hopkins University Press.

Hondagneu-Sotelo, Pierette. 1994. *Gendered Transitions.* Berkeley and Los Angeles: University of California Press.

Hondagneu-Sotelo, Pierrette, and Ernestina Avila. 1997. I'm Here, but I'm There: The Meanings of Latina Transnational Motherhood. *Gender and Society* 11 (5): 548–69.

Hughes, H.S. 1975. *The Sea Change.* New York: Harper and Row.

Hume, I. 1973. Migrant Workers in Europe. *Finance and Development* 10: 2–6.

Ignatiev, Noel. 1995. *How the Irish Became White.* New York: Routledge.

Inter-American Development Bank (IDB). 1987. *Economic and Social Progress in Latin America.* Washington, D.C.: Inter-American Development Bank.

International Monetary Fund. 1998. *Balance of Payments Statistics Yearbook Annual.* Washington, D.C: International Monetary Fund.

Itzigsohn, José, Carlos Dore Cabral, Esther Hernández Medina, and Obed Vázquez. 1999. Mapping Dominican Transnationalism: Narrow and Broad Transnational Practices. *Ethnic and Racial Studies* 22 (2): 216–40.

Jacobs, Margaret. 1998. Legal Beat: World Court Orders U.S. to Stay Virginia Execution of Paraguayan. *Wall Street Journal.* 10 April.

Jacobson, David. 1996. *Rights Across Borders: Immigration and the Decline of Citizenship.* Baltimore: Johns Hopkins University Press.

Janofsky, Michael. 1999. Legal Immigrants Would Regain Aid in Clinton's Plan. *New York Times.* 25 January.

Jezierski, Louise. 1994. Latinas in New England at Work and in Politics. Paper presented at the 89th meeting of the American Sociological Association, 5–9 August, Los Angeles, California.

Jones, Richard. 1982. Channelization of Undocumented Mexican Migrants to the U.S. *Economic Geography* 58: 156–76.

Jones-Correa, Michael. 1998a. *Between Two Nations: The Political Predicament of Latinos in New York City.* Ithaca and London: Cornell University Press.

———. 1998b. Commentary presented at the Transnationalism and the Second Generation Conference, April, Harvard University, Cambridge, Massachusetts.

Kasarda, John. 1989. Urban Industrial Transition and the Underclass. *The Annals of the American Academy of Political and Social Science* 501: 26–47.

Kasinitz, Philip. 1992. *Caribbean New York: Black Immigrants and the Politics of Race.* Ithaca and London: Cornell University Press.

Kastoryano, Riva. 1994. Mobilisations des migrants en Europe: du national au transnational. *Revue Européenne des Migrations Internationales* 10 (1): 169–80.

Katzenell, Jack. 1999. Israel's Supreme Court Blocks Sheinbein's Extradition. Associated Press, 25 February.

Kayal, Philip. 1978. The Dominicans in New York: Part II. *Migration Today* 6: 10–15.

Kearney, Michael. 1993. Borders and Boundaries of State and Self at the End of the Empire. *Journal of Historical Sociology* 4 (1): 52–74.

———. 1995. The Local and the Global: The Anthropology of Globalization and Transnationalism. *Annual Review of Anthropology* 24: 547–65.

Kibria, Nazli. 1993. *Family Tightropes.* Princeton: Princeton University Press.

———. 1998. The Ties of Blood and Homeland Trips: Transnationalism and Identity Among Second-Generation Chinese and Korean Americans. Paper presented at the Transnationalism and the Second Generation Conference, Weatherhead Center for International Affairs, Harvard University, Cambridge, Massachusetts.

Kleinekathoefer, M. 1987. *El sector informal: integración o transformación.* Santo Domingo: Fundación Freidrich Ebert.

Kritz, Mary, Charles Keely, and Sylvio Tomasi, eds. 1981. *Global Trends in Migration: Theory and Research on International Population Movements.* New York: Center for Migration Studies.

Kymlicka, Will. 1995. *Multicultural Citizenship.* New York: Oxford University Press.

Laguerre, Michel. 1998. *Diasporic Citizenship.* New York: St. Martin's Press.

Landolt, Patricia, Lilian Autler, and Sonia Baires. 1999. From Hermano Lejano to Hermano Mayor: The Dialectics of Salvadoran Transnationalism. *Racial and Ethnic Studies* 22 (2): 290–316.

Levitt, Peggy. 1994. The Social Basis for Latino Small Businesses: The Case of Dominican and Puerto Rican Entrepreneurs. In *Latinos, Poverty and Public Policy in Massachusetts,* edited by Edwin Meléndez and Miren Uriarte. Boston: University of Massachusetts Press.

———. 1995. A Todos Les Llamo Primo: The Social Base for Latino Small Businesses. In *Immigrant Entrepreneurship in Massachusetts,* edited by Marilyn Halter. Boston: University of Massachusetts Press.

———. 1996. Transnationalizing Civil and Political Change: The Case of Transnational Organizational Ties Between Boston and the Dominican Republic. Ph.D. diss., Massachusetts Institute of Technology.

———. 1997. Transnationalizing Community Development: The Case of Migration Between Boston and the Dominican Republic. *Nonprofit and Voluntary Sector Quarterly* 26: 509–26.

———. 1998a. Local-Level Global Religion: The Case of U.S.–Dominican Migration. *Journal for the Scientific Study of Religion* 3: 74–89.

———. 1998b. Forms of Transnational Community and Their Impact on the Second Generation: Preliminary Findings. Paper prepared for the Transnationalism and the Second Generation Conference, April, Harvard University, Cambridge, Massachusetts.

———. 1999. Social Remittances: A Local-Level, Migration-Driven Form of Cultural Diffusion. *International Migration Review* 32 (124): 926–49.

Levitt, Peggy, and Rafael de la Dehesa. 1998. States' Roles in Shaping Transnational Participation. Paper prepared for the Annual Meetings of the Latin American Studies Association, September, Chicago.

Levitt, Peggy, and Erin Collins. 2000. Transnational Practices Among Irish Americans: Past and Present. Paper prepared for the Boston College Seminar on Irish American History, March, Boston College, Boston.

Light, Ivan, and Edna Bonacich. 1988. *Immigrant Entrepreneurship.* Berkeley and Los Angeles: University of California Press.

London Daily Telegraph. 1998. State to Defy World Court, Execute Killer, Judges Have No Jurisdiction: Virginia. 11 April.

López, David, and Ricardo Stanton-Salazar. 1999. The Mexican American Generation: Yesterday, Today, and Tomorrow. Paper prepared for the University of California Comparative Immigration and Integration Program Research Workshop, February, San Diego, California.

Louie, Andrea. 1998. Still Transnational After All These Years: Chinese Americans and the Chinese Motherland. Paper presented at the Transnationalism and the Second Generation Conference, Weatherhead Center for International Affairs, Harvard University, Cambridge, Massachusetts

MacDonald, Christine. 1998. Latino Community Celebrates Close Ties to the Caribbean. *Boston Globe,* 30 August.

Mahler, Sarah. 1996. *American Dreaming.* Princeton: Princeton University Press.

———. 1998. Theoretical and Empirical Contributions Toward a Research Agenda for Transnationalism. In *Transnationalism from Below: Compar-*

ative Urban and Community Research, Vol. 6, edited by M.P. Smith and Luis Guarnizo. New Brunswick, New Jersey, and London: Transaction Publishers.

Margolis, Maxine. 1994. *Little Brazil: An Ethnography of Brazilian Immigrants in New York City.* Princeton: Princeton University Press.

Marshall, T.H. 1950. *Citizenship and Social Class and Other Essays.* Cambridge: Cambridge University Press.

Massey, Douglas. 1995. The New Immigration and Ethnicity in the United States." *Population and Development Review* 21 (3): 631–52.

Massey, Douglas, Rafael Alarcón, Jorge Durand, and Humberto González. 1987. *Return to Aztlan: The Social Process of International Migration in Western Mexico.* Berkeley and Los Angeles: University of California Press.

Massey, Douglas, Joaquín Arango, Graeme Hugo, Ali Kouaouci, Adela Pellegrino, and J. Edward Taylor. 1993. Theories of International Migration: A Review and Appraisal. *Population and Development Review* 19: 431–65.

Mato, Daniel. 1997. On Global Agents, Transnational Relations, and the Social Making of Transnational Identities and Associated Agents. In *Identities: Global Studies in Culture and Power* 4 (2): 33–47.

Matthei, Linda, and David A. Smith. 1998. Belizean 'Boyz N the Hood?' Garifuna Labor Migration and Transnational Identity. In *Transnationalism from Below: Comparative Urban and Community Research, Vol. 6,* edited by Luis Guarnizo and Michael P. Smith. New Brunswick, New Jersey, and London: Transaction Press.

McNaught, Sarah. 1999. Alien Ballot: A Novel Idea in Cambridge: Give Noncitizen Immigrants the Vote. *Boston Phoenix,* 18–25 February.

Messina, Milton. 1988. *Memorias del ajuste de una economía en crisis.* Santo Domingo: Fondo para el Avance de las Ciencias Sociales.

Mexican Ministry of Foreign Affairs and U.S. Commission on Immigration Reform. 1998. *Migration Between Mexico and the United States: A Binational Study.* Austin, Texas: U.S. Government Printing Office.

Meyer, John, and Brian Rowan. 1983. Institutionalized Organizations: Formal Structure as Myth and Ceremony. *American Journal of Sociology* 83: 340–63.

Meyer, John, John Boli, and George Thomas. 1994. Ontology and Rationalization in the Western Cultural Account. In *Institutional Environments and Organizations,* edited by W. Richard Scott and John Meyer. Thousand Oaks, California, and London: Sage Publications.

Migration News. 1998. "Remittances: Dominican Republic." Electronic document available at http://migration.ucdavis.edu/data/remit.on.www.DomRep.html.

Miller, Mark. 1989. Political Participation and Representation of Noncitizens. In *Immigration and the Politics of Citizenship in Europe and North America,* edited by W. Rogers Brubaker. Lanham, Maryland, and New York: University Press of America and the German Marshall Fund.

Mitchell, Christopher. 1992. U.S. Foreign Policy and Dominican Migration to the United States. In *Western Hemisphere Immigration and United States Foreign Policy,* edited by Christopher Mitchell. University Park: Pennsylvania State University Press.

Mittleberg, David, and Mary C. Waters. 1992. The Process of Ethnogenesis among Haitian and Israeli Immigrants in the United States. *Ethnic and Racial Studies* 15: 412–35.

Morawska, Ewa. 2001a. The New-Old Transmigrants, Their Transnational Lives, and Ethnicization: A Comparison of 19th/20th- and 20th/21st-Century Situations. In *Immigrants, Civic Culture, and Modes of Political Incorporation,* edited by Gary Gerstle and John Mollenkopf. New York: Russell Sage Foundation.

———. 2001b. International Migration and Consolidation of Democracy in East Central Europe: A Problematic Relationship in a Historical Perspective. In *Democratic Consolidation in Eastern Europe: International and Transnational Factors,* edited by Alex Pravda and Jan Zielanka. New York and London: Routledge Press.

———. 2001c. Becoming Ethnic, Becoming American: Different Patterns and Configurations of the Assimilation of American Jews, 1890–1940. In *Divergent Centers: Shaping Jewish Cultures in Israel and America,* edited by Deborah Dash Moore and Ilan Troen. New Haven: Yale University Press.

Moreno, Sylvia. 1992. Dinkins Scores with Visit. 1992. *Newsday,* 22 May.

Morokvasic, Mirjana. 1984. Birds of Passage Are Also Women. *International Migration Review* 18 (4): 886–907.

Mountz, Alison, and Richard Wright. 1996. Daily Life in the Transnational Migrant Community of San Agustin, Oaxaca, and Poughkeepsie, New York. *Diaspora* 5: 403–26.

Moya Pons, Frank. 1981. Dominican National Identity and Return Migration. Working Paper. University of Florida at Gainesville Center for Latin American Studies.

———. 1995. *The Dominican Republic Today.* New Rochelle, New York: Hispaniola Books.

Nagel, Joanne. 1994. Constructing Ethnicity: Creating and Recreating Ethnic Identity and Culture. *Social Problems* 41 (1): 152–176.

Nagengast, Carol, and Michael Kearney. 1990. Mixed Ethnicity: Social Identity, Political Consciousness, and Political Activism. *Latin American Research Review* 25: 61–91.

Nonini, Donald, and Aihwa Ong. 1997. Chinese Transnationalism as an Alternative Modernity. In *The Cultural Politics of Modern Chinese Transnationalism,* edited by Aihwa Ong and Donald Nonini. New York: Routledge Press.

Nugent, Walter. 1992. *Crossings: The Great Transatlantic Migrations, 1870–1914.* Bloomington, Indiana University Press.

Ong, Aihwa. 1993. On the Edge of Empires: Flexible Citizenship among Chinese in Diaspora. *Positions* 1 (3): 745–78.

Osterman, Paul. 1990. In the Midst of Plenty: A Profile of Boston and Its Poor. Boston: The Boston Foundation.

Ostrander, Susan, and Paul Schervish. 1994. Giving and Getting: Philanthropy as a Social Relation. In *Critical Issues in American Philanthropy: Strengthening Theory and Practice,* edited by J. Van Til. San Francisco: Jossey-Bass.

Pachón, Harry, and Louis DeSipio. 1994. *New Americans by Choice: Political Perspectives of Latino Immigrants.* Boulder, Colorado: Westview Press.

Pan, Philip. 2000. La Nueva Vida, the Road to Citizenship. *Washington Post.* 4 July: A-1.

Papastergiadis, Nikos. 1998. *Dialogues in the Diaspora.* London: Rivers Oram Press.

Park, Robert E. 1950. *Race and Culture.* Glencoe, Illinois: Free Press.

Patterson, Orlando. 1988. The Emerging West Atlantic System: Migration, Culture, and Underdevelopment in the United States and the Circum-Caribbean Region. In *Population in an Interacting World,* edited by William Alonso. Cambridge, Massachusetts: Harvard University Press.

Peña, Javier, and Miguel Parache. 1971. Emigración a New York de tres comunidades: Janico, Baitoa, y Sabana Iglesias. Master's thesis, Universidad Católica Madre y Maestra.

Pérez, G. 1981. The Legal and Illegal Dominican in New York City. Paper presented to the Conference on Hispanic Migration to New York City: Global Trends and Neighborhood Change, December, New York University, New York.

Pessar, Patricia. 1999. The Role of Gender, Households, and Social Networks in the Migration Process: A Review and Appraisal. In *The Handbook of International Migration,* edited by Charles Hirschman, Philip Kasinitz, and Josh DeWind. New York: Russell Sage Foundation.

Phillips, Julie, and Douglas Massey. 1998. Engines of Immigration: Stocks of Human and Social Capital in Mexico. Paper presented to the Annual Meetings of the Eastern Sociological Association, March, Philadelphia.

Pinkus, Noah, ed. 1998. *Immigration and Citizenship.* Lanham, Maryland, and Boulder, Colorado: Rowan and Littlefield.

Piore, Michael. 1979. *Birds of Passage.* New York: Cambridge University Press.

Popkin, Eric. 1999. Guatemalan Mayan Migration to Los Angeles: Constructing Transnational Linkages in the Context of the Settlement Process. *Ethnic and Racial Studies* 22 (2): 378–99.

Portes, Alejandro. 1999. Conclusion: Towards a New World: The Origins and Effect of Transnational Activities. *Ethnic and Racial Studies* 22 (2): 463–78.

————, ed. 1995. *The Economic Sociology of Immigration: Essays on Networks, Ethnicity, and Entrepreneurship.* New York: Russell Sage Foundation.

Portes, Alejandro, and John Walton. 1981. *Labor, Class and the International System.* New York: Academic Press.

Portes, Alejandro, and Robert Manning. 1986. The Immigrant Enclave: Theory and Empirical Examples. In *Competitive Ethnic Relations,* edited by Susan Olzak and Joanne Nagel. Orlando, Florida: Academic Press.

Portes, Alejandro, and Jozsef Borocz. 1989. Contemporary Immigration: Theoretical Perspectives on Its Determinants and Modes of Incorporation. *International Migration Review* 23: 606–30.

Portes, Alejandro, and Luis Guarnizo. 1991. Tropical Capitalists: U.S.-bound Immigration and Small-Enterprise Development in the Dominican Republic. In *Migration, Remittances, and Small Business Development: Mexico and Caribbean Basin Countries,* edited by S. Díaz-Briquets and S. Weintraug. Boulder, Colorado: Westview Press.

Portes, Alejandro, and Julia Sensenbrenner. 1993. Embeddedness and Immigration: Notes on the Social Determinants of Economic Action. *American Journal of Sociology* 98 (5): 1320–50.

Portes, Alejandro, and Min Zhou. 1993. The New Second Generation: Segmented Assimilation and Its Variants. *Annals of the American Academy of Political Science* (530): 74–96.

Portes, Alejandro, and Patricia Landolt. 1996. The Downside of Social Capital. *The American Prospect* 26: 18–25.

Portes, Alejandro, Luis Guarnizo, and Patricia Landolt. 1999. Introduction: Pitfalls and Promise of an Emergent Research Field. *Ethnic and Racial Studies* 22 (2): 217–38.

Profamilia, ONAPLAN, IRD/Macro International, Inc. 1992. *Encuesta demográfica y de salud (ENDESA).* Santo Domingo: IRD/Macro.

Putnam, Robert. 1993. *Making Democracy Work: Civic Traditions in Modern Italy.* New Jersey: Princeton University Press.

————. 2000. *Bowling Alone: The Collapse and Revival of American Community.* New York: Simon and Schuster.

Rhoades, Robert E. 1978. Intra-European Return Migration and Rural Development: Lessons from the Spanish Case. *Human Organization* 37: 136–47.

Rivera-Salgado, Gaspar. 1999. Political Organizing Across the U.S.-Mexican Border: The Experience of Mexican Indigenous Migrant Workers. Paper presented to the University of California Comparative Immigration and Integration Program Research Workshop, February, San Diego.

Roberts, Bryan, Reanne Frank, and Fernando Lozano-Ascencio. 1999. Transnational Migrant Communities and Mexican Migration to the U.S. *Ethnic and Racial Studies* 22 (2): 238–67.

Rodriguez, Cindy. 1999. From Island Politics to Local Politics: Dominicans Making Gains in City Offices. *Boston Globe,* 14 November.

Rohter, Larry. 1996a. New York's Dominicans Taking Big Role in Island Elections. *New York Times,* 26 June.

———. 1996b. New York Dominicans Strongly Back Candidates on Island. *New York Times,* 29 June.

Rouse, Roger. 1989. Mexican Migration to the United States: Family Relations in the Development of Transnational Circuits. Ph.D. diss., Stanford University.

———. 1991. Mexican Migration and the Social Space of Postmodernism. *Diaspora* 1: 8–24.

———. 1992. Making Sense of Settlement: Class Transformation, Cultural Struggle, and Transnationalism Among Mexican Migrants in the United States. In *Towards a Transnational Perspective on Migration: Race, Class, Ethnicity, and Nationalism Reconsidered,* edited by N. Glick-Schiller, L. Basch, and C. Blanc-Szanton. New York: New York Academy of Sciences.

Rumbaut, Rubén. 1996. Origins and Destinies: Immigration, Race and Ethnicity in Contemporary America. In *Origins and Destinies: Immigration, Race and Ethnicity in America,* edited by Silvia Pedraza and Ruben Rumbaut. Belmont, California: Wadsworth Publishers.

———. 1997. Ties That Bind: Immigration and Immigrant Families in the United States. In *Immigration and the Family,* edited by Alan Booth, Ann C. Crouter, and Nancy Landale. Mahwah, New Jersey: Lawrence Erlbaum Associates.

———. 1998. Coming of Age in Immigrant America. *Research Perspectives on Migration* 1 (6): 1–14.

Sáez, Jose Luis. 1987. *Cinco siglos de Iglesia Dominicana.* Santo Domingo: Editora Amigo del Hogar.

Safa, Helen. 1995. *The Myth of the Male Breadwinner: Women and Industrialization in the Caribbean.* Boulder, Colorado: Westview Press.

Sagás, Ernesto. 1999. From Ausentes to Dual Nationals: The Incorporation of the Diaspora into Dominican Politics. Unpublished manuscript.

Sales, Teresa. 1999. *Brasileiros Longe de Casa.* Sao Paulo, Brazil: Editora Cortês.

Sánchez, Arturo Ignacio. 1997. Transnational Political Agency and Identity Formation Among Colombian Immigrants. Paper presented to the Conference on Transnational Communities and the Political Economy of New York, 19 October, New School for Social Research, New York.

Sassen, Saskia. 1991. *The Global City.* New Jersey: Princeton University Press.

———. 1996. *Losing Control? Sovereignty in an Age of Globalization.* New York: Columbia University Press.

Sassen-Koob, Saskia. 1978. The International Circulation of Resources and Development: The Case of Migrant Labor. *Development and Change* 9: 509–45.

———. 1992. Formal and Informal Associations: Dominicans and Colombians in New York. In *Caribbean Life in New York City: Sociocultural Dimensions*, edited by Constance Sutton and Elsa Chaney. New York: Center for Migration Studies.

Schervish, Paul. 1996. Consumption Philanthropy: Taking Care of Your Own Business First. In *Charity and Strategy: The Meaning of Philanthropy and Its Practice among the Wealthy*, edited by Paul Schervish. San Francisco: Jossey-Bass.

Schervish, Paul, and Herman, A. 1988. Empowerment and Beneficence: Strategies of Living and Giving among the Wealthy. In *Final Report: The Study on Wealth and Philanthropy*. Boston: Social Welfare Research Institute: Boston College.

Schoultz, Lars. 1992. Central America and the Politicization of U.S. Immigration Policy. In *Western Hemisphere Immigration and United States Foreign Policy*, edited by C. Mitchell. University Park: Pennsylvania State University Press.

Schuck, Peter H. 1998. *Citizens, Strangers, and In-Betweens*. Boulder, Colorado: Westview Press.

Schudson, Michael. 1998. *The Good Citizen: A History of American Civic Life*. New York: Martin Kessler Books.

Scott, W. Richard. 1995. *Institutions and Organizations*. Thousand Oaks, California, and London: Sage Publications.

Shand-Tucci, Douglass. 1998. *Built in Boston: City and Suburb, 1800–1950*. Amherst: University of Massachusetts Press.

Sharpe, Kenneth. 1977. *Peasant Politics: Struggle in a Dominican Village*. Baltimore: Johns Hopkins University Press.

Sikkink, Kathryn. 1991. *Ideas and Institutions: Developmentalism in Brazil and Argentina*. Ithaca and London: Cornell University Press.

Sjaastad, L.A. 1962. The Costs and Returns of Human Migration. *Journal of Political Economy* 7: 80–93.

Skocpol, Theda. 1999. "Advocates without Members: The Recent Transformation of American Civic Life." In *Civic Engagement in American Democracy*, edited by Theda Skocpol and Morris P. Fiorina. Washington, D.C.: Brookings Institute Press and New York: Russell Sage Foundation.

Smart, Alan, and Josephine Smart. 1998. Transnational Social Networks and Negotiated Identities in Interactions between Hong Kong and China. In *Transnationalism from Below: Comparative Urban and Community Research, Vol. 6*, edited by Michael Peter Smith and Luis Guarnizo. New Brunswick, New Jersey, and London: Transaction Publishers.

Smith, Christian. 1996. *Disruptive Religion: The Force of Faith in Social Movement Activism*. New York: Routledge.

Smith, Michael Peter, and Luis Guarnizo, eds. 1998. *Transnationalism from Below: Comparative Urban and Community Research, Vol. 6*. New Brunswick, New Jersey, and London: Transaction Publishers.

Smith, Robert. 1995. Los Ausentes Siempre Presentes: The Imagining, Making and Politics of a Transnational Community between Ticuani, Puebla, Mexico and New York City. Ph.D. diss., Columbia University.

———. 1997. Transnational Localities: Community, Technology, and the Politics of Membership within the Context of Mexico-U.S. Migration. In *Transnationalism from Below: Comparative Urban and Community Research, Vol. 6.*, edited by Michael Peter Smith and Luis Guarnizo. New Brunswick, New Jersey: Rutgers University Press.

———. 1998a. Reflections on Migration, the State and the Construction, Durability, and Newness of Transnational Life. In *Soziale Welt.* Sonderband 12. Transnationale Migration NOMOS Verlagsgesellschaft, Baden-Baden, Germany.

———. 1998b. Transnationalism in the Second Generation Among Mexican Americans in Brooklyn. Paper prepared for the Transnationalism and the Second Generation Conference, April, Harvard University, Cambridge, Massachusetts.

Sontag, Deborah. 1992. New York Dominicans to Vote in Homeland Elections. *New York Times,* 15 November.

———. 1997. Advocates for Immigrants Exploring Voting Rights for Noncitizens. *New York Times,* 31 July.

———. 1998. A Mexican Town That Transcends All Borders. *New York Times,* 21 July.

Sontag, Deborah, and Celia Dugger. "New Immigrant Tide: Shuttle Between Worlds. *New York Times,* 19 July.

Sorensen, Ninna Nyberg. 1998. Narrating Identity Across Dominican Worlds. In *Transnationalism from Below: Comparative Urban and Community Research, Vol. 6,* edited by Michael Peter Smith and Luis Guarnizo. New Brunswick, New Jersey, and London: Transaction Publishers.

Soysal, Yasemin. 1994. *Limits of Citizenship: Migrants and Postnational Membership in Europe.* Chicago and London: University of Chicago Press.

Spiro, Peter. 1999. The Citizenship Dilemma. *Stanford Law Review* 51 (3): 597–639.

Stark, Oded. 1991. *The Migration of Labor.* Cambridge, Massachusetts: Basil Blackwell.

Strang, David, and John Meyer. 1994. Institutional Conditions for Diffusion. In *Institutional Environments and Organizations,* edited by W. Richard Scott and John W. Meyer. Thousand Oaks, California: Sage Publications.

Suárez-Orozco, Marcelo. 1998. Commentary presented at the Transnationalism and the Second Generation Conference, Weatherhead Center for International Affairs, Harvard University, Cambridge, Massachusetts.

Thomas, William, and Florian Znaniecki. 1927. *The Polish Peasant in Europe and America.* New York: Alfred A. Knopf.

Tölölyan, Khachig. 1998. (Re)Thinking Diasporas: Stateless Power at the Transnational Moment. *Diaspora* 5 (1): 3–37.

Torres-Saillant, Silvio. 1995a. The Dominican Republic. In *No Longer Invisible: Afro-Latin Americans Today,* edited by Minority Rights Group. London: Minority Rights Group.

———. 1995b. The Tribulations of Blackness: Stages in Dominican Racial Identity. *Latin American Perspectives* 100 (25): 126–46.

Torres-Saillant, Silvio, and Ramona Hernández. 1998. *The Dominican Americans.* Westport and London: Greenwood Press.

Turner, Bryan. 1990. Outline of a Theory on Citizenship. *Sociology* 24 (2): 189–218.

Ugalde, Antonio, Frank Bean, and Gilbert Cárdenas. 1979. International Migration from the Dominican Republic: Findings from a National Survey. *International Migration Review* 13: 253–54.

Ugalde, Antonio, and T. Langham. 1980. International Return Migration: Socio-Demographic Determinants of Return Migration to the Dominican Republic. Paper prepared for the Caribbean Studies Association.

United Nations Statistical Yearbook, 72nd edition. 1997. Department of Economic and Social Affairs and Statistics Division. New York: United Nations.

U.S. Bureau of the Census. 1992. *Census of the Population: General Social and Economic Characteristics.* PC(1)-C23.1. Washington, D.C.: U.S. Government Printing Office.

U.S. Department of State. 1999. *1998 Human Rights Report,* released by the Bureau of Democracy, Human Rights, and Labor, 26 February.

U.S. Immigration and Naturalization Service. 1960. *Immigration Statistics: Fiscal Year 1959.* Washington, D.C.: U.S. Government Printing Office.

U.S. Immigration and Naturalization Service. 1970. *Immigration Statistics: Fiscal Year 1969.* Washington, D.C.: U.S. Government Printing Office.

U.S. Immigration and Naturalization Service. 1980. *Immigration Statistics: Fiscal Year 1979.* Washington, D.C.: U.S. Government Printing Office.

U.S. Immigration and Naturalization Service. 1990. *Immigration Statistics: Fiscal Year 1989.* Washington, D.C.: U.S. Government Printing Office.

U.S. Immigration and Naturalization Service. 1993. *Immigration Statistics: Fiscal Year 1989.* Washington, D.C.: U.S. Government Printing Office.

Vecoli, Rudolph. 1972. European Americans: From Immigrants to Ethnics. *International Migration Review* 6: 403–35.

Vedovato, Claudio. 1986. *Politics, Foreign Trade and Economic Development: A Study of the Dominican Republic.* London: Croom Helm.

Verba, Sidney, Kay Lehman Scholzman, and Henry Brady. 1995. *Voice and Equality.* Cambridge, Massachusetts: Harvard University Press.

Vicens, L. 1982. *Crisis económica 1978–1982.* Santo Domingo: Alfa y Omega.

Wade, Peter. 1997. *Race and Ethnicity in Latin America.* London and Chicago: Pluto Press.

Waldinger, Roger. 1997. Comments on paper presented to the Conference on Transnational Communities and the Political Economy of New York City in the 1990s, February, New School for Social Research, New York City.

Waldinger, Roger, Howard Aldrich, and Robin Ward. 1990. *Ethnic Entrepreneurs.* Newbury Park, California: Russell Sage.

Walker, Adrian. 1998. Mapping Out Road to Power. *Boston Globe,* 10 December.

Warren, Robert. 1998. Legalization Data and Other Statistical Information about Dominican Migration to the United States. Paper presented to the Conference on Dominican Migration, Fundación Friedrich Ebert, Santo Domingo.

Waters, Mary. 1990. *Ethnic Options.* Berkeley and Los Angeles: University of California Press.

————. 1999. *Black Identities: West Indian Immigrant Dreams and American Realities.* Cambridge, Massachusetts: Harvard University Press.

Waters, Mary, Philip Kasinitz, and John Mollenkopf. 1998. Transnationalism and the Children of Immigrants in the Contemporary United States: What Are the Issues? Paper presented at the Transnationalism and the Second Generation Conference, Weatherhead Center for International Affairs, Harvard University, Cambridge, Massachusetts.

Weist, Raymond. 1979. Implications of International Labor Migration for Mexican Rural Development. In *Migration Across Frontiers: Mexico and the United States.* Contributions of the Latin American Anthropology Group, Vol. 3. Albany, New York: Institute for Mesoamerican Studies.

Westney, D. Eleanor. 1987. *Imitation and Innovation: The Transfer of Western Organizational Patterns to Meiji, Japan.* Cambridge, Massachusetts, and London: Harvard University Press.

Weyland, Karin. 1999. Dominican Women *con un pie aquí yotro allá:* International Migration, Class, Gender and Cultural Change. Ph.D. diss., New School for Social Research, New York.

Wiarda, Howard. 1975. *Dictatorship, Development, and Disintegration: Politics and Social Changes in the Dominican Republic.* Ann Arbor, Michigan: Xerox University Microfilms.

————. 1979. The Dominican Republic: The Politics of a Frustrated Revolution II. In *Latin American Politics and Development,* edited by Howard Wiarda and Harvey Kline. Boston: Houghton Mifflin.

Wiarda, Howard, and Michael Kryzanek. 1982. *The Dominican Republic: A Caribbean Crucible.* Boulder, Colorado: Westview Press.

Wiltshire, Rosina. 1992. Implications of Transnational Migration for Nationalism: The Caribbean Example. In *Towards a Transnational Perspective on Migration,* edited by Nina Glick-Schiller, Linda Basch, and Cristina Blanc Szanton. New York: New York Academy of Sciences.

Wolf, Diane. 1997. Family Secrets: Transnational Struggles Among Children of Filipino Immigrants. *Sociological Perspectives* 40 (3): 457–82.

World Almanac and Encyclopedia. 1920. New York: The Press Publishing Company.

World Bank. 1986. *World Development Report.* New York: Oxford University Press.

Wyman, M. 1993. *Round Trip to America: The Immigrants Return to Europe 1880–1930.* Ithaca and London: Cornell University Press.

Yuval-Davis, Nina. 1997. *Gender and Nation.* London and Thousand Oaks, California: Sage Publications.

Zabin, Carol, and Luis Escala-Rabadan. 1998. Mexican Hometown Associations and Mexican Immigrant Political Empowerment in Los Angeles. Working Paper. The Aspen Institute Nonprofit Sector Research Fund Working Paper Series.

Zhou, Min, and Carl Bankston. 1998. *Growing Up American.* New York: Russell Sage Foundation.

Index

Designer: Steve Renick
Compositor: G & S Typesetters, Inc.
Text: 11/13.5 Caledonia
Printer: Thomson-Shore, Inc.
Binder: Thomson-Shore, Inc.